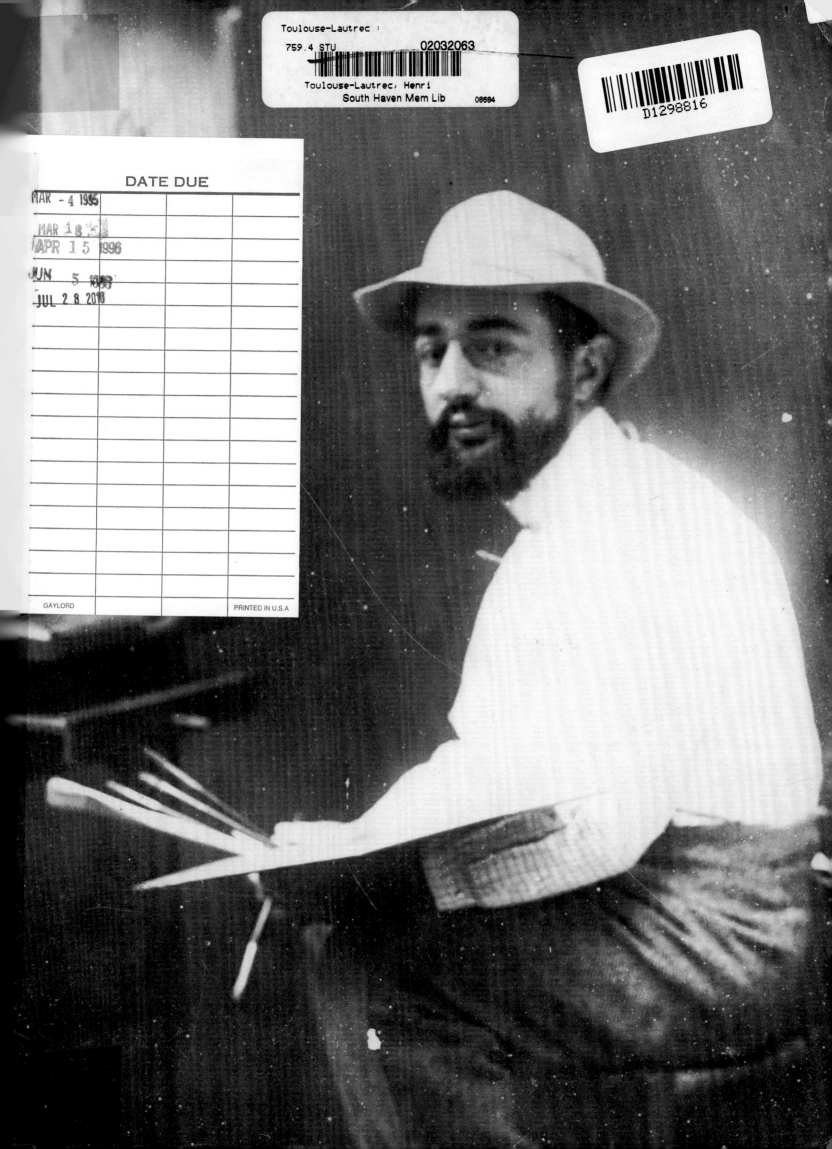

This project was supported in part by the
National Endowment for the Arts and the City of Chicago

COVER:
Au Moulin Rouge, 1892-1895
The Art Institute of Chicago
Helen Birch Bartlett Collection

Photograph by Toulouse-Lautrec in 1894 (Roger-Viollet)

TOULOUSE-LAUTREC: PAINTINGS

Charles F. Stuckey

with assistance of Naomi E. Maurer

Fig. 1
Lautrec painting Berthe la sourde in the garden of Mr. Forest
1890

Contents

Foreword

The Art Institute of Chicago is pleased and honored to bring to our public the exhibition *Toulouse-Lautrec: Paintings,* a retrospective made possible by the Musée Toulouse-Lautrec in Albi and the generosity of fourteen other museums and thirty-two private collectors in the United States, France, Japan, Canada, England and Switzerland.

This exhibition extends an enviable record of the past 36 years in which the Art Institute has initiated exhibitions by the major artists of the Impressionist and Post-Impressionist Schools. The most recent of these were the splendid exhibitions of works by Renoir (1973), Monet (1975) and Bazille (1978).

Toulouse-Lautrec has been a favorite of visitors to the Art Institute for many years. Our own collection of eight paintings and many superb graphics comprises an excellent representation of this great French artist.

During the period of the exhibition, our Print and Drawing Department will exhibit a selection of its outstanding collection of etchings, lithographs and posters which should add importantly to the excitement of this exhibition.

The Trustees of the Musée Toulouse-Lautrec d'Albi and their Chairman, Mr. Jean-Alain Méric, have been most gracious in their willingness to send us forty paintings, many of which are visiting the United States for the first time. For making it possible that these be shown in America we are extremely pleased and appreciative. Our thanks go also to the many other lenders whose paintings assure the completeness and distinction of the exhibition.

Finally, we are deeply grateful to Charles F. Stuckey, Guest Curator, who is responsible for arranging the exhibition and preparing the catalogue.

ARTHUR M. WOOD
Chairman, Board of Trustees

Preface

I am delighted that my seniority grants me the opportunity to introduce the present magnificent exhibition. Lautrec has been very much discussed, and he will be discussed again, forever. It is hardly necessary to assert that his personal style was that of a genius. Everyone recognizes that. Thus I will limit myself to the recollection of a few memories. Having been associated with the Musée d'Albi from its foundation, I have played a role, along with Maurice Joyant, its creator, in the presentation of its treasures.

And since that time I have consecrated myself to Lautrec's work, for which I prepared the general catalogue, as well as to the museum and its functions.

My first memory of a Toulouse-Lautrec exhibition at The Art Institute of Chicago was that of December 1930-January 1931 in which it was impossible for the Musée d'Albi to participate, since the museum was still obliged (so shortly after its foundation) to certain regulations which prevented the removal of any works on any pretext. This exhibition entitled "Loan exhibition of paintings, drawings, prints and posters by Henri de Toulouse-Lautrec" contained 31 paintings, 10 drawings, 7 dry-points, 197 lithographs and 13 posters, which were easier to bring together at that time than today. In the preface to the catalogue Daniel Catton Rich, the director, analyzed the essence of Lautrec's art:

"The case of Toulouse-Lautrec is a challenge to the school of criticism which demands that art have no traffic with subject matter but remain 'pure' and aloof. For here was a man, frankly infatuated with life, a man who felt an immense curiosity about other men, who became, nevertheless, a powerful creator, admired as much for the forms of his art, as for its psychological content."

Then there was the great success of an important exhibition of Toulouse-Lautrec shared by the Philadelphia Museum of Art and The Art Institute of Chicago in 1955-1956 with the collaboration of the Musée d'Albi which lent no fewer than 37 works. Daniel Catton Rich was director of The Art Institute of Chicago, if my memory is correct, and Carl O. Schniewind was curator.

In 1955-1956 a travelling exhibition of "French Drawings: Masterpieces" included the magnificent drawing from the Musée d'Albi "Portrait of the Countess de Toulouse-Lautrec, the artist's mother."

And now I can permit myself to look toward the immediate future and the opening of this prodigious exhibition which will add still more to Lautrec's glory. I cannot forget that the exhibition at the Musée d'Albi in 1980 of master paintings from The Art Institute of Chicago will equally give prestige to Albi. May we look forward to a long collaboration of working together for Lautrec and for our beloved museums.

M. G. DORTU, *Trustee, Musée d'Albi*
President, Société des Amis de Toulouse-Lautrec

Preface

Je suis ravie que mon grade d'ancienneté me confie l'avantage de présenter la magnifique exposition actuelle. On a beaucoup parlé de Lautrec, on en parlera encore et toujours. Point n'est donc besoin de répéter que son trait bien personnel était génial. Désormais chacun le reconnaît. Aussi vais-je me borner à évoquer quelques souvenirs puisque, attachée au musée d'Albi depuis sa création, j'ai participé déjà, au côté de Maurice Joyant, son fondateur, à la présentation de ses richesses.

Et, depuis lors, je me suis consacrée à l'oeuvre de Lautrec dont j'ai fait le catalogue général, ainsi qu'au musée d'Albi et à ses activités.

Mon premier souvenir d'une exposition Toulouse-Lautrec à l'art institute de Chicago est celle de décembre 1930 à janvier 1931, à laquelle le musée d'Albi n'a pu participer, étant encore tenu (si peu de temps après sa fondation), à certains engagements de ne décrocher aucune oeuvre de ses murs sous aucun pretexte. Cette exposition intitulée "Loan exhibition of paintings, drawings, prints and posters by Henri de Toulouse-Lautrec" comprenait 31 tableaux, 10 dessins, 7 pointes sèches, 197 lithographies et 13 affiches, plus faciles à réunir il est vrai, à cette époque-là que maintenant. Le directeur Daniel Catton Rich dans la préface du catalogue a analysé comme but l'art de Lautrec:

"The case of Toulouse-Lautrec is a challenge to the school of criticism which demands that art have no traffic with subject matter but remain 'pure' and aloof. For here was a man, frankly infatuated with life, a man who felt an immense curiosity about other men, who became, nevertheless, a powerful creator, admired as much for the forms of his art, as for its psychological content."

Puis, une importante exposition Toulouse-Lautrec jumelée Philadelphia du 29 octobre au 11 décembre 1955 et Chicago 2 janvier au 15 fevrier 1956, avec la collaboration du musée d'Albi qui ne prêta pas moins de 37 oeuvres, eut un grand succès; Daniel Catton Rich était directeur de l'art institute si mes souvenirs sont bons et Carl O. Schniewind curator.

En 1955-1956 une exposition itinérante "French Drawings: Masterpieces" comprenait le magnifique dessin du musée d'Albi "Portrait de la comtesse de Toulouse-Lautrec, mère de l'artiste."

Et maintenant, puis-je me permettre de me pencher sur l'avenir dont le plus proche est cette prodigieuse manifestation qui en ouvrant ses portes ajoutera encore à la gloire de Lautrec. Je n'oublie pas qu'en 1980 l'exposition à Albi des chefs-d'oeuvre de Chicago donnera également un grand prestige à Albi. Puissions-nous longtemps encore par notre collaboration oeuvrer ensemble pour Lautrec et pour nos musées qui nous sont chers.

M. G. DORTU, *Administrateur du Musée d'Albi*
Présidente de la Société des Amis de Toulouse-Lautrec

Acknowledgements

This exhibition and catalogue are the product of the self-less collaborative efforts of a large group of people whom it is my pleasure to acknowledge.

Naomi E. Maurer was more than a research assistant and editor. Her insights and expertise improved every aspect of the catalogue and exhibition to which she tirelessly dedicated herself, and the extent of her contribution is only fractionally indicated by her initialled catalogue entries.

It was a special honor and a great pleasure to have the guidance and hospitality of my dear personal friend, Evan M. Maurer, who shared his incomparable knowledge of art and museology with me for months on end.

Mary Kuzniar's secretarial assistance was both devoted and flawless. The success of this entire project is in many ways the direct result of her caring efforts.

My heartfelt thanks to many individuals at The Art Institute of Chicago whose cooperation with me during my guest curatorship was essential for the realization of this exhibition:

Arthur M. Wood, *Chairman of the Board of Trustees*

James W. Alsdorf, *Trustee and former Chairman of the Board of Trustees*

Leigh B. Block, *Life Trustee and former Chairman of the Board of Trustees*

Charles A. Meyer, *Trustee*

E. Laurence Chalmers, Jr., *President*

Helen Becker, *Secretary to the President*

Robert E. Mars, *Vice President for Administrative Affairs*

Larry Ter Molen, *Vice President for Development and Public Relations*

Linda Starks, *Secretary*

Wallace Bradway, *Registrar*

Mary Braun, *Assistant Registrar*

Dominique Vasseur, *Secretary, Registrar's Office*

Timothy Lennon, *Associate Conservator*

Harold Joachim, *Curator, Department of Prints and Drawings*

Anselmo Carini, *Associate Curator, Department of Prints and Drawings*

Suzanne McCullagh, *Assistant Curator, Department of Prints and Drawings*

Louise Berge, *Assistant Curator, Department of Classical Art*

Susan Wise, *Assistant Curator, Department of Earlier Paintings*

Lorraine Schaefer, *Secretary, Department of Earlier Paintings*

Osamu Ueda, *Associate Curator, Department of Oriental Art*

Milo Naeve, *Curator, Department of American Art*

Peter S. Reed, *Secretary, Department of Primitive Art*

Cecilia Chin, *Associate Librarian, Head of the Reference Department, Ryerson Library*

Daniel Starr, *Reference/Catalogue Librarian, Ryerson Library*

Deborah Ezzio, *Senior Library Assistant, Ryerson Library*

Howard Kraywinkel, *Director of Museum Photography*

John Mahtesian, *Associate Director of Museum Photography*

Linda Cohn, *Rights and Reproductions Coordinator*

Maebetty Langdon, *Rights and Reproductions*

Gene Yates, *Chief Printer, Department of Museum Photography*

Anne Benolken, *Coordinator, Department of Museum Photography*

Jaroslav Kobylecky, *Photographer, Department of Museum Photography*

Katherine Shaw, *Department of Museum Photography*

Edith Gaines, *Director of Annual Programs*

Leslie Huff, *Membership Programs Coordinator*

Margaret Blasage, *Director of Publications*

Sharon Burge, *Assistant Director of Publications*

Helen Lethert, *Director of Public Relations*

P. C. Noble, *Assistant Exhibition Secretary*

Reynold Bailey, *Supervisor, Art Installation Department*

Barbara Mengel, *Volunteer Coordinator*

Rex Moser, *Executive Director, Museum Education*

Celia Marriott, *Staff lecturer*

Ray Carlson, *Audio-visual assistant*

Lou Malozzi, *Audio-visual assistant*

Jane Clark, *Consultant-writer, Junior Museum*

Katherine Hannaford, *Catalogue Assistant*

Paula Prokopoff-Giannini, *Catalogue Assistant*

Dorothy Rudzki, *Catalogue Assistant*

Cheryl Tolbert, *Catalogue Assistant*

Marc Vincent, *Catalogue Assistant*

John Vinci, *Architect, A.I.A.*

Mr. and Mrs. H. George Mann

I also wish to extend sincere gratitude to professional colleagues in this country and abroad for their generous cooperation and help:

William Acquavella, *Acquavella Galleries, Inc., New York;*

Hélène Adhémar, *Conservateur en chef, Musée du Jeu de Paume;*

William Agee, *Director, Museum of Fine Arts, Houston;*

Elizabeth Anderson, *Coordinator of Public Programs, Philadelphia Museum of Art;*

Rutgers Barclay, *Acquavella Galleries, Inc., New York;*

Vivian Barnett, *Curatorial Assistant, The Solomon R. Guggenheim Museum, New York;*

The Honorable David Bathurst, *Christie's of London;*

William L. Beadleston, *New York;*

W. A. L. Beeren, *Director, Museum Boymans-van-Beuningen, Rotterdam;*

Jean Sutherland Boggs, *Director, Philadelphia Museum of Art;*

Marc Boscus, *Conservateur, Musée du 19e siècle, Paris;*

David S. Brooke, *Director, Sterling and Francine Clark Art Institute;*

Victor Carlson, *Curator, Department of Prints and Drawings, Baltimore Museum of Art;*

Hermine Chivian-Cobb, *Sotheby Parke-Bernet, New York;*

Desmond L. Corcoran, *Alex Reid & Lefevre Ltd., London;*

Lili Couvée, *Conservateur, Rijksmuseum Vincent van Gogh, Amsterdam;*

Caroline Cummings, *Christie's of London;*

Annette Field, *Sotheby Parke-Bernet, New York;*

M. Roy Fisher, *Wildenstein & Co., New York;*

Tom L. Freudenheim, *Director, National Endowment for the Arts;*

Peter Fusco, *Curator, Department of European Painting and Sculpture, Los Angeles County Museum of Art;*

Lawrence Gowing, *Director, Slade School of Art, University of London;*

Marco Grassi, *New York;*

Phillip Johnston, *Chief Curator, Wadsworth Atheneum, Hartford;*

John House, *University College, London;*

Peter Lasko, *Director, Courtauld Institute of Art, London;*

Nancy Little, *Research Librarian, M. Knoedler & Co., New York;*

Marion McCaughan, *Cambridge, Massachusetts;*

William McNaught, *Director, New York Office, Archives of American Art;*

Charles Millard, *Chief Curator, Hirschhorn Museum and Sculpture Garden, Washington, D.C.;*

Charles S. Moffett, *Curator, Department of European Painting, The Metropolitan Museum of Art, New York;*

Christopher P. Monkhouse, *Curator of Decorative Arts, Museum of Art, The Rhode Island School of Design, Providence;*

Charles Parkhurst, *Assistant Director, National Gallery of Art, Washington, D.C.;*

David Parrish, *Registrar, Wadsworth Atheneum, Hartford;*

John W. Payson, *Hobe Sound Gallery, Florida;*

Ann Percy, *Curator, Department of Prints and Drawings, Philadelphia Museum of Art;*

John Rewald, *New York;*

Brenda Richardson, *Assistant Director, Baltimore Museum of Art;*

Joseph Rishel, *Curator of Paintings, Philadelphia Museum of Art;*

John R. Sale, *Wake Forest University, North Carolina;*

Mrs. Sam Salz, *New York;*

Robert Schmit, *Galerie Schmit, Paris;*

Karen Skubich, *Newberry Library, Chicago;*

Richard Sonn, *Itasca, Illinois;*

Marianne Stevens, *University of Kent;*

Jackie Stewart, *Sotheby Parke-Bernet, London;*

Martin Summers, *Alex Reid & Lefevre, Ltd., London;*

Louise Averill Svendsen, *Senior Curator, The Solomon R. Guggenheim Museum, New York*

John T. Tancock, *Sotheby Parke-Bernet, New York;*

Eugene Thaw, *New York;*

John Walsh, Jr., *Baker Curator of Paintings, Museum of Fine Arts, Boston;*

Mark Weil, *Washington University, St. Louis;*

Daniel Wildenstein, *Membre de l'Institut;*

Marke Zervudachi, *Director, Niarchos Limited, London.*

I am also indebted to the Reference Department Staff Joseph Regenstein Library, University of Chicago, and the Staff of the Interlibrary Loan Department and Special Collections Department, Northwestern University Library.

Lastly I wish to give special thanks to the trustees of the Société des Amis du Musée Toulouse-Lautrec in Albi and to the staff of the museum: Philippe Brame, Trustee; Jean Devoisins, Conservateur; Mlle. Volle, Secretary. Very special thanks are due Jean-Alain Méric and M. G. Dortu, the President of the Société, who shared their connoisseurship of Lautrec's work with me and contributed in fundamental ways to bring about the present exhibition.

CHARLES F. STUCKEY

The loan exhibition of paintings by Toulouse-Lautrec is supplemented by a group of prints and drawings, exclusively from the collection of the Art Institute.

Out of 365 prints listed by Loys Delteil (omitting 3 monotypes), The Art Institute owns 329, including all the major color lithographs. The collection was started in 1927 by Charles F. Glore with a gift of 93 lithographs. In the 1940's and 1950's, Carter H. Harrison, five times elected Mayor of Chicago, became the most enthusiastic and generous donor to that collection.

Carter Harrison was also among the donors of drawings by Toulouse-Lautrec, along with Leigh and Mary Block, Margaret Day Blake, B.E. Bensinger, and Helen Regenstein.

Harold Joachim
Curator of Prints and Drawings

PRINTS

1.* **Tristan Bernard,** 1898
Drypoint on zinc printed in brown, Delteil 9
No. 15 of 28 in the first edition
The Charles F.Glore Collection,
1946.452

2. **At the Moulin Rouge, La Goulue and her sister,** 1892
Lithograph, Delteil 11
The Charles F. Glore Collection
1946.449

3. **The Englishman at the Moulin Rouge,** 1892
Lithograph, Delteil 12
Gift of the Print and Drawing Club
1931.67

4. **The Theatre Box with the Gilded Mask,** 1893
Lithograph, Delteil 16, first of two states
Gift of Mrs. Gilbert W. Chapman
in Memory of Charles B. Goodspeed
1947.871

5. Cover of **L'Estampe Originale,** 1893
Lithograph, Delteil 17
The Charles F. Glore Collection
1932.1326

6. **For you!...**
Plate 2 of the series *Vieilles Histoires,* 1893
Lithograph, Delteil 19, first of two states
The Mr. and Mrs. Carter H. Harrison Collection
1931.27

7. **Jane Avril,** from the portfolio *Café Concert,* 1893
Lithograph, Delteil 28
The Albert H. Wolf Fund
1935.49

8. **Madame Abdala,** from the portfolio *Café Concert,* 1893
Lithograph, Delteil 33
The Mr. and Mrs. Carter H. Harrison Collection
1931.42

9. **Caudieux,** from the portfolio *Café Concert,* 1893
Lithograph, Delteil 35
Gift of Horace Swope
1931.20

10. **Miss Loie Fuller,** 1893
Lithograph, Delteil 39
The Joseph Brooks Fair Collection
1931.451

11.* **Sarah Bernhardt in "Phaedra,"** 1893
Lithograph, Delteil 47
Gift of Carl O. Schniewind
1944.459

12. **At the Opera: Mme Caron in "Faust,"** 1894
Lithograph, Delteil 49
The John H. Wrenn Memorial Collection
1953.366

13.* **Brandès and Leloir in "Les Cabotins,"** 1894
Lithograph, Delteil 62
The Charles F. Glore Collection
1927.902

14. **Une Redoute au Moulin Rouge,** 1894
Lithograph, Delteil 65
The Charles F. Glore Collection
1927.893

15. **At the Ambassadeurs,** 1894
Lithograph, Delteil 68
The Mr. and Mrs. Carter H. Harrison Collection
1951.7

16. **La Goulue,** 1894
Lithograph, Delteil 71, first of two states
The Charles Deering Collection
1927.6442

17. **Yvette Guilbert,** plates for the publication by
Gustave Geffroy of 1894
Eight lithographs in the first state before letters,
Delteil 81, 82, 84, 85, 86, 89, 91, and 96
The Mr. and Mrs. Carter H. Harrison Collection
1952.10-16 and 1950.1384

18. **Mlle Marcelle Lender, en buste,** 1895
Lithograph, Delteil 102, second of three states
The Charles F. Glore Collection
1927.986

19. **Mlle Marcelle Lender, Standing,** 1895
Lithograph printed from three stones, Delteil 103
(one of 12 impressions printed in color)
The Clarence Buckingham Collection
1959.544

20. **Cecy Loftus,** 1895
Lithograph, Delteil 116
The Charles F. Glore Collection
1927.988

21. **Miss May Belfort with Long Hair,** 1895
Lithograph, Delteil 118 (one of 20 impressions)
The Charles F. Glore Collection
1927.941

22. **Miss May Belfort** (The Large Plate), 1895
Lithograph, Delteil 119, first of two states
The John H. Wrenn Memorial Collection
1941.37

23.* **The Waltz of the Rabbits,** 1895
Lithograph, Delteil 143
The Charles F. Glore Collection
1935.53

24. **La Goulue before the Tribunal,** 1895
Lithograph, Delteil 148
The Charles F. Glore Collection
1927.965

25. **La Loge** (Faust), 1896
Lithograph, Delteil 166
The Charles F. Glore Collection
1927.912

26. **Leaving the Theatre,** 1896
Lithograph, Delteil 169
The Charles F. Glore Collection
1927.963

27. **Le Sommeil (Sleep),** 1896
Lithograph, Delteil 170, no. 6 of 12 impressions
The Mr. and Mrs. Carter H. Harrison Collection
1954.110

28. **Blanche et Noire,** 1896
Lithograph, Delteil 171, no. 9 of 12 impressions
The Clarence Buckingham Collection
1959.545

29. Frontispiece for the series *Elles,* 1896
Lithograph, Delteil 179
The Mr. and Mrs. Carter H. Harrison Collection
1927.972

30. **La clownesse assise** (Mlle Cha-u-ka-o),
from the series *Elles,* 1896
Lithograph, Delteil 180
The Charles F. Glore Collection
1927.970

31. **Woman with a Tray (Mme Baron and Mlle Popo),**
from the series *Elles,* 1896
Lithograph, Delteil 181
The Charles F. Glore Collection
1927.977

32. **Woman in Bed,** from the series *Elles,* 1896
Lithograph, Delteil 182
The Charles F. Glore Collection
1927.973

33. **Woman At the Tub,** from the series *Elles,* 1896
Lithograph, Delteil 183
The Charles F. Glore Collection
1927.978

34. **Woman Washing Herself,** from the series *Elles,* 1896
Lithograph, Delteil 184
The Charles F. Glore Collection
1927.975

35. **Woman with a Mirror,** from the series *Elles,* 1896
Lithograph, Delteil 185
The Charles F. Glore Collection
1927.979

36. **Woman Combing Her Hair,** from the series *Elles,* 1896
Lithograph, Delteil 186
The Charles F. Glore Collection
1927.976

37. **Woman in Bed,** from the series *Elles,* 1896
Lithograph, Delteil 187
The Charles F. Glore Collection
1927.971

38. **Woman Lacing her Corset,** from the series *Elles,* 1896
Lithograph, Delteil 188
The Charles F. Glore Collection
1927.974

39. **Woman Reclining,** from the series *Elles,* 1896
Lithograph, Delteil 189
The Charles F. Glore Collection
1927.980

40.* **Oscar Wilde and Romain Coolus,** 1896
Lithograph, Delteil 195, fourth of four states
Gift of Guy Mayer
1950.1390

41. **The Crocodile Menu,** 1896
Lithograph, Delteil 200, second of two states
The Charles F. Glore Collection
1927.903

42. **The Automobilist,** 1896
Lithograph, Delteil 203
The Charles F. Glore Collection
1927.915

43. **La Grande Loge,** 1897
Lithograph, Delteil 204,
no. 12 of 12 published impressions
The Mr. and Mrs. Carter H. Harrison Collection
1949.937

44. **La Clownesse au Moulin-Rouge,** 1897
Lithograph, Delteil 205,
no. 12 of 20 published impressions
The Mr. and Mrs. Carter H. Harrison Collection
1949.938

45. **Idylle Princière,** 1897
Lithograph, Delteil 206,
one of 16 published impressions
The William McCallin McKee Memorial Collection
1930.134

46. **Elsa, The Viennese,** 1897
Lithograph, Delteil 207,
no. 8 of 17 published impressions
The Mr. and Mrs. Carter H. Harrison Memorial Collection,
1958.529

47. **La Petite Loge**, 1897
Lithograph, Delteil 209, second of two states,
no. 5 of 12 published impressions
The Mr. and Mrs. Carter H. Harrison Collection
1940.948

48. **A la Souris (Mme Palmyre)**, 1897
Lithograph, Delteil 210, second of two states,
no. 4 of 25 published impressions
The William McCallin McKee Memorial Collection
1949.939

49. **The Tandem**, 1897
Lithograph with additions of watercolor, Delteil 218
The Olivia Shaler Swan Collection
1940.797

50. **Partie de Campagne**, 1897
Lithograph, Delteil 219
The John H. Wrenn Memorial Collection
1948.399

51. **In Bed**, 1898
Lithograph, Delteil 226
The Robert A. Waller Fund
1950.1447

52.* **La Fillette Nue, Menu**, 1898
Lithograph, Delteil 233
The Charles F. Glore Collection
1927.964

53.* **The Horse Connoisseur**, 1898
Lithograph, Delteil 234
Gift of Mrs. Cyrus H. Adams
1959.547

54.* **Yvette Guilbert**, Cover, 1898
Lithograph, Delteil 250
The William McCallin McKee Memorial Collection
1930.123

55. **The Dog and the Parrot**, 1899
Lithograph, Delteil 277, first of two states
The Charles F. Glore Collection
1927.896

56. **The Jockey**, 1899
Lithograph, Delteil 279, printed in color
The Mr. and Mrs. Carter H. Harrison Collection
1931.46

57. **The Jockey Returning to the Paddock**, 1899
Lithograph, Delteil 282, second of three states,
unique proof printed in color
The William McCallin McKee Memorial Collection
1930.135

58. **The Swoon**, 189?
Lithograph, Delteil 294, proof of an unpublished print
The Clarence Buckingham Collection
1959.548

59. **Moulin Rouge (La Goulue)**, 1891
Lithograph, Delteil 339, second of two states
The Mr. and Mrs. Carter H. Harrison Collection
1954.1193

60. **The Hanged Man**, 1892
Lithograph, Delteil 340, first of two states
The Mr. and Mrs. Carter H. Harrison Collection
1950.1465

61. **Divan Japonais**, 1892
Lithograph, Delteil 341
The Mr. and Mrs. Carter H. Harrison Collection
1949.1002

62. **Jane Avril**, 1893
Lithograph, Delteil 345
The Mr. and Mrs. Carter H. Harrison Collection
1949.1004

63. **Aristide Bruant dans son Cabaret**, 1893
Lithograph, Delteil 348, second of two states
The Mr. and Mrs. Carter H. Harrison Collection
1949.1005

64. **L'Artisan Moderne**, 1894
Lithograph, Delteil 350, third of three states
The Clarence Buckingham Collection
1932.1320

65. **Babylone d'Allemagne**, 1894
Lithograph, Delteil 351, second of two states
The Mr. and Mrs. Carter H. Harrison Collection
1949.1025

66. **Confetti**, 1894
Lithograph, Delteil 352
The Charles F. Glore Collection
1927.924

67. **The Photographer Sescau**, 1894
Lithograph, Delteil 353
The Clarence Buckingham Collection
1959.549

68. **La Revue Blanche**, 1895
Lithograph, Delteil 355, first of two states
The Clarence Buckingham Collection
1932.1322

69. **May Milton**, 1895
Lithograph, Delteil 356, second of two states
The Mr. and Mrs. Carter H. Harrison Collection
1948.451

70. **Napoléon**, 1895
Lithograph, Delteil 358
The Albert H. Wolf Memorial Collection
1941.127

71. **The Troupe of Mlle Eglantine**, 1896
Lithograph, Delteil 361, third of three states
The Mr. and Mrs. Carter H. Harrison Collection
1936.220

72. **Irish and American Bar, Rue Royale** (The Chap Book), 1896
Lithograph, Delteil 362, second of two states
The Mr. and Mrs. Carter H. Harrison Collection
1931.48

73. **La Vache Enragée**, 1896
Lithograph, Delteil 364, second of two states
The William McCallin McKee Memorial Collection
1947.121

74. **The Passenger in Chair 54** (or **Yachting**), 1896
Lithograph with additions of watercolor, Delteil 366,
first of two states
The John H. Wrenn Memorial Collection
1949.936

75. **The Passenger in Chair 54** (or **Yachting**), 1896
Lithograph, Delteil 366, first of two states
The Mr. and Mrs. Carter H. Harrison Collection
1938.1254

DRAWINGS

76. **The Model Nizzavona,** ca. 1882-83
    Charcoal with estompe, on white laid paper
    The Mr. and Mrs. Carter H. Harrison Collection
    1933.881

77. **Bar of the Café de la Rue de Rome,** ca. 1886
    Charcoal with estompe and scraping, heightened
    with white chalk, on ivory wove paper
    The Mr. and Mrs. Carter H. Harrison Collection
    1933.879

78. **At the Door,** ca. 1887
    Blue crayon and brush with black wash, heightened
    with white gouache, on buff wove paper
    The Helen Regenstein Collection
    1965.22

79. **Le Père Cotelle, the Lithographer,** ca. 1893
    Charcoal with red and blue crayons,
    on tan wove paper
    The Mr. and Mrs. Carter H. Harrison Collection
    1933.880

80. **La Macarona in the Costume of a Jockey,** 1893
    Watercolor and oil, over charcoal,
    on tan tracing paper
    Gift of Mrs. Leigh B. Block
    1954.22

81.* **Head of Yvette Guilbert,** ca. 1894
    Graphite, on ivory wove paper
    The Albert H. Wolf Memorial Collection
    1941.132

82. **The Cortege of the Rajah,** ca. 1895
    Black and blue crayons, on cream wove paper
    The Worcester Sketch Fund
    1959.81

83. **The King's Card Game,** ca. 1895
    Brush and gray wash with watercolor and
    black crayon, on ivory wove paper
    The Helen Regenstein Collection
    1969.271

84. **Mlle Polaire,** 1895
    Brush with black ink, over charcoal, heightened
    with white gouache, on tan tracing paper
    Gift of Robert Allerton
    1925.1547

85.* **Sailboats,** 1899
    Brush and gray wash, on ivory wove paper
    The Mr. and Mrs. Lewis L. Coburn Memorial Collection
    1933.528

86. **At the Circus; Work in the Ring,** 1899
    Colored pencil with pastel and black crayon,
    on ivory wove paper
    Gift of Mr. and Mrs. B.E. Bensinger
    1972.1167

87. **At the Circus; Trained Pony and Baboon,** ca. 1899
    Black chalk with estompe, colored crayons
    and graphite, on ivory wove paper
    The Margaret Day Blake Collection
    1944.581

88. **Mlle Cocyte,** 1900
    Red chalk and graphite, heightened with white chalk,
    on ivory wove paper
    The Helen Regenstein Collection
    1965.146

*Due to unexpected space limitations, these pieces have
been eliminated from the exhibition.

Lenders

Aberdeen Art Gallery and Museum
Musée d'Albi
Albright-Knox Art Gallery, Buffalo
The Honorable Walter H. Annenberg
The Art Institute of Chicago
Baldwin M. Baldwin Foundation Collection
Kunstmuseum, Bern
Mr. and Mrs. Leigh B. Block, Chicago
Maître Maxime Blum, Paris
Museum of Art, Carnegie Institute, Pittsburgh
Columbus Museum of Art
Mr. Nathan Cummings, New York
Mr. Alain Delon, Paris
The Denver Art Museum
The FORBES Magazine Collection, New York
Mr. Léon Fromer, New York
Former Hahnloser Collection, Winterthur
The Armand Hammer Collection
Alan and Simone Hartman
Joseph H. Hazen, New York
The Alex Hillman Family Foundation
The Museum of Fine Arts, Houston
Mr. Harold F. Johnson, Southampton
The Los Angeles County Museum of Art

Musée du Louvre, Galerie du Jeu de Paume, Paris
The Metropolitan Museum of Art, New York
The Museum of Modern Art, New York
Dr. Peter Nathan, Zurich
Neue Pinakothek, Munich
The Newark Museum
Stavros S. Niarchos Collection
Henry and Rose Pearlman Foundation
Musée du Petit Palais
Philadelphia Museum of Art
The Phillips Family Collection
Rijksmuseum Kröller-Müller, Otterlo
Rijksmuseum Vincent van Gogh, Amsterdam
Museum of Art, Rhode Island School of Design, Providence
Mrs. Paul Sampliner
Sterling and Francine Clark Art Institute, Williamstown, Massachusetts
Steven Straw Company, Inc., Newburyport
Mr. Yasuo Suita
Mrs. C. van der Waals-Koenigs
Wadsworth Atheneum, Hartford
Kunsthaus, Zurich
Private Collectors

Bibliographic References

All bibliographic references in the text and catalogue entries have been abbreviated for convenience. The following list indicates our abbreviations along with complete references to those works.

We have omitted full bibliographic information and exhibition histories from our catalogue entries, because that information is available in M.G. DORTU's catalogue of Lautrec's works cited below. To refer to works of art not included in our exhibition we have used her system of classification: "P.," "S.P.," "A.," "D.," or "S.D.,"followed by a number. For example, "D.467" refers to the work so designated in Dortu's catalogue.

ADHÉMAR — Adhémar, Jean. *Toulouse-Lautrec: His Complete Lithographs and Drypoints*. New York, 1965.

COMTESSE ATTEMS — Attems, Comtesse. *Notre Oncle Lautrec*. Geneva, 1963.

COOPER — Cooper, Douglas. *Henri de Toulouse-Lautrec*. New York, 1956.

COQUIOT — Coquiot, Gustave. *Lautrec ou quinze ans de moeurs parisiennes, 1885-1900*. Paris, 1921.

CORR. — *Unpublished Correspondence of Henri de Toulouse-Lautrec*. Edited by Lucien Goldschmidt and Herbert Schimmel. Introduction by Jean Adhémar and Theodore Reff. London, 1969.

L.D. — Delteil, Loys. *Le Peintre-graveur illustré*. Vols. IX and X: *Henri de Toulouse Lautrec*. Paris, 1920.

DORTU — Dortu, M. G. *Toulouse-Lautrec et son oeuvre*. Six vols. New York, 1971.

DORTU, GRILLAERT AND ADHÉMAR — Dortu, M. G., Grillaert, Madeline, and Adhémar, Jean. *Toulouse-Lautrec en Belgique*. Paris, 1955.

DURET — Duret, Théodore. *Lautrec*. Paris, 1920.

GAUZI — Gauzi, Francois. *Lautrec et son temps*. Paris, 1954.

GEORGES-MICHEL — Georges-Michel, Georges. *Les Peintres que j'ai connus*. Paris, 1954.

JOHNSON — Johnson, Lincoln F. "Time and Motion in Toulouse-Lautrec" *College Art Journal*. Vol. XVI (1956-1957), pp. 13-22.

JASPER — Jasper, Gertrude R. *Adventure in the theatre: Lugné-Poë and Théâtre de l'Oeuvre to 1899*. New Brunswick, 1947.

JEDLICKA — Jedlicka, Gotthard. *Henri de Toulouse-Lautrec*. Berlin, 1929.

JOURDAIN AND ADHÉMAR — Jourdain, Francis and Adhémar, Jean. *Toulouse-Lautrec*. New York, 1952.

JOYANT — Joyant, Maurice. *Henri de Toulouse-Lautrec*. Two vols. Paris, 1926-1927.

LECLERCQ — Leclercq, Paul. *Autour de Toulouse-Lautrec*. Geneva, 1954.

MACK — Mack, Gerstle. *Toulouse-Lautrec*. New York, 1938.

MATRINCHARD — Matrinchard, Robert. *Princeteau 1843-1914*. No publisher or date.

MATISSE — Matisse, Henri. *Ecrits et propos sur l'art*. Paris, 1972.

MURRAY — Murray, Gale B. "Review of M. G. Dortu, *Toulouse-Lautrec et son oeuvre*." *The Art Bulletin*. Vol. LX, March 1978, pp. 179-182.

NATANSON, 1950 Natanson, Thadée. "Toulouse-Lautrec: The Man." *Art News Annual.* November, 1950, pp. 77-84.

NATANSON, 1951 Natanson, Thadée. *Un Henri de Toulouse-Lautrec.* Geneva, 1951.

PERRUCHOT Perruchot, Henri. *Toulouse-Lautrec.* Translated by Humphrey Ware. New York, 1962.

POLÁŜEK Poláŝek, Jan. *Toulouse-Lautrec, Drawings.* New York, 1975.

RENARD Renard, Jules. *The Journal.* Edited and translated by Louise Bogan and Elizabeth Roget. New York, 1964.

RIVOIRE, 1901 Rivoire, André. "Henri de Toulouse." *Revue de l'art.* December 1901, pp. 391-400.

RIVOIRE, 1902 idem., *Revue de l'art.* April 1902, pp. 247-262.

ROTHSTEIN Rothenstein, William. *Men and Memories, 1872-1900.* New York, 1931.

SCHAUB-KOCH Schaub-Koch, Emile. *Psychanalyse d'un peintre moderne: Henri de Toulouse Lautrec.* Paris, 1935.

SERT Sert, Misia. *Two or Three Muses.* trans. by Moura Budbers. London, 1953.

SUGANA Sugana, G. M. *L'opera completa di Toulouse-Lautrec.* Milan, 1977.

SUTTON Sutton, Denys. "Some Aspects of Toulouse-Lautrec." *Connoisseur Yearbook,* 1956, pp. 71-76.

SYMONS Symons, Arthur. *From Toulouse-Lautrec to Rodin with some personal impressions.* New York, 1930.

VAN GOGH van Gogh, Vincent. *The Complete Letters of Vincent van Gogh.* Three vols. Translated by C. de Dood, Amsterdam. New York, 1953.

VUILLARD Vuillard, Edouard, as told to Germain Bazin. "Lautrec raconté par Vuillard." *L'Amour de l'art.* Vol. 12, April 1931, pp. 141-142.

WAGNER Wagner, Hugo. "Madame Misia Natanson au piano, 1897." *Berner Kunstmitteilungen.* Vol. 184, August-September 1978, pp. 8-10.

WATTENMAKER Wattenmaker, Richard J. *Puvis de Chavannes and The Modern Tradition.* Art Gallery of Ontario, 1975.

WEINTRAUB Weintraub, Stanley. *Beardsley, a biography.* New York, 1967.

WICK Wick, Peter, introduction. *Yvette Guilbert.* Text by Gustave Geffroy. Illustrated by Henri de Toulouse-Lautrec. New York, 1968.

Models and Spectators in the Art of Lautrec

Henri de Toulouse-Lautrec was born in 1864 into one of France's most ancient and distinguished families. His Christian name was chosen out of respect for the Comte de Chambord, that lingering pretender to the monarchy founded by Henri IV in the sixteenth century. If his family stubbornly hoped for the reestablishment of a discarded social order, however, the artist celebrated the spectacle of ordinary life in modern France and glorified even the most vulgar members of its Republic in stately designs and precious tapestries of color fit for counts and countesses. The "bohemian" artist both enjoyed and spoofed his incongruous ancestry. For example, he signed one of his portraits "H. Quatre" ("H. Four"), as if the Roman numeral "IV" were a common French surname (cat. no. 48).

Lautrec himself claimed that he would have been more of a nobleman and far less of an artist if he were not crippled. His legs ceased to develop after the age of thirteen, when accidental bone fractures revealed that he suffered from a disfiguring genetic abnormality, the cruel heritage of parents who were first cousins. The stunted child increasingly devoted himself to art and achieved a virtuosity which would bring him far greater respect than any aristocratic title. As the author Jules Renard noted in his diary (p. 69) early in 1895: "Toulouse-Lautrec. The oftener you see him, the taller he grows. He ends up by being taller than average." The towering impression he made was partly the result of his curiosity and the piercing scrutiny with which he satiated it. Partly it was the intensity with which he participated in life's revels and sorrows. But Lautrec's sense of his own physical insufficiency and his sympathy for human sadness led him to feed on alcohol, which quickly disabled and then destroyed him at the age of thirty-seven. His life was short, but his art remains far "taller than average."

Lautrec began formal art studies in 1882. Under the guidance of Bonnat and Cormon, award-winning Academic artists, he learned how to render proportionally correct three-dimensional models with carefully modulated tonal gradations (cat. nos. 14, 15). He mastered these fundamentals quickly and proceeded to the next stage of Academic instruction, the invention of harmoniously composed allegorical scenes, such as *The spring of life* (cat. no. 16). But Lautrec was inclined by nature against idealistic art. In 1881 he had confided to a childhood friend, "I have tried to draw something real, not something ideal" (Mack, p. 32).

Exposed to the controversies of the Parisian art world during the following years, Lautrec's disposition sympathized with such maverick artists as Manet, Degas and Renoir, whose individualistic styles ignored the inflexible Academic standards of compositional organization, finish, and elevated subject matter. Like so many students of his generation, Lautrec became convinced that the finest art was based upon principles unacknowledged in art schools. He therefore supplemented his education with the advice of independent painters who introduced him to exciting new directions in art. A close association with

Jean-Louis Forain (Gauzi, p. 144) sensitized Lautrec to the pictorial richness of sordid dressing room and cabaret scenes (fig. 1). And at Renoir's invitation, Lautrec made frequent visits to his atelier, where he encountered the bold colors and simple everyday subjects which the Impressionists had developed outside of official sanctions (Natanson, 1951, p. 14). Renoir and such colleagues as Manet and Degas immediately became touchstones for Lautrec's own unique insights and the unconventional pictorial means he developed in order to express them. As his companion Arthur Symons (p. 2) noted, Lautrec was "the Painter who has learnt from Manet and Degas: who yet remains insolently original."

Like his new associates, Lautrec insisted that artistic truth was necessarily predicated on familiarity with and participation in whatever scenes an artist chose to depict. He proclaimed his irreverant disapproval of idealized truths when he organized his fellow students to parody Puvis de Chavannes' *The sacred wood* (cat. no. 21), the most highly acclaimed work exhibited at the state-sponsored Salon in 1884. In their version of Puvis' pastorale, a group of top-hatted artists and gadabouts trespass on the Muses' sacrosanct grove, and an anachronistic clock added to the monumental arch at the center of the picture suggests the absurdity of timeless subject matter.

During the same year Lautrec began a dedicated study of tough Montmartre cabarets, even though he found them distasteful at first. He was motivated by important convictions which had been systematically formulated by Baudelaire in the early 1860s. In his persuasive essay "The Painter of Modern Life," Baudelaire encouraged artists to leave their secluded studios and go into the midst of crowds where they could study the customs, gestures and appearances of modern times, the beauties of make-up and the elegant pretense of fashions. According to Baudelaire, art could express truth and beauty only if it was based upon the direct experience of life, for the transient aspects of observed reality formed the basis of all enduring artistic values. In order to capture contemporary life directly from personal experience, without the prejudice of particular canons of taste, Baudelaire wanted artists to look at life with the wonder of a child instead of with the presumptions of an adult. Sincere art should record a visual world in which the artist participated on equal terms with his models and patrons. If that world did not stand still to pose, the artist might have to abbreviate his techniques and style, as newspaper illustrators did.

Lautrec's earliest cabaret subjects (fig. 2; cat. nos. 24, 25) are rendered with rapid, sketchy strokes like those used by commercial illustrators unconcerned with Academic conventions. Writing to his grandmother, Lautrec characterized his new artistic activities as "outside the law" (Huisman and Dortu, p. 45). His phrase refers both to the unacceptable moral standards of Montmartre society and to his departure from the rules which were the basis of formal art education. These rules were codified to guarantee the illusionistic description of physical reality. The harshly drawn forms and jarring colors of

Fig. 1
Forain, *At the café* , undated, 0.24 x 0.34 m., watercolor
Private collection

Fig. 2
Toulouse-Lautrec, *In a café*
1887, 0.50 x 0.44 m., peinture à l'essence on board
Private collection

Lautrec's unorthodox pictures, however, both describe the scene and evoke its vice-charged atmosphere through expressive distortions.

Lautrec's fundamental artistic goal would always be the pictorial expression of emotional realities which underlie human experience. It was a goal shared by many of Lautrec's extraordinary contemporaries, particularly van Gogh and Gauguin, and they were fascinated by Seurat and Signac's systematic investigation of the inherent emotional forces in individual colors, lines and shapes, which in themselves expressed a spectrum of distinct moods. They agreed, for example, that green, blue and purple evoked melancholy and inhibition, whereas red, orange and yellow suggested warmth and joy. They also attributed abstract emotional content to the directional orientation of lines: upward slanting or rising lines conveyed pleasure, and descending lines depression.

As did Lautrec, Seurat and his associates sought to intensify colors so as to represent the full vibrancy of the lighting conditions they observed, a fundamental goal inherited from the Impressionists. Seurat advocated both the juxtaposition of areas of complementary colors and the general interweaving of complementaries into any given area of a picture. Since complementaries intensify one another, Seurat's theories made it possible to imitate more closely than before the coloristic vibrancy of observed reality. Juxtaposed complementaries likewise enhance the psychological properties of colors chosen to define distinct emotional states. Inspired by Seurat's investigations, Lautrec explored a new repertoire of expressive means beginning in the mid-1880s. For example, he used a predominantly blue-green tonality to describe the melancholy of *At the Moulin de la Galette* (cat. no. 38). The few carefully placed complementary orange-red accents intensify the dreary mood, as does the plunging diagonal in the foreground.

Lautrec's understanding of the expressive qualities of line and color was enriched by his interest in non-Academic representational conventions. He was a connoisseur of Japanese graphics, which he appreciated for their expressive distortions of anatomy and space, their decorative juxtapositions of high-valued colors and their simplified compositions. In comparison with Academic art, Japanese stylistic devices, as well as medieval and early Renaissance ones, or those of provincial and commercial artists, were generally characterized as "naïve" or "primitive." These diverse representational systems tended to simplify and synthesize complicated visual experiences into decorative compositions. "Naïve" artists accentuated significant characteristics of their subjects, eliminated extraneous details and artfully distorted space, form and color for expressive ends. Unconcerned with photographic illusionism, "naïve" art emphasized the flatness of forms. Lautrec deeply admired a portrait previously attributed to Piero della Francesca (fig. 3), for example, because of its simplified, flattened silhouette, which he compared with the bold painted panels fashioned by artisans for carriage doors (Joyant, I, p. 172).

Fig. 3
Baldovinetti, *Portrait of a lady in yellow*
c. 1450, 0.63 x 0.41 m., tempera on panel
National Gallery, London

He used the profile idiom of Piero's portrait and similar "naïve" works increasingly during the later 1880s (figs. 4, 5), a preference which was shared by his closest associates. Indeed, models with particularly striking features reappear in pictures by different painters, each of whom recognized the heraldic elegance of "primitive" art in the same distinguished profile. For example, the most prominent figure in Lautrec's *At the Moulin Rouge: the dance* (fig. 6) also posed in profile for his friend Anquetin (fig. 7).

If the profile pose is inherently simple and decoratively abstract, it is also emotionally blank, because profile views severely limit the observation of facial expressions. Lautrec's preference for the pose, therefore, seems to contradict his fundamental aim to find pictorial means to represent psychological truths. Lautrec's art, however, is rich in seeming contradictions. Judging from a group of portraits taken in profile, Lautrec adopted the pose precisely for its neutrality, which placed the burden of emotional characterization entirely upon his organization of the abstract visual details he chose for costumes and settings (cat. nos. 13, 26, 31).

Stiffly formal, the profile pose is hardly the best idiom with which to convey the random appearance of candidly observed realities. Since Lautrec placed a premium on candor, it would seem at first that he should have avoided profiles. But he realized that contrasted informality and formality intensify one another as surely as juxtaposed complementary colors heighten vibrancy. *At the Moulin Rouge: the dance* (fig. 6) is illustrative of his developed thought about the interrelationship of unrehearsed behavior and pose in his art. The model's bright pink dress stands out amidst the generally drab cabaret clientele, none of whom appears to take notice of her. The other figures taken together represent a cross-section of directly observed cabaret activities, dancers, passersby, and clusters of friends. It is as if Lautrec chose to reproduce a random scene, no matter who entered or departed from his field of vision, since the men on the left are arbitrarily cropped by the frame. Yet no matter how candidly observed her counterparts may appear, the woman in pink seems intrusively posed, a note of calculated artifice in what otherwise pretends to be an unadjusted record of contemporary life. The apparent discrepancy, however, was purposeful.

Lautrec did not interject meaningless anomalies into his art. The nature of poses raised profound questions: whether art could depict observed reality truthfully, and how it might succeed in doing so. Painters who sought to capture directly observed experience could not unfold an easel at a cabaret and depend upon the clientele to stay put for however long an artist needed to finish a painting. Consequently, any picture unavoidably falsified observed experience. Although Lautrec sketched copious notes for even the most minute details of a work (fig. 8) prior to beginning it, he had to execute the final version at his studio, and to rely upon memory, photographs and hired models. Since he and his associates desired truth in

Fig. 4
Toulouse-Lautrec, *Gabrielle, the dancer*
1891, 0.67 x 0.53 m., peinture à l'essence on board
National Gallery, London

Fig. 5
Toulouse-Lautrec, *Hélène Vary*
1888, 0.75 x 0.50 m., peinture à l'essence on board
Kunsthalle, Bremen

Fig. 7
Anquetin, *Girl reading a newspaper*
1890, 0.54 x 0.44 m., pastel
The Tate Gallery, London

Fig. 6
Toulouse-Lautrec, *At the Moulin Rouge: the dance*
1890, 1.15 x 1.50 m., oil on canvas
Henry P. McIlhenny Collection, Philadelphia

Fig. 8
Toulouse-Lautrec, *Dancers and feet*
undated, ink on graph paper
Courtesy of The Boston Public Library, Print Department

their art, hiring models to dress and pose as if they were at a specific locale amounted to a hypocrisy that adulterated their elusive goal. Lautrec, who went so far as to equip his studio with cabaret tables for props, had pangs of conscience about tricks of the trade which made a travesty of candor, and he determined to unmask his props and poses, at least in part. For pictures such as *Waiting at Grenelle* (cat. no. 29) he troubled to pose a model collapsed in boredom, as if one saw her at a café in Montmartre. But behind her he included studio bric-a-brac unlike any ever seen in a café. Similarly, for *The seated dancer* he hired a model to pose dressed as a ballerina, and then painted her seated purposelessly on his studio couch (cat. no. 23). These paintings seem to depict two mutually exclusive realities or what is called absurdity, which may often be the most respectable truth. Lautrec's art is seasoned with provocative "mistakes." It is preposterous for *Berthe la sourde* (cat. no. 41) to be wearing a hat and clutching an umbrella inside Lautrec's studio, where their only rationale is that of props. Henri Dihau's portrait (cat. no. 43) is no less eccentric. Saluting a hypothetical being not included in the picture, it is as if Dihau has lost his senses, as if everyone has left him holding an empty gesture.

It is Lautrec's sense of humor which distinguished his art from that of his great contemporaries, Gauguin and van Gogh. Lautrec's humor gives his work an extra fullness, a tenderness, and an extra degree of insight into human nature. Absurdities and paradox magnetized him, as they do all philosophers and poets. In their earnest searches after truth both Gauguin and van Gogh with-

drew from Paris where it seemed to them that fashions and rehearsed behavior obscured the candor of basic emotions. Neither of them could appreciate, as Lautrec could, the paradox of a fashionably dressed woman who poses while participating in a real-life situation, like the woman in *At the Moulin Rouge: the dance* (fig. 6). They preferred the less urbane models of provincial Arles or Tahiti, where they felt they could better study unpretentious human nature. For Lautrec, however, truth and deceit were integrated indivisibly. Like Degas and Manet, he preferred subjects which were at once candid and posed. They understood that observed truth is characteristically alloyed with delusion, and that masks and postures reveal something of what they cover.

Models in unlikely settings and unmotivated poses upset habitual expectations, and the artificial locales Lautrec chose to depict exaggerate the candor of the emotions he observed there. Lost in meditation at crowded cabarets or brothels, Lautrec's figures are seldom fully conscious of their surroundings and often emotionally disassociated from them. Jane Avril (cat. no. 50) paces somnambulistically outside of the Moulin Rouge where the sparkling setting mocks her somber mood. The other figures in the painting, whose presence should alleviate the emptiness, instead magnify it by turning their backs to walk away. Lautrec's portrait of his favorite cousin Gabriel (fig. 9) is founded on a similar rupture between character and setting, as Denys Sutton (p. 76) has noticed: "Is it only one's fancy, or is it symbolical of his nature, that he leaves the theatre at such a moment? As if to suggest the life—the life of the theatre—can proceed without him? The stridency of the red carpet, the theatre's ordinary drugget, lends weight to the painting's inner meaning: the emotional discord between the departing figure and his surroundings." Most extraordinary of all is Lautrec's portrait of the caustic humorist Tristan Bernard planted before the endless circular track at the Velodrome Buffalo (cat. no. 76). He faces the empty grandstand as if listening to some distant echo of spectators who have gone away, and their absence haunts his presence. The influential critic Octave Mirbeau recognized this poetry in Lautrec's art and dubbed him "the painter of uneasy conscience" (Schaub-Koch, p. 99).

Close friends reported that Lautrec thoroughly familiarized himself with any given sitter or milieu and plotted every detail of a picture in his mind, sometimes over a period of years, before beginning to paint (for example, Rivoire, 1901, p. 398). The result of his extensive analysis is an art charged with innuendo. The saucers carelessly stacked in the immediate foreground of *At the Moulin de la Galette* (cat. no. 38) are as expressive as any of the isolated figures. Each saucer counts a drink, reordered and emptied to fill the boring hours of unalleviated anticipation. The coat hanging limply behind Jane Avril (fig. 10) seems to escort her, but with emptiness. Lautrec's writer friend Jules Renard claimed that a book could be written on the back of each of Lautrec's portraits. (Schaub-Koch, p. 128). Although Lautrec's pictures are seldom

Fig. 9
Toulouse-Lautrec, *Doctor Tapié de Céleyran in a theater corridor*
1894, 1.10 x 0.56 m., oil on canvas
Musée d'Albi

Fig. 10
Toulouse-Lautrec, *Jane Avril entering the Moulin Rouge*
1892, 1.02 x 0.55 m., peinture à l'essence on board
The Courtauld Institute of Art, London

Fig. 11
Cranach, *Portrait of Johannes Scheuring*
1529, 0.52 x 0.35 m., oil on panel
Musées Royaux des Beaux-Arts de Belgique, Brussels

anecdotal or narrative, his uncanny pictorial descriptions of cabarets, brothels and theaters are comparable to chapters in "naturalist" novels, and his output taken as a whole is comparable to panoramic modern-life literary epics like Balzac's *Comédie Humaine* and Zola's *Rougon-Macquart*. His companions, many of them writers, were impressed with Lautrec's complete familiarity with modern literature, in particular the works of Balzac.

Lautrec had a connoisseur's knowledge of all kinds of art and tirelessly studied in museums. Frequently locales or individuals reminded him of his favorite images, and when they did, his pictures amount to double perceptions, as if memory transfigured his immediate visual experience. Jane Avril's fur collar recalled a portrait by Cranach (fig. 11) which he admired deeply, and the memory of it dominated Lautrec's portrait of her (fig. 12), even if a later addition to the picture (fig. 10) diminished the similarities which initially sparked his imagination. Natanson (1950, p. 81) remembered that "Lautrec loved to do take-offs on other artists and, if he had an audience, he would produce them on request." When the painter indulged himself in renditions of other artists' compositional idiosyncracies he did so lightheartedly, but with respect. Degas was his favorite artist, and his favorite target (cat. nos. 22, 44, 95). Occasionally Lautrec "quoted" poses from respected masterpieces to dignify subject matter which contemporaries found vulgar. For example, almost all of his brothel pictures are related to well-known images by old masters, such as Carpaccio (cat. no. 75), Rembrandt (cat. no. 72), Velasquez (cat. no. 79) and Goya (figs. 13, 14).

Superimposing memories of art upon his observations of brothel routine is but one aspect of Lautrec's sense of masquerade. According to Natanson (1950, p. 81) and other witnesses, he loved "Mardi Gras disguises." Although his impish fun disturbed Mallarmé, who was insulted by Lautrec's impersonation of him (Sert, p. 41), the playfulness amused most friends, and several were drawn into his games. Joyant, for example, agreed to pose as an American fisherman (cat. no. 104). Leclercq evidently never fulfilled Lautrec's desire to paint him as a marquis from the time of Louis XIV, however, a role for which the artist found him to be ideally suited (Natanson, 1951, p. 14). Lautrec delighted in casting friends in inappropriate roles: his dignified cousin Gabriel, for instance, had to endure posing as an unrestrained womanizer (cat. no. 99). Lautrec summoned delusions like an alchemist to transmute reality, and his world is populated with impostors, actors, clowns, and faces distorted into grotesque masks.

Lautrec was a tireless spectator of the human comedy and his deepest sympathy often went out to fellow spectators, like himself vulnerable to hopeful misperceptions. Their glances and stares scatter desire, jealousy and introspection throughout his pictures. Lautrec observed jealous men watching other men take the notice of a desirable woman (fig. 2), and jealous women helplessly witnessing

Fig. 12
Toulouse-Lautrec, *Jane Avril entering the Moulin Rouge,*
detail of painting before addition at the bottom
1892, peinture à l'essence on board
The Courtauld Institute of Art, London

Fig. 13
Goya, *It is nicely stretched*
1799, 0.25 x 0.15 m., etching, burnished aquatint and burin
The Art Institute of Chicago, The Clarence Buckingham Collection

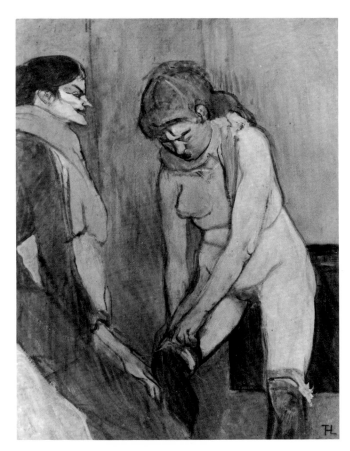

Fig. 14
Toulouse-Lautrec, *Woman adjusting her stocking*
1894, 0.60 x 0.50 m., peinture à l'essence on board
Musée du Louvre, Paris

friends who fall prey to mesmerizing lechery (fig. 15). He watched women looking at men who were turned to look at other women, themselves oblivious to being watched, hypnotized by someone else, somewhere else in a crowded hall. In Lautrec's pictures glances are only seldom acknowledged or returned. Instead, he diagrams the routines of curiosity and anticipation he observed at public places. Turned, magnetized by something that they see, Lautrec's figures are alter egos to his own unnoticed scrutiny. As for his paintings' eventual viewers, their act of observation is ultimately mimicked by that of the figures they look upon.

Lautrec frequently set figures at tables placed immediately in his paintings' foregrounds, as if to suggest that the spectator sits or stands across from them, joins them in imagination and fulfills the otherwise unresolved circumstances in which Lautrec posed them. "Cropped" subjects, fragments of activity, pointedly energize the passive role assumed by people looking at pictures. In his portrait, Mr. Fourcade (fig. 16) seems to be absent-mindedly approaching the painting's foremost plane, unaware of the invisible barrier separating his pictorial world from our own. His face presses forward and confronts the spectator's at close range, an implied relationship which repeats the face-offs in which all the other figures in the picture are engaged. Mr. Fourcade's portrait is an attempted intrusion of painted fiction into the traditional hegemony of spectators.

In other cases, Lautrec filled his foregrounds with participants and spectators seen from the rear, and beyond them depicted whatever spectacle they observe. Looking at these pictures involves imaginary participation as part of an audience at a theater, side-show (fig. 17), or medical demonstrations (fig. 18). Implied spectator participation was a fundamental goal of almost every "realist" or "naturalist" artist, including, of course, Manet, the Impressionists and the Neo-Impressionists (fig. 19). Most often they, too, attained the goal of heightened illusionism with "cropped" themes, or points of view associated by habit with specific locales where an observer could imagine himself to be. For example, a picture of a performer on stage observed from below or above not only depicts the performer but also simultaneously "implies" the point of view of someone in the audience. Imagining a specific point of view inevitably extends the illusion of a viewer's on-the-spot observation. The background of *Au Cirque Fernando* (cat. no. 32) is the opposite side of an arena where members of the audience "reflect" the activity and physical locale presumed by any observer of the picture.

All of these conceits allowed Lautrec to incorporate observers into his paintings as themselves, in their role as observers. Since visual experience incorporates that which is seen and the awareness of seeing it, art which does not take the context of experience into account is only a half-truth. Looking at looking is perhaps the basic theme of Lautrec's art. Mr. Samary, the actor, addresses an audience, the absence of which suggests that the viewer is part of that missing audience and therefore part of the picture (cat. no. 37). Eyeing the audience through his

Fig. 15
Toulouse-Lautrec, *The Englishman at the Moulin Rouge*
1892, 0.86 x 0.66 m., peinture à l'essence on board
The Metropolitan Museum of Art, New York

Fig. 16
Toulouse-Lautrec, *Mr. Fourcade*
1889, 0.77 x 0.62 m., oil on board
Musée d'art, São Paulo

Fig. 18
Toulouse-Lautrec, *Dr. Péan performing a tracheotomy*
1891, 0.74 x 0.50 m., oil on board
Sterling and Francine Clark Art Institute, Williamstown

Fig. 17
Toulouse-Lautrec, *Decorative painting for La Goulue's side show tent*
1895, 3.00 x 3.00 m., oil on canvas
Musée du Louvre, Paris

Fig. 19
Seurat, *Invitation to the side show (La parade)*
1888, 1.00 x 1.50 m., oil on canvas
The Metropolitan Museum of Art, New York

monocle, Mr. Samary is typical of Lautrec's figures posed in the visual act. In theaters, cabarets or brothels, Lautrec's models regard their surroundings and are transfixed by what they observe. Sometimes their stares testify to basic motives, such as desire or jealousy; and Lautrec seldom missed the opportunity to suggest symbolically how observation arouses fantasy. Canes protruding from men's laps are emblems for hidden reactions of voyeurism. Other figures preen at mirrors (fig. 20 and cat. no. 99), like deceitful narcissists setting traps for voyeurs, or they pause at mirrors, stunned by the impact of self-awareness (cat. nos. 3, 96). The most abject of Lautrec's characters stare blankly at nothing (cat. nos. 97, 108). Unaware that they are being observed, their private meditation is witnessed but not understood. Lautrec had the profound insight to scrutinize people looking, or as they follow their thoughts along the paths of glances over shoulders and across rooms, or tracked backwards into private reveries. Confronting the visual act increases our awareness of all that it can mean to see, and this was Lautrec's poetry.

CHARLES F. STUCKEY

Fig. 20
Toulouse-Lautrec, *Prostitute adjusting her chignon*
1893, 0.65 x 0.31 m., peinture à l'essence on board
Private collection, New York

Color Plates

PLATE I   Nude in black stockings, 1882

PLATE 2 Count Alphonse, 1883

PLATE 3   At the Moulin de la Galette, 1885

PLATE 4   The laundress, 1886-87

PLATE 5   Madame the countess, 1887

PLATE 6   Mr. Samary, 1889

PLATE 7   At the Moulin de la Galette, 1889

PLATE 8   Redhead in Mr. Forest's garden, 1889

PLATE 9   Dr. Bourges, 1891

PLATE 10 At the Nouveau Cirque: the clowness before five shirtfronts, 1892

PLATE 11   Woman at the window, 1893

PLATE 12   Interior in the rue des Moulins, 1894

PLATE 13   Abandon, 1895

PLATE 14   Dancer, 1896

PLATE 15   Misia at the piano, 1897-98

PLATE 16   Woman in a nightgown, 1898

PLATE 17   Interval at a masked ball, 1899

PLATE 18   Mr. Viaud, 1900

PLATE 19 The milliner, 1900

PLATE 20   Woman adjusting her nightgown, 1900

Catalogue

Height precedes width in all entries. Rather than include extensive bibliographic references and exhibition histories, we refer the specialized reader to M. G. Dortu, *Toulouse-Lautrec et son oeuvre,* Six vols., New York, 1971, where such information is available.

Entries are initialled by:
E.M.M. Evan M. Maurer
N.E.M. Naomi E. Maurer
C.F.S. Charles F. Stuckey

01

Artilleur sellant son cheval

Gunner saddling his horse

1879

0.505, 0.375 m.; 19⅞, 14⅞ in.

Oil on canvas

Dortu, 1971: P.13

Musée d'Albi

Lautrec's earliest works, executed when he was fourteen and fifteen years old, are primarily representations of horses, riders and carriages. This choice of themes is hardly surprising, given his country upbringing and his father's obsession with the hunt. Indeed, Lautrec's great-grandfather, father and uncle were all amateur artists who had attempted similar scenes, and the family numbered several contemporary artists among its friends. One of these was Princeteau (cat. no. 6), a specialist in animal pictures with whom Lautrec had begun informal studies in this year. In addition, it is frequently surmised that these themes held a particular allure for the youthful Lautrec, since congenital frailties had prevented him from participating in active sports and games from early in his childhood. The extraordinary delight with which Lautrec studied and sought to express the sensation of vitality and movement throughout his career surely derived in part from his own frustrating limitations.

Artilleur sellant son cheval is one of the most successfully composed and executed of his early works. In it, Lautrec reveals a predilection for placing a strong image centrally against a generalized background, a motif he would develop in many important later works (for example, cat. nos. 37, 97). The large centralized mass of the horse dominates the indistinct background of grey-green foliage, yet figures and ground are harmoniously unified by Lautrec's limited palette of cool, muted tones. The boldness and individuality of his color sense is apparent as well here. He has defined all the shadows in brilliant blue and enlivened an otherwise homogeneous surface of cool tonalities with a few carefully disposed bravura strokes of red and yellow. Both forms and setting quiver with vitality. The energy of the horse's arched neck, pricked ears, and widely planted hind legs is reinforced by the muscular tension of the rider's bending, twisting body, rendered with a simplification and vigor of outline characteristic of all Lautrec's mature work. The entire effect of lively movement is augmented by Lautrec's loose and highly energized brushwork. With a freedom unusual for one his age, he has manipulated broad passages of paint to evoke the sensation of form with the least possible detail, dragging the stick end of his brush across the canvas to add to its textural interest.

N.E.M.

02

Un coupé attelé vu d'arrière

A horse-carriage viewed from the rear

1879

0.235, 0.14 m.; 9¼, 5½ in.

Oil on panel

Dortu, 1971: P.17

Musée d'Albi

Executed when Lautrec was fifteen, this diminutive painting of a carriage is one of his most original and daring early works. Although many nineteenth-century artists had painted carriage scenes, most notably Constantin Guys and Degas, there seem to be no prototypes for the unusual point of view from which Lautrec chose to study this motif. He returned to a similar *perspective plongeante* only once, in his paintings and lithograph for *Babylone d'Allemagne* of 1894 (cat. nos. 66, 67).

Glimpsed from an upper-storey window, the dark square mass of the coupé dominates the center of the composition. Lautrec has anchored the carriage firmly into place with the shadow that extends from it down to the bottom of the picture, and by the vertical and diagonal lines of architecture and road which lock it into a geometric framework. Even if the carriage is stationary, the steep diagonal of the roadway suggests a rapidly accelerating movement into the distance. This implication of the vehicle's potential enlarges the visual and psychological experience that Lautrec has carefully composed. The elongated shadow and the subdued colors evoke the stillness of dawn or twilight, while the line of the building clipped abruptly at the left, as well as the wrought iron lamp fixture, enhance the sense of the viewer's distance and isolation from the scene below.

N.E.M.

03

Portrait de Lautrec devant une glace

Self-portrait in front of a mirror

1880

0.405, 0.325 m.; 16, 12⅞ in.

Peinture à l'essence on board

Dortu, 1971: P.76

Musée d'Albi

At the age of sixteen Lautrec painted the only straight-forward self-portrait of his career. Although he was occasionally to incorporate his own image into a larger scene (cat. no. 52) and often caricatured himself in drawings or lithographs, he never again devoted a painting to serious self-examination. Self-portraiture is always a meaningful and revealing undertaking for the artist. Even at this youthful age, Lautrec's solution to its problems was original and suggestive of the thoughtful manner with which he approached his subjects throughout his life.

Always aware of himself as an observer, because of his physical frailties somewhat detached from the active life of others, he chose to paint himself in the act of regarding his own mirrored image. All artists must use a mirror to render their own likenesses, but few painters prior to Lautrec indicated this prop, usually portraying themselves directly as if confronting a spectator. Lautrec's decision to include the mirror reveals a concern for expressing experiences as truthfully as possible, for exposing the process of intense introspection and self-scrutiny that underlies all self-portraits. But the inclusion of the mirror also enables Lautrec to communicate his inner sense of detachment more palpably, since the mantlepiece objects are a substantial barrier between his reflected image and his own or a spectator's gaze. Looming large in the foreground, they dominate the small figure behind them in scale and in the vividness of their colors, which taken together comprise the strongest accents in the picture.

The distancing of his image achieved by the devices of mirror and mantle creates an effect of the artist's isolation and objectivity. This mood is further emphasized by Lautrec's rendering of his features. Blurred and generalized, conveying only an impression of selected details of his face, they imply the impossibility of ever seeing oneself clearly. Lautrec evidently felt that the depiction of his likeness was secondary to the evocation of his feelings about himself. In the tilt of the dark brows and the downward-pulled corner of a mouth rendered in strong streaks of crimson, Lautrec has suggested his underlying seriousness and melancholy. His mouth was reportedly unusually red, wet, and loose-lipped, and with characteristic candor he has accented it boldly to make this disfigurement his dominant feature.

N.E.M.

04

Champ de courses

Racetrack

1881

0.164, 0.238 m.; 6½, 9⅜ in.

Oil on panel

Dortu, 1971: P.116

Musée d'Albi

Lautrec was from birth surrounded by horses, which became his favorite pictorial subjects under the influence of his father, uncle, and first art instructor, Princeteau (cat. no. 6). Nevertheless, Lautrec seldom drew or painted scenes of the fashionable world of the racetrack until the later 1890s (cat. no. 98), although the theme had obsessed French painters since the time of Géricault, when the English sport was imported to France. The subject would seem to be ideally suited to Lautrec's predilections for depicting contemporary life and particularly movement, yet only three early race track paintings survive to record his brief period of interest around 1881-1882.

Champ de courses, the smallest of Lautrec's race-track pictures, is a rapid oil sketch of extraordinary energy. The nearly empty foreground, where several summarily executed figures are waiting, plunges abruptly into the distance along the track. The grandstand to the right is barely indicated, as if Lautrec wanted to describe the blur of his vision as his glance raced down the track toward the oncoming pack. Lautrec represented the distant horses rounding the bend with pinpoints of color that suggest the jockeys' silks.

Lautrec's uncanny expression of movement and suspense would be unimaginable without the examples of two of his favorite artists, Degas and Manet, both of whom studied racetrack scenes beginning in the early 1860s. In particular, Lautrec could have known Manet's *Racetrack near Paris* (fig. 1) in its lithographic version.

Interestingly, it was in 1881, the year Lautrec painted this sketch, that the great equestrian artist Meissonier invited the photographer Muybridge to his atelier to lecture on the topic of the appearance of equine locomotion, and Lautrec's first academic master, Bonnat, was in the audience (Johnson, p. 13).

C.F.S.

Fig. 1
Manet, *Racetrack near Paris*
c. 1864, 0.44 x 0.85 m., oil on canvas
The Art Institute of Chicago

05

Un wagon

A wagon

1881

0.224, 0.141 m.; 8⅞, 5½ in.

Oil on panel

Dortu, 1971: P.119

Musée d'Albi

In 1881 Lautrec traveled by train from his family home at Céleyran to Nice in the south of France, jotting down his impressions along the way both verbally and in the form of quick visual sketches for his *Cahier Zig-Zags*. One of these rapidly executed images portrayed a man sitting next to the window of his compartment in the train. At some point later in the year, Lautrec painted a diminutive panel with a similar motif, transforming the "monsieur très chic" of his captioned drawing into a woman seated at a table near the compartment's partially curtained window.

Lautrec has manipulated the pictorial elements of this little work with typical precision, organizing a few salient features into a format of almost abstract geometric power. Three light areas stand out boldly from the enveloping darkness of the car's interior, creating the dominant accents of the painting. Window and tablecloth are carefully disposed to balance each other and unify the upper and lower portions of the picture. Their strong diagonal sweep is broken midway by the horizontal band of the tabletop and window sash, a device which anchors the composition firmly and accentuates the light areas even more dramatically. Lautrec has posed the woman's head delicately against the empty wall near the window, the third element of counterpoint in the overall gloom. Tilted gently to the right, her head acts as a subtle balance to the angle of the window made trapezoidal by the line of the curtain.

Within this play of almost abstract pictorial elements, Lautrec has contrived a strong evocation of the train's movement and the monotony of travel. The blurred sweep of the passing landscape and the woman's closed eyes and nodding head fill this vignette with the very sensation of his train trip. The close juxtaposition of illuminated window and head posed against a dark ground has the intensity of similar images by Odilon Redon, but in their generalized treatment they create a psychological effect that is Lautrec's own.

N.E.M.

06

Princeteau dans son atelier

Princeteau in his studio

1881

0.73, 0.54 m.; 28¾, 21⅜ in.

Oil on canvas

Dortu, 1971: P.131

Collection of Alan and Simone Hartman

René Princeteau was a deaf-mute artist who practised in Paris beginning in the late 1860s. He became a friend of Lautrec's father, whose Parisian lodgings were near his studio and who, as an avid sportsman, must have been attracted to Princeteau's subject matter. A specialist in animal paintings, especially scenes of the hunt, farm and racetrack, Princeteau had achieved a considerable commercial success by the 1880s.

In 1872, when Lautrec came to Paris to attend the Lycée Condorcet, his father introduced him to Princeteau, who developed a paternal love for the seven-year-old Lautrec and welcomed the child into his studio (Martrinchard, p. 63). In 1879, at the age of 14, Lautrec became an informal pupil and began to make copies from Princeteau's pictures and take general instruction. Although Princeteau remained on friendly terms with Lautrec until the latter's death, their student-teacher relationship ended when Lautrec entered the studio of Bonnat early in 1882.

In 1881, while on vacation in Nice, Lautrec practised caricature drawings in a journal he kept, the *Cahier Zig-Zags*. One of the images he invented in this notebook was a picture of himself at his easel (D. 2.067). When he returned to Paris, Lautrec amplified the caricature sketch into witty drawings of Princeteau in his studio (for example, D. 2077), later developing these into two paintings of which this is the larger and more interesting.

Lautrec depicted Princeteau seated casually amongst the taxidermist-like trappings of his atelier. The top hat and gangling limbs with which Lautrec characterized his teacher are reminiscent of Daumier's sardonic character, Ratapoil (fig. 1), and details of the picture reveal that Lautrec's irreverance extended beyond the caricaturing style he employed here. The wolf's head, rendered in profile like Princeteau's, seems engaged in a silent *tête-à-tête* with the artist. Even the sculptured bust in the background repeats the dominant profile formula. The use of the compositional device of isocephalic profiles, often turned face to face to introduce dynamic tension into a motif, would become a striking feature of Lautrec's mature work (see cat. no. 38). Evidently he was at least partially indebted to Princeteau for the formulation of this compositional device, since the older artist was well known for his paintings of animals in silhouette (Matrinchard, p. 60), one of which Lautrec has included on an easel in the background of this portrait. Through the repetition of this idiosyncratic motif of Princeteau's and the humorous evocation of animal-human dialogue, Lautrec gently lampoons his teacher's personality and artistic practices, while caricaturing his physical appearance.

C.F.S.

Fig. 1
Daumier, *Ratapoil*
c. 1850-1851, 0.44 m., plaster
Albright-Knox Art Gallery, Buffalo
Elisabeth H. Gates Fund

07

Cuirassier

1881

0.73, 0.60 m.; 28¾, 23⅝ in.

Oil on canvas

Dortu, 1971: P.100

Private collection, Japan

One of the first works Lautrec produced after beginning his informal studies with Princeteau (cat. no. 6) was this painting of a mounted cuirassier. Princeteau specialized in pictures of horses and riders, and the fact that this canvas is signed "D'après Princeteau" (after Princeteau) indicates that Lautrec copied a work by his teacher.

The genre had been a common theme since it was developed by artists like Géricault, Gros, Charlet and Raffet in the early nineteenth century. Princeteau, who worked in the academic tradition, must have been influenced by these artists and, more particularly, by his contemporary Meissonier. In fact, in 1880 Meissonier had painted a picture called *The outpost* (fig. 1), to which Princeteau's painting and Lautrec's copy bear a startling similarity. Lautrec reveals his anti-academic attitude toward pictorial expression, however, in his simplification of forms, his avoidance of illusionistic details, and the vigorous freedom of his scumbled brushwork.

N.E.M.

Fig. 1
Meissonier, *The outpost*
1880, 1.05 x 0.91 m., oil on canvas
The Art Institute of Chicago

08

Tête d'homme-M. Etienne Devisme

Mr. Etienne Devisme

1881

0.61, 0.51 m.; 24⅛, 19¾ in.

Oil on canvas

Dortu, 1971: P.124

Musée d'Albi

Etienne Devisme and Lautrec were childhood friends who corresponded and collaborated on illustrated stories (Mack, pp. 26-35). Presumably the sitting took place at the Lautrec family estate at Céleyran, where the young artist often posed his models in the gardens. The various deep green tones of the foliage provide a rich decorative backdrop against which the model's head is silhouetted. The decorative backdrop and profile pose are characteristic of many of Lautrec's portraits and always reminiscent of so-called "primitive" fifteenth-century portrait conventions. In this case, however, Lautrec modified the formality of those conventions somewhat. Seated sideways on a chair, the back of which props his arm, the model seems rather relaxed. He wears a casual gray shirt with pale red stripes, complementary accents to the dominant gray-green tones. Lautrec's assured handling of the portrait is proof of precocious artistic virtuosity.

C.F.S.

09

Vieille femme assise sur un banc, à Céleyran

Elderly woman seated on a bench, at Céleyran

1882

0.53, 0.44 m.; 20⅞, 17¼ in.

Oil on canvas

Dortu, 1971: P.148

Musée d'Albi

Lautrec posed a family servant for this garden portrait taken in profile. Her peasant dress and weary pose recall an early work by Degas, although Lautrec's compositional substructure is more complex, and it is unlikely that he could have seen the earlier work.

Lautrec's flair for composition is fully developed in this work. He organized a decorative interplay of grays and greens, and counteracted the stiffness of the profile pose by observing the bench obliquely. Its graceful s-curve form boldly fills the immediate foreground to the left, emphasizing a corner as Lautrec so often would do in subsequent works. The curves of the bench are repeated and varied in almost every line of the model's pose, and the result is among Lautrec's finest early portraits.

C.F.S.

10

Un travailleur à Céleyran

A laborer at Celeyran

1882

0.60, 0.49 m.; 23⅝, 19⅜ in.

Oil on canvas

Dortu, 1971: P.147

Musée d'Albi

During the summer of 1882, Lautrec posed one of the laborers on the family estate at Céleyran in a meadow. The resulting picture is unusual in the context of Lautrec's total oeuvre because it includes a large expanse of landscape. With his lively interest in human nature and his penetrating sensitivity to psychological and emotional realities, Lautrec in his maturity rejected pure landscape painting as unsuitable for great art, and generally restricted his outdoor settings to a minimally indicated backdrop for his figures.

The extensive landscape background in this picture forms an essential part of an idea that Lautrec wished to convey. The lush meadow, its vibrant greens and gold softened with dappling shadows, spreads out like a carpet around the central figure of the obviously posing worker. Unlike earlier artists such as Millet, who depicted peasants in the midst of their labor to express the romantic notion of the nobility of toil, Lautrec seems to be suggesting a subtler and more insightful truth. The rich splendor of nature so expansively displayed contrasts meaningfully with the stiffly seated laborer. The awkwardness of his upright posture and the expression of tight-lipped seriousness on his worn face are eloquent testimony to the harshness of a life spent working the soil. Lautrec enhances this symbolic meaning by playing off the glowing colors of the fields and flowers with the dusty earth tones of the model's apparel. This subtle interweaving of vivid and subdued colors enlivens the simple compositional balance of vertical figure with horizontal setting, as does Lautrec's vigorous brushwork. It is interesting to note that in the quality of brushwork and color as well as in the type of subject portrayed, this painting anticipates the work Van Gogh was to produce beginning around 1887.

N.E.M.

11

Le jeune Routy à Céleyran

The young Routy at Céleyran

1882

0.61, 0.51 m.; 24⅛, 19¾ in.

Oil on canvas

Dortu, 1971: P.149

Musée d'Albi

According to Joyant (I, p. 75-6), Lautrec painted this picture at his family's estate in Céleyran during 1882. At that time Lautrec had just begun classes with Bonnat, and perhaps the careful studies preparatory to this picture testify to the discipline of Bonnat's atelier. The model Routy was apparently one of several field workers on the estate whom Lautrec used as models, sometimes without variation in pose (cat. no. 10).

Lautrec first made a careful drawing of Routy seated whittling a stick (fig. 1), an activity only imprecisely rendered in the final painting for which it was used. Before proceeding to our picture, Lautrec investigated its general composition in a full-size oil sketch, which has darker tonalities as if it were left incomplete at an early stage. For the final painting Lautrec used a subdued but nevertheless light palette, perhaps to accentuate the figure's blue apparel. The composition is elegantly simple. A thinly painted foreground is left empty except for the exquisite scumble of gray-green shadows on the sandy soil. The diagonal line of a weathered wall upon which Routy is seated gently counters his leftwards orientation, and he is framed by balanced small trees to either side. Lautrec's touch is precociously delicate. His colors are so thinly brushed that the relatively few evenly loaded strokes stand out like accents in impasto.

It is impossible to know whether Lautrec painted the final version out-of-doors, but it seems likely. Such garden settings would continue to attract Lautrec, but after the summer of 1882, he returned only once, in 1900, to the subject of a rural worker (cat. no. 105).

C.F.S.

Fig. 1
Toulouse-Lautrec, *The young Routy at Céleyran*
1882, 0.61 x 0.47 m., charcoal
Musée d'Albi

12

Madame la Comtesse A. de Toulouse-Lautrec

The Countess A. de Toulouse-Lautrec

1882

0.41, 0.35 m.; 16¼, 12⅞ in.

Oil on canvas

Dortu, 1971: P.180

Musée d'Albi

In the spring of 1882, Lautrec painted this lovely portrait of his mother seated on a garden bench at the family estate at Céleyran. The motif was one which the "Impressionist" painters had begun exploring in the 1870s as an extension of their preoccupation with modern life subjects and *plein-air* lighting effects, and it is possible that by this date, after his first season as an art student in Paris, Lautrec might have been familiar with images similar to Manet's *Woman in a garden* or Monet's *In the park* (fig. 1). It is interesting to note that Renoir, for whose work Lautrec was later to develop a deep admiration, painted a picture that same summer which was very similar to and no more advanced than the one conceived independently by the teenage Lautrec (fig. 2). Lautrec himself obviously found the motif so appealing that he later posed a variety of models seated with umbrella across the knees in a garden setting (fig. 3 and P.360).

As was so often the case with Lautrec, even at a youthful age he has handled a common contemporary subject with originality and invested it with a mood reflective of his uniquely penetrating sensibility. Lautrec, whose eccentric father largely ignored him, was adored by his mother and always cherished a tender regard for her. In many of the portraits he executed of her during the 1880s he represented her with downcast eyes and pensive face (fig. 4 and cat. no. 31) in an attempt to capture her abiding quality of gentle resignation. Whereas his older colleagues ignored the potential for the psychological interpretation of their models, treating them purely as

Fig. 2
Renoir, *Among the roses—Portrait of Madame Léon Clapisson*
1882-1883, 1.0 x 0.8 m., oil on canvas
Private collection, New York

Fig. 1
Monet, *In the park*
c. 1874, 0.73 x 1.0 m., oil on canvas
The Tate Gallery, London

Fig. 3
Toulouse-Lautrec, *Young woman*
1889, 0.69 x 0.69 m., oil on board
Private collection, New York

visual motifs and foils for the depiction of *plein-air* effects, Lautrec has imbued his portrait with a subtle evocation of character. He positioned his mother in the immediate foreground, bringing her closer to the spectator to obtain a greater sense of intimacy, and using the spreading foliage to dapple her face and body with softening, transfiguring shadows. The rippling decorative quality of deep shade and sparkling, sunlit highlights is enhanced by Lautrec's vigorous brushwork and his application of a flickering range of cool greens and blues.

With his uncanny ability to create balanced effects through his manipulation of a simplified prop, Lautrec used the bench to structure his loose, splotchy patterns of leaves and pockets of light and shadow. The wide horizontal slats balance the upright figure of the Countess in perfect equilibrium and contribute to the painting's entire air of tranquility and repose, but with the incorporation of one further detail Lautrec relieved the composition from an overly emphatic flatness and formality. The little addition of the end of another bench viewed obliquely in the bottom right-hand corner opens the picture out, gives the figure breathing space, and anticipates Lautrec's later development of diagonal *repoussoir* elements (cat. no. 38).

N.E.M.

Fig. 4
Toulouse-Lautrec, *The Countess A. de Toulouse-Lautrec*
1881, 0.92 x 0.80 m., oil on canvas
Musée d'Albi

13
Etude de nu
Study of a nude
1882
0.55, 0.46 m.; 21⅝, 18⅛ in.
Oil on canvas
Dortu, 1971: P.170
Musée d'Albi

In 1882, having just enrolled in Bonnat's studio, the eighteen-year-old Lautrec executed his first painting of a nude model. Wearing black stockings, she is seated in profile on his studio bed with head bent and finger raised to her mouth in a gesture of unselfconscious reflection. In contriving this pose, the precocious Lautrec created an image new in the history of nineteenth-century art. Courbet and Manet had both painted unidealized images of contemporary nude models in the 1860s, but they were posed in the grand style of sixteenth-century Venetian representations of classical goddesses. Renoir's sensuous female nudes, many partially draped, also had the flavor of antique classical sculpture or traditional Venetian painting. When Manet and Degas began to study nudes more consistently in the period between 1879 and 1883, both were drawn to create more strictly "naturalist" images capturing women in the midst of various boudoir activities, such as stepping out of tubs or dressing themselves (fig. 1).

Lautrec's first painting of a female nude already establishes characteristics of both mood and composition which would permeate much of his mature work. Where his naturalist predecessors had pursued an effect of immediacy by suggesting unposed action, Lautrec portrayed his model frankly posing and sought to convey a mood of introspective meditation. Placed centrally and in profile, this figure lost in reverie achieves a sense of iconic dignity which cancels out the provocative sensuality of the black stockings. Indeed, Lautrec has minimized the sensual potential of figure and setting in every way. The model's body seems slight in comparison with the voluptuous, fleshy nudes of Courbet, Manet, Degas or Renoir, and Lautrec has posed her unseductively with slouched posture and bent arm chastely covering her chest. The setting is reduced to the essential element of the studio bed covered with a near-Eastern rug, a prop Lautrec was to use repeatedly in later years (for example, P.223) and which provides a subtle decorative foil for the sober simplicity of the woman's body and the plain wall. Lautrec's limited palette of muted neutral tones also accentuates the effect of reflective repose.

Lautrec repeated this motif of a centrally positioned semi-nude woman portrayed in dreamy profile by a bed in several important later works, most notably *Le coucher* of 1899 (cat. no. 97) and *Femme retroussant sa chemise* of 1901 (cat. no. 108), one of the last paintings he realized before his death. In all of these pictures he balances the inherent sexuality of the model's bare body with the emotional and psychological overtones of the reflective face and pose, summarizing the physical and mental aspects of human nature in images as profound and evocative as those of Rembrandt.

The motif of a nude in stockings became increasingly popular in the late nineteenth and early twentieth centuries. For example, a figure similar in pose to Lautrec's appeared at the right of Seurat's *Les poseuses* of 1888

Fig. 1
Manet, *Woman adjusting her garter*
1879, 0.53 x 0.44 m., pastel
Ordrupgaard Collection, Copenhagen

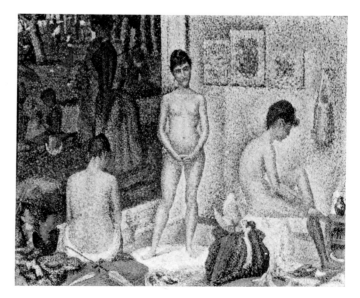

Fig. 2
Seurat, *The models*
1888, 0.39 x 0.49 m., oil on canvas
Private collection

(fig. 2), but in the context of the painting it is more a "naturalist" vignette and decorative motif than a psychological characterization. Lautrec himself returned to the theme once again in 1897 (fig. 3), by which time his style had altered considerably under the influence of Japanese prints. This late work has become much more simplified, flat, linear, and decorative, capturing the same erotic effect as the Shunga prints Lautrec loved and collected. This strain of decorative eroticism became a significant feature of much early twentieth-century painting, from the raw bawdiness of Picasso to the exquisite sensuality of Egon Schiele (fig. 4). Whether or not these artists were familiar with similar images by Lautrec, it is evident that he was the first painter of his time to capture this aspect of modern mood and sensibility.

N.E.M.

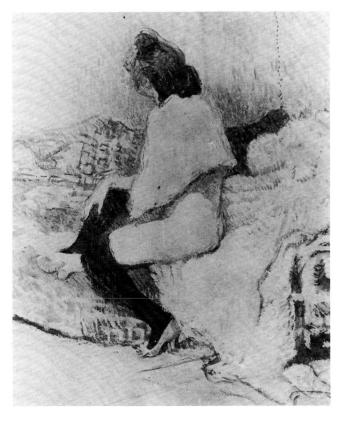

Fig. 3
Toulouse-Lautrec, *Red-headed woman seated on a divan*
1897, 0.59 x 0.48 m.
Private collection

Fig. 4
Schiele, *Nude with violet stockings*
1912, 0.32 x 0.47 m., watercolor, pencil, brush and ink
The Museum of Modern Art, New York

14

Le polisseur de marbre

The marble polisher

1882

0.65, 0.81 m.; 25⅝, 32 in.

Oil on canvas

Dortu, 1971: P.184

The FORBES Magazine Collection,
New York

Unknown to Joyant, this is the largest of Lautrec's surviving *académies,* a term for painted (or drawn) studies from nude models which were executed in the initial phases of traditional art instruction in France during the nineteenth century. Judging from the timid rendering of the model's anatomy and the casually brushed background curtain, *Le polisseur de marbre* may be the earliest of Lautrec's *académies.* He began painting them under the supervision of Léon Bonnat, the teacher with whom he went to study early in 1882 at the advice of Princeteau (cat. no. 6) and Henri Rachou, a young painter friend from Toulouse. A highly regarded portraitist, Bonnat was a severe teacher, who remarked of Lautrec's work (in May 1882) "Your painting is not bad; it is chic, yet that is not bad, but your drawing is quite honestly atrocious." (Joyant, I, p. 58).

The model is in a common classroom pose of a man polishing a block of marble. Interestingly, Lautrec painted this early academic exercise from an angle which presents the model's platform on a sharp diagonal. As a result, the lower left corner of *Le Polisseur* prefigures one of Lautrec's most abiding compositional predilections: a strong diagonal accent at the corner (see cat. nos. 52 and 56).

C.F.S.

15
Académie d'homme nu: buste
Study of a nude man: bust
1883
0.80, 0.64 m.; 31½, 25¼ in.
Oil on canvas
Dortu, 1971: P.208
Private collection

This relaxed half-length *académie* was painted in 1883 according to Joyant, who did not indicate whether Lautrec painted it early in the year under Bonnat, or later under Cormon. Although the figure casts no shadow on the draped background, his body is highlighted dramatically from the right, as if he was posed to demonstrate basic principles of light-dark modelling (chiaroscuro).

That Lautrec took satisfaction in this studio exercise is clear not simply from his having spared the picture from destruction late in his life, but from its depiction several years after it was painted among the studio paraphernalia he organized as a background for *La rousse au caraco blanc* (fig. 1). In that painting, chosen for an exhibition in Brussels in 1888, he propped this *académie* on the floor next to the model Carmen Gaudin (cat. nos. 28, 39). In its new context, the nude male takes on the aspect of a spectator gazing up at the seated woman. Given Lautrec's warm attraction to Carmen and the wry amusement he took in satirizing aspects of himself in some of his pictures, one can see the inclusion of this half-length study of a naked, bearded model as a witty reference to the diminutive Lautrec's unrequited love for his model. Thadée Natanson reported the following poignant anecdote regarding Lautrec's tendency to supplicate women for their favors at parties. After pestering the mistress of a friend all evening, he finally proposed to her: "Wait . . . I'm going to sit behind you . . . I'll be able to speak to you well enough . . . I'll be close enough . . . no need to see you . . . I know you by heart . . I even prefer that you won't look at me" (Natanson, 1951, p. 123).

C.F.S.

Fig. 1
Toulouse-Lautrec, *Woman in a studio, The redhead in a white blouse.*
1887, 0.56 x 0.46 m., oil on canvas
Museum of Fine Arts, Boston
Bequest of John T. Spaulding

16

Allégorie: Le printemps de la vie

Allegory: The spring of life

1883

0.50, 0.75 m.; 19¾, 29½ in.

Oil on canvas

Dortu, 1971: P.205

Musée d'Albi

Painted in 1883, according to Joyant, *Allégorie* is a rapid oil sketch or *esquisse* possibly intended for a larger picture. Its subject was almost undoubtedly suggested by Cormon, the celebrated young painter under whom Lautrec had just begun two years of study. Like the highly admired murals of Puvis de Chavannes (1824-1895), Lautrec's *Allégorie* depicts a mythical scene from pre-history in a simplified style reminiscent of Poussin and classical art.

The figures in the chariot probably represent Bacchus, crowned with vines, and Ariadne, who embrace while their team of tigers relaxes. One of the tigers is playing snappishly with a baby satyr, whose adult counterparts, all devotees of Bacchus, dance a lively round in the middle distance. The appeal of this type of poetic and gracefully simplified subject matter, especially for decorative mural ensembles, continued well into the twentieth century. The dancers in *Allégorie* are strikingly similar to those created by Matisse for his *Joie de vivre* and its eventual evolution into *La danse*.

The correspondence between Lautrec's mother and grandmother during the summer of 1884 (Huisman and Dortu, pp. 51-54) indicates that on several occasions Cormon invited Lautrec to assist him with special projects, including the illustrations for a monumental edition of Victor Hugo's works. Although Lautrec did not sign any of the illustrations, Huisman and Dortu suggested (pp. 237-244) that he may have contributed to the engraving which accompanies the poem, "Le Satyre." There are certainly strong similarities between Lautrec's sympathetic depiction of the baby satyr in *Allégorie* and the Hugo illustration. Given the frequency with which Lautrec satirized his own size and sexual desires in drawings and prints throughout his career, it is also quite possible that the mythological subhuman is a gentle allusion to himself. Indeed, according to one witness, Lautrec expressed the wish "to be a faun and walk about the woods naked" (Perruchot, p. 107).

C.F.S.

17
Peuplade primitive
Ancient tribe
1883
0.48, 0.62 m.; 19, 24½ in.
Peinture à l'essence on board
Dortu, 1971: P.215
Musée d'Albi

In 1882 Lautrec entered Cormon's newly formed atelier, where he remained a student until 1886 (Corr., p. 306-7). Cormon, an artist who specialized in history paintings, had just achieved new fame for his picture *The flight of Cain,* which was purchased by the state and exhibited at the prestigious Palais Luxembourg. During the first year of their relationship, Cormon was working on a series of paintings representing the Stone Age (Polášek, p. 18). The subject matter of his teacher's work obviously affected Lautrec, who in 1883 produced a series of allegorical sketches featuring a siren (P.212) and two centaurs (P. 211, P.213), both subjects from classical mythology. The only two works on historic themes that Lautrec painted during this period were an interior with costumed figures entitled *Scène Merovingienne* (P.214) and this more ambitious composition called *Peuplade primitive.*

Dortu lists an unidentified drawing of exactly the same dimensions that is obviously a full-scale study for this painting. It represents a busy camp where the members of this early tribe go about their daily tasks. In this instance and during the period in general, the adjective "primitive" carried no pejorative meaning, but rather referred to the uncorrupted and essential nature of an early people's lifestyle as a positive and admirable state of existence.

On the right Lautrec grouped four women in a stiff yet evenly balanced arrangement of two standing and two lying figures. In the right background two horsemen look back over their shoulders as they ride past the scene. An equally conventional academic figural group dominates the center of the work, forming a rising diagonal from the child playing with a dog in the foreground to a mother holding her baby above her head so that it meets the horizon line.

The powerful figure of a man controlling two large bullocks dominates the left half of the composition. This is certainly the most engaging and energetic section of the picture. Its relative vitality is probably the result of Lautrec's having encountered it in real life and not arranged it in the studio. In that same year he drew a vintner with his team of oxen pulling a large farm cart, called "Vendanges à Céleyran: Boeufs" (Polášek, p. 9, D. 1.631, where it is dated 1880). While the figures and the two straining animals are facing in the opposite direction in this quick study from life, it is obvious that the scene was Lautrec's inspiration for the lefthand section of this odd little history piece painted in Cormon's studio.

E.M.M.

18
Etude d'après le plâtre
Study of a plaster bust
1883
0.61, 0.50 m.; 24, 19¾
Oil on canvas
Dortu, 1971: P.216
Musée d'Albi

Paintings after plaster casts of antique and Renaissance sculptures constituted typical exercises during the early course of formal art education in late nineteenth-century France. *Etude d'après le plâtre*, in the background of which a paint box and other studio debris are visible, is such an exercise. Sugana (no. 150) identified the sculpture as a reproduction of Pollaiuolo's *Bust of a warrior* (fig. 1), a model Lautrec also studied in a charcoal and crayon drawing (fig. 2).

It is noteworthy that despite the frontal orientation of the sculpture, Lautrec painted it in strict profile. Lautrec's mature portrait work was frequently conceived in terms of profile views, as if inspired by the Italian quatrocento portraits he greatly admired for their forthright simplicity. This predilection for simplified and characteristic silhouette was shared by most of the symbolist painters as they evolved during the late 1880s. Artists as diverse as Odilon Redon, Seurat, and Gauguin venerated the clarity and decorative beauty of early Italian Renaissance portraiture, but Lautrec's early student picture has a characteristically subtle humor. He has transformed a routine academic exercise by rendering a frontally oriented Renaissance bust in the profile convention of Renaissance painted portraiture, thereby emphasizing his understanding of the period's aesthetic.

C.F.S.

Fig. 2
Toulouse-Lautrec, Drawing for *Study of a plaster bust*
1883, 0.61 x 0.47 m., charcoal and crayon
Musée d'Albi

Fig. 1
Pollaiuolo, *Bust of a warrior*
n.d., 0.50 m., bronze
Bargello, Florence

19

Le Comte Alphonse de Toulouse-
Lautrec

Count Alphonse de Toulouse-Lautrec

c. 1883

0.92, 0.65 m.; 36⅜, 25⅝ in.

Oil on canvas

Dortu, 1971: P.221

Mr. Harold F. Johnson

Count Alphonse de Toulouse-Lautrec-Monfa (1838-1912), the artist's father, was a singularly eccentric nobleman whose family had ruled in the region of Languedoc since the ninth century. Count Alphonse graduated from Saint-Cyr and was commissioned as an officer in the sixth regiment of lancers. At the age of twenty-five he married his cousin, Adèle Tapié de Céleyran, and left the Army to devote himself to the pleasures of the sporting life, if not to his new bride and future family. An expert and daring horseman, the Count seems to have genuinely admired the animals that carried him to the hunt as well as those which were their prey. Alphonse continued his ancestors' sense of chivalry by his strict and whole-hearted adherence to the traditions and rules of the hunt which seemed to furnish one of the only elements of structure and order in an otherwise eccentric personality. When Alphonse's expectations that his son would continue the family tradition of the active, athletic life were shattered by the development of Henri's physical condition, he could not hide his disappointment and drifted further apart from his wife and child.

Joyant provides a series of anecdotes indicative of Alphonse's lack of self-consciousness and his sometimes bizarre behavior, which was often an embarrassment to members of his family. After his marriage he indulged some of his romantic yearnings by appearing at home and abroad in an interesting variety of costumes. Sometimes he wore the fringed buckskins and fur cap of a Canadian trapper, or the exotic garb of a Kirghiz horseman. However, his favorite costume seems to have been that of a Scottish Highlander complete with kilt and sporan. Occasionally the heavily bearded Alphonse would appear at family dinners in his Highland outfit, only substituting a dancer's frilled tutu for the kilt (Mack, pp. 15-16).

The Count's favorite sport was falconry, and Henri's first equestrian portraits of his father in 1881 show him riding in Cossack dress holding a falcon in his upraised left hand (P.91). Two previously unidentified watercolor portraits of Alphonse on his horse, wearing the same costume but shown from the rear and facing right, can be dated to the same year and serve to illustrate the young artist's interest in this theme (A. 78, A. 164).

This elegant equestrian portrait from 1883 reveals a thorough understanding of the anatomy and dynamic relationship of horse and rider. The twist of the Count's body and his alertly held head signal the potential movement of his mount and create a tension which is emphasized by the white of his collar and cuffs. With his excellent grasp of complicated structure and mass, Lautrec rendered this theme with economy and elegance, making this exquisite portrait among the most powerful examples of his early work. The thin washes of ground color which Lautrec used here presage his development of a technique which he would utilize throughout his career.

Lautrec knew and emulated rather similar images by artists of the previous generation whom he admired, for example an incredibly sure equestrian portrait by Manet (fig. 1), whose posed horse and rider and general composition are very close to those used by the nineteen-year-old student. When this portrait was painted Lautrec was a pupil of René Princeteau (cat. no. 6), a well-known artist who specialized in pictures of horses. Their mutual love of equine themes was shared by the painter John Lewis Brown who had a studio in the same building as Princeteau and who specialized in military and hunting scenes.

E.M.M.

Fig. 1
Manet, *M. Arnaud on horseback*
c. 1875, 2.20 x 1.57 m., oil on canvas
Galleria Civica d'Arte Moderna, Milan

20

Jeanne

1884

0.64, 0.555 m.; 25¼, 21⅞ in.

Oil on canvas

Dortu, 1971: P.231

Rijksmuseum Kröller Müller, Otterlo

This lovely seated nude was painted by Lautrec in the studio of his fellow students, Henri Rachou and Henri Grenier, according to Joyant (I, p. 260), who also recorded the model's name. Although academic (cat. nos. 14, 15) in mood, Lautrec's picture is modelled in the manner of Manet, especially the left arm. If neither daring nor compositionally inventive, Lautrec's pictorial idea developed unexpected vigor when he painted *La grosse Maria*, probably shortly afterwards. The latter painting (fig. 1), for which a different model posed, is among the most powerful female nudes of the entire century.

Seven years later, Lautrec included *Jeanne* in the background of one of his portraits of the poet George-Henri Manuel (fig. 2). Posed rigidly, hands in his lap, Manuel is juxtaposed to the picture of the naked woman in a witty dialogue common to Lautrec's portrait compositions (cat. nos. 15, 86). Manuel and the woman in the picture face one another as gentleman and sex object. Consequently, Lautrec's portrait of the poet spoofs the numerous dressing room rendezvous in the works of Manet, Degas (fig. 3) and many other artists, including Lautrec himself (see cat. no. 80, figs. 1 and 5).

C.F.S.

Fig. 2
Toulouse-Lautrec, *M. Georges-Henri Manuel*
1891, 0.45 x 0.49 m., pastel on board
Private collection

Fig. 1
Toulouse-Lautrec, *La grosse Maria*
1884, 0.79 x 0.64 m., oil on canvas
Van der Heydt Museum, Wuppertal

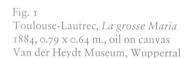

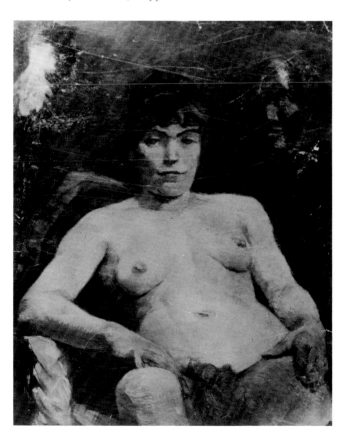

Fig. 3
Degas, *Nude woman combing her hair*
1877-1879, 0.21 x 0.16 m., pastel on monotype
Private collection

21

**Parodie du <u>Bois sacré</u> de Puvis de
Chavannes**

A parody of *The Sacred Grove* by Puvis
de Chavannes

1884

1.72, 3.80 m.; 67⅞, 149⅜ in.

Oil on canvas

Dortu, 1971: P.232

The Henry and Rose Pearlman
Foundation

In 1884 Lautrec and his fellow students at Cormon's saw Puvis de Chavannes' *Le bois sacré* (fig. 1) exhibited at the annual Salon. The picture provoked a storm of dispute and impassioned discussions in the studio as to whether it was a poetic dream surpassing material reality, or a pallid and facile decoration (Gauzi, p. 116). Although the young artists of this period admired Puvis' unconventionally flat and simplified style, so reminiscent of medieval art and Japanese prints, they often found his traditional mythological subject matter and literary references as antiquated and remote as his classically garbed figures. In agreement with their "naturalist" predecessors Courbet, Manet, and Degas, and like the great poet and critic Baudelaire, Lautrec's circle believed that the art of the modern age could only be meaningful if it was based on actual experience and study of the real, contemporary world. This conviction motivated Lautrec and his friends to paint a parody of Puvis' picture in which they satirized its symbolic content with witty irreverence.

By this period there was already a long established tradition of caricaturing Salon pictures or traditional masterpieces. Manet in particular had become notorious in 1863 for his paintings *Déjeuner sur l'herbe* and *Olympia*, both spoofs on Renaissance themes and compositions. Lautrec's parody was intended more as a private joke, however, executed by a group effort in two afternoons, and when Lautrec acquired his own studio in 1886 he hung it high on the wall (see cat. no. 32, fig. 1) where it remained until 1897 (Gauzi, p. 116).

Puvis' painting is an allegorical homage to artistic inspiration, representing the classical personifications of the muses in a tranquil, idyllic natural setting and emphasizing the meditative nature of artistic creativity. Lautrec has removed two of Puvis' figures and instead intruded a procession of casual contemporary characters into this remote and peaceful scene, including a roughly dressed worker in checked overalls, a policeman to keep the queue in order, and an irreverent rear-facing self-portrait whose stance suggests Lautrec is relieving himself on the grass. The presence of a Japanese gentleman at the far right could be a humorous allusion to Puvis' flat, reduced style, which in artistic circles was associated with Japanese graphics. Lautrec has adorned Puvis' chaste classical frieze with a clock whose specific time, 9:05, undermines the original artist's intention of producing an effect of timeless universality, and the figures flying through the air now carry a gigantic tube of paint in place of a lyre.

In one last alteration, Lautrec replaced the reflective woman at the far left with a figure inspired by an earlier painting of Puvis', his *Prodigal son* of 1879. Accompanied by the pigs always associated with this theme, the prodigal sits with reverently crossed arms before an easel propped with two canvases on which are written the names Meissonier and MacKay. Meissonier was a popular contemporary artist who worked in the traditional academic style against which Lautrec and his friends were rebelling, and MacKay was a patron who rejected Meissonier's commissioned portrait (Wattenmaker, p. 98). Perhaps this small vignette symbolizes all the group of young men at Cormon's who rejected banal academic conventions in favor of the cruder but more provocative characteristics of modern-life painting. Although they spoofed Puvis' allegory mercilessly, the friends have left one feature of the original picture intact, in fact have made it even more emphatic. The reduction and flattening of forms, for which Puvis was venerated by the Symbolists, has been retained and accentuated, and in this alone the young artists revealed that this criticism also contained elements of conscious homage (Gauzi, p. 117).

N.E.M.

Fig. 1
Puvis de Chavannes, *The sacred grove*
c. 1884, 0.93 x 2.31 m., oil on canvas
The Art Institute of Chicago

22

Scène de ballet

A scene from a ballet

1885

1.50, 1.50 m.; 59⅛, 59⅛ in.

Fresco transferred to canvas

Dortu, 1971: P.241

The Art Institute of Chicago

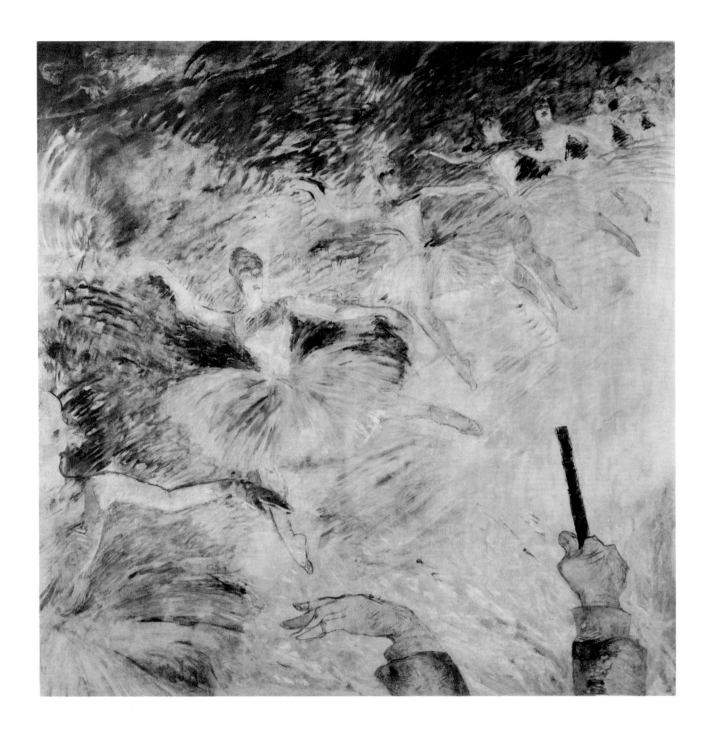

Scène de ballet is one of four related mural decorations Lautrec painted for an inn at Villiers-sur-Morin, where he visited his friends, the Greniers. The other three (P.239, P.242, and fig. 1) depict a ballet dancer at a mirror in her dressing room, a stagehand ringing a call to stage with a bell, and the gallery of a theater where Lautrec painted himself among the spectators. Several of the pictures, including *Scène de ballet*, were painted directly on plaster walls. They were subsequently removed and transferred to new supports, probably after 1913 when Coquiot divulged their existence and Lautrec's work had achieved a high market value. Unfortunately, the delicate removal process was done unprofessionally, and the original surface was badly cracked and chipped. Consequently, the painting needed extensive retouching. Although much of the present surface is, therefore, restored, the composition and color scheme are Lautrec's. Despite its poor condition, The Art Institute of Chicago's picture is a rare historical record, not only of an early phase of Lautrec's work, but of all the bold, humorous murals, long lost, which so many nineteenth-century artists obligingly executed under similar circumstances.

Scène de ballet is clearly indebted for its humor to Daumier (fig. 2) and for its compositional eccentricities to Degas. On several occasions (for example, fig. 3) Lautrec parodied the latter's work, which was often distinguished by bold diagonal groupings and figures cropped

Fig. 1
Toulouse-Lautrec, *Dancer in her dressing room*
1885, 1.15 x 1.01 m., oil on plaster transferred to canvas
Private collection

Fig. 2
Daumier, *The annoyed dancer*
1857, 0.22 x 0.25 m., lithograph
The Art Institute of Chicago

suddenly at the borders (figs. 4, 5). Lautrec extended the repeated forms of a line of dancers along a diagonal from the bottom left to upper right corner, bluntly dividing his composition into two equal triangular zones seen in a cockeyed perspective. The eccentric composition leaves two relatively empty areas, each of which Lautrec filled with an amusing detail. Below he included the hands of the orchestra leader. They amount to a spoof of the intrusive heads, instruments and fans frequently featured at the border of Degas' works, and those of other modern artists under the influence of Japanese graphics. In the upper triangle Lautrec depicted the distorted face of what must be a stagehand watching the dance from behind a flat. Duret (1920, p. 119) claimed that Lautrec painted two *pompiers* (firemen) here, but Duret must be mistaken, for this section is in a relatively good state of preservation. In any event, the presence of a leering face, distorted by artificial lighting and lodged in a corner of a composition, was a motif Lautrec repeated throughout his career, culminating in the additions he made for *Au Moulin Rouge* (cat. no. 52).

C.F.S.

Fig. 3
Toulouse-Lautrec, *Dancers*
1885, 1.0 x 1.52 m., oil on canvas
Private collection

Fig. 4
Degas, *Dancing school: the rehearsal*
1879, 0.47 x 0.61 m., oil on canvas
The Frick Collection, New York

Fig. 5
Degas, *The ballet*
1878, 0.40 x 0.50 m., pastel
Private collection

23

Danseuse assise sur un divan rose

Ballerina seated on a rose sofa

1886

0.475, 0.36 m.; 18¾, 14¼ in.

Oil on canvas

Dortu, 1971: P.248

From the collection of Mr. Nathan
Cummings, New York

Lautrec was just beginning to digest the achievement of avant-garde artists when he painted this somewhat muted and saccharine picture, which was owned by Lautrec's conservative uncle Odon. It is as if Lautrec wished to depict a Renoiresque model set out à la Degas. The concoction may appear awkward, but Lautrec nevertheless garnished it with interesting pictorial ideas of his own.

Whereas Degas would paint a ballerina in her accustomed rehearsal room or stage milieu, and Renoir would choose an altogether neutral setting, Lautrec depicted his ballerina amidst the clutter of the studio into which he moved in 1886. His decision to do so was a decision to reveal his actual process of painting and evidently to question the importance of an "appropriate" or "realistic" setting in a picture. Indeed, the model is seated rather limply and the odd shape of her tutu spread on Lautrec's studio cot is perversely graceless. The details suggest that Lautrec wished to indicate that the model was resting rather than posing and that he had transformed a rehearsed situation into a candid one. At this time, Lautrec frequently set "genre" scenes in his studio without troubling to disguise it, perhaps to avoid accusations of "romanticizing." For example, the bamboo pole in the corner of this picture also appears in the background of *Poudre de riz* (cat. no. 30) and a canvas propped against the wall appears in that of *A Grenelle: L'attente* (cat. no. 29), both of which are primarily café scenes. By including recognizable studio props in his "genre" subjects, Lautrec underlined that even if they evoked actual contemporary life, they were of necessity fabricated under studio conditions beneficial for making art, an often inescapable truth which Corot had stressed in his later works. Lautrec's abiding interest in the borderline area between pose and candor, deception and representation, is evident in this ballerina.

His composition is typically inventive. The slashing diagonals create a visual energy which is out of keeping with the model's repose, just as the setting is out of keeping with her clothes.

C.F.S.

24
Artilleur et femme
Soldier and woman
1885
0.57, 0.46 m.; 22½, 18⅛ in.
Gouache on tracing paper
Dortu, 1971: P.272
Musée d'Albi

Although never realized as a finished oil, Lautrec's final colored tracing after his drawing of a man ogling a woman at a café table is the earliest complete example of that boldness of draughtsmanship and color which characterizes Lautrec's best works. With its rude melodrama of lust and allure, it also is the first manifestation of one of Lautrec's favorite themes.

The psychological tensions between lovers began to receive serious attention from artists no later than the seventeenth century and was a genre of particular interest to mid-nineteenth century artists in England and France. Lautrec's officer and prostitute explore a theme close to that of Degas' *Le viol* (1874, McIlhenny Collection, Philadelphia) and Caillebotte's *Intérieur, femme à la fenêtre* (1880), for example, indicating Lautrec's growing interest in works by the avant-garde of modern life painting. Gauzi (pp. 44-45) recalled that when Lautrec showed him the composition, he complained that oblique allegories of sex, such as "Mars and Venus," were not "riffraffish" (*canaille*) enough for his tastes.

The half dozen separate stages culminating in this work testify that this important new departure was the result of serious and conscientious study. Although within a few years Lautrec's reputation would be founded on his uncanny ability to capture the fleeting events of Parisian nightlife first hand, all of his earliest work, including this investigation of the theme, was premeditated and precisely staged. Judging from the initial pencil drawing (fig. 1), Lautrec posted Frédéric Wenz (cat. no. 35), a fellow student at Cormon's atelier, in his artillery volunteer's uniform.

Wenz's bulky stature and aggressively set, block-like head afforded Lautrec the salient details with which to create an emblem of brutish male sexuality. Posed with one hand hooked swaggeringly in his waistband and the other suggestively near his crotch, jacket hiked back to emphasize his outthrust abdomen, Wenz epitomizes the open, indiscreet desires commonly witnessed in the rowdy Montmartre cafés Lautrec had recently begun to frequent in pursuit of just this type of raw, modern-day subject matter. Although Lautrec at first juxtaposed the soldier with a woman rendered in emotionally neutral profile and less blatantly sexual detail, from the outset he emphasized the nature of their interaction by drawing her head close to and on the same level with his genitals.

Lautrec made a tracing of his drawing to which he added highlights of local color, and then proceeded to a second tracing, the work discussed here. Gauzi (p. 25) describes this process as typical of Lautrec's working methods, although any examples of these preliminary tracings for other works seem to have been lost. In this final tracing, Lautrec not only developed his garish, emotionally-charged color scheme more fully but also completed important changes in the seated female figure. Although keeping her original shape, he readjusted his internal drawing to turn her body slightly away from the soldier. This device opens the composition towards the

viewer, inviting him to share the spectacle enjoyed by Wenz. The high vantage point intensifies the sense of spectator participation, forcing the viewer to gaze down at the seated whore precisely as Wenz does.

A far more powerful figure than Lautrec's initial profile sketch, the final conception of the woman intensifies the new diagonal activity of the composition. By transforming the woman into a brazen whore, chest exposed, lips painted blood, green shadows haunting her face, Lautrec not only rivets the spectator's attention but creates a more dynamically unified composition. His studied adjustments for this abandoned painting typify the meticulous organization of detail by which Lautrec achieved such expressive power.

C.F.S.

Fig. 1
Toulouse-Lautrec, *Soldier and woman*
1887, 0.70 x 0.48 m., color sketch
Musée d'Albi

25

Au Moulin de la Galette

At the Moulin de la Galette

1885

0.61, 0.50 m.; 24⅛, 19¾ in.

Peinture à l'essence on board

Dortu, 1971: P.281

Formerly Hahnloser Collection

La Goulue (cat. no. 51) and Valentin le Désossé (the boneless) were, very roughly speaking, the Ginger Rodgers and Fred Astaire of Montmartre during the second half of the 1880s and early 1890s. Both naturally gifted dancers, their collaborative virtuosity brought crowds to dance halls—the Elysée Montmartre, the Moulin de la Galette, and beginning in 1890, the Moulin Rouge. The high-kicking style of dance, of course, followed rousing music by Offenbach and his imitators.

Lautrec was drawn to Montmartre as a source of artistic inspiration in the mid-1880s. Somewhat ill at ease there at first, Lautrec claimed he was pursuing an art that was "outside the law" (Comtesse Attems, pp. 114-115). Apparently he hoped to become for the cabaret world what Degas was for the ballet. From as early as 1885 he made paintings of Montmartre entertainment celebrities, initiating a class of subjects which preoccupied him for the remainder of his career.

Judging from works done around 1885-1886, Lautrec adopted a bold, coarse style to capture this smoke-filled, working-class milieu. He was reputedly critical of gratuitously elegant conventions of style and composition (Gauzi, p. 118) and dismissed unchallenging art as merely commercial (Joyant, I, pp. 53-54). For this painting and its related study (P.282) which probably began as rapid, precise sketches taken on-the-spot (e.g. D. 2.973, 2.977), Lautrec adopted an abbreviated caricature-like idiom. This style, ultimately based upon illustrations made for popular periodicals (fig. 1), was as highly improvisatory as the self-taught choreographies of Valentin and La Goulue. Valentin's figure is naïvely rendered, his face crudely modelled. Uncommonly thin and long-legged, he appears to be drawn disproportionately. His relaxed demeanor contrasts with La Goulue's concentrated dancing, skirts hiked, black-stockinged legs in motion. Her down-turned head is only an area of yellow streaked with blue-green shadows for hair and a red jab for her neck or ear. Both figures are dimly spotlighted, yet their drab garments merge into the gloomy, indistinct background from where spectators look on at the dancers. Rapid parallel hatchings in blue, green and black indicate the floor, figures, and light caged in drifting smoke.

Although Lautrec made several spirited pictures of the famous dancers in the second half of the 1880s (P.261, P.311), it was only beginning in 1890, by which time he had largely abandoned the self-consciously crude style apparent in this picture, that Lautrec's ambitions to paint cabaret subjects culminated in a brilliant series of dance hall works (P.361, P.399). Many of them, such as his monumental Moulin Rouge poster of 1891, depict the performance of Valentin and La Goulue. Consequently, this painting contains the kernel of the pictorial idea which obsessed Lautrec for the subsequent five or six years.

Lautrec seemingly took satisfaction in this early composition, since he readapted it for one of the curtains which he supplied for La Goulue's street fair tent (fig. 2) in 1895, by which date she no longer enjoyed cabaret celebrity. Although Murray (p. 181) feels that this work was done at the later date as a study for the tent, its raw stylistic idiom supports a much earlier dating.

C. F. S.

Fig. 1
Steel engraving after Guys, *Dance-hall scene*
c. 1860
New York Public Library

Fig. 2
Toulouse-Lautrec, *Dance at the Moulin Rouge: La Goulue's tent*
1895, 3.00 x 3.00 m., oil on canvas
Musée du Louvre, Paris

26

A Grenelle, buveuse d'absinthe

At Grenelle, absinthe drinker

1886

0.55, 0.458 m.; 21¾, 19¼ in.

Oil on canvas

Dortu, 1971: P.308

Joseph H. Hazen Collection

Lautrec first exhibited publicly in 1886, when Aristide Bruant began to borrow pictures to decorate his cabaret *Le Mirleton* on the boulevard Rochechouart. Bruant's was one of several Montmartre nightspots which Lautrec began to frequent around 1884 to find and study scenes from modern life suitable for pictures. Presumably his interest was motivated by Cormon's advice (Corr., p. 70) to paint outside of his studio, as well as by the inclinations of his fellow students at Cormon's and the example of the sardonic illustrator Jean-Louis Forain, a neighbor of Princeteau's. Initially, or so at least Lautrec wrote his relatives, he went to the Montmartre bars out of artistic duty, for he claimed to find them boring and distasteful (Corr., p. 85; Comtesse Attems, p. 115). Lautrec wrote of his difficulty in adjusting to experiences so "outside the law" as those he witnessed in Montmartre (Huisman and Dortu, p. 45), but the sense of pursuing the unconventional in life as well as in art must have been ultimately appealing.

Bruant wrote and sang bittersweet ballads, one of which, "À Grenelle," was published in his cabaret newsletter (Mirleton, no. 18, May 15, 1886). The ballad evokes the memories of a prostitute, who upon seeing younger girls remembers her happier past. Gauzi reports that Lautrec frequently sang Bruant songs while at Cormon's (p. 23-4), and in a small sketchbook of 1886 he drew a woman seated at a table and inscribed the page "1886 à Grenelle, Mirleton" (D.2.947). The sketch was surely the basis for this painting, which according to Joyant was executed in 1888 and put on permanent exhibition along with works by other artists at Bruant's cabaret. But it is unlikely that Lautrec would have waited two years between hearing the song and producing the sketch to executing the painting for Bruant. Stylistically the picture relates far more to other works of 1886 than to the compositionally more complex and delicately painted pictures of 1888. Gauzi relates that Bruant hung the picture over the piano at the Mirleton (p. 45) and that Lautrec reclaimed it from him in 1889, when his fellow student Wenz (cat. no. 35) suggested he submit a picture to the *L'Union artistique* exhibition in Rheims, where Wenz's parents lived. Gauzi further relates that Wenz's father, although he did not admire Lautrec's picture, bought it to present it to his son, and that this was Lautrec's first sale (pp. 44-45). But this painting was among those sold with Bruant's estate in 1905, and therefore could not have been sold to Wenz. It is known, however, that Lautrec did submit a picture called *À Grenelle* depicting an absinthe drinker to the Rheims exhibition, where it was bought by Wenz's father (cat. no. 29). Gauzi must have confused the pictures, for it is unlikely that Lautrec would retract a gift from his good friend Bruant.

Lautrec's admiration for Renoir, whose studio he visited regularly (Natanson, 1951, p. 15), seems apparent in *À Grenelle* (fig. 1). Lautrec adopted Renoir's open style of hatched brushstrokes, although not his typically hightoned palette. He must have realized that the brighter colors would have been inappropriate to express the depressed sentiment of Bruant's ballad, which he captured

Fig. 1
Renoir, *Young girl reading*
1887, 0.34 x 0.27 m., oil on canvas
Private collection

through his predominate use of olive-toned browns highlighted with iron grays. He intensified the mood further with shadows tinted an acid green and with dull red strokes around the woman's tearful eyes, a technique of building up colored accents over a canvas established in *gris coloré* which he learned from Cormon (Huisman and Dortu, p. 242). The expressive use of color adds pathos to the dignified neutrality understandably associated with figures rendered in profile. As Gauzi wrote of Lautrec's attitude toward color: "He loathes gloss: grey predominates in his work, and many of his portraits are primarily drawings enhanced by color. He paints on cardboard, on canvas sized only so as to subdue the color and imbue the pictures with the restraint which he considers essential to every work of art." (Huisman and Dortu, p. 62).

Lost in sad reverie, isolated figures seated before a glass of yellowish absinthe or some other alcoholic beverage entered the repertoire of avant-garde French painters when Degas exhibited his extraordinary *L'absinthe* (see cat. no. 95, fig. 1) at the second Impressionist exhibition. Manet and Renoir quickly followed his lead with versions of their own, and the theme became a staple of contemporary modern painters such as Jean-Louis Forain (fig. 2). Perhaps it was Lautrec's admiration for these artists which led him to re-introduce the moody theme, which was further developed in the hands of Van Gogh (fig. 3), Beardsley (fig. 4) and Picasso (fig. 5), to cite only a few examples of the artists for whom the solitary woman at a cabaret became an emblem of Parisian life.

N.E.M. & C.F.S.

Fig. 2
Forain, *Café scene*
1878, 0.31 x 0.20 m., gouache
The Brooklyn Museum, Gift of a Friend

Fig. 3
Van Gogh, *Seated woman at the Café Tambourin*
1887, 0.55 x 0.46 m., oil on canvas
Rijksmuseum Vincent Van Gogh, Amsterdam

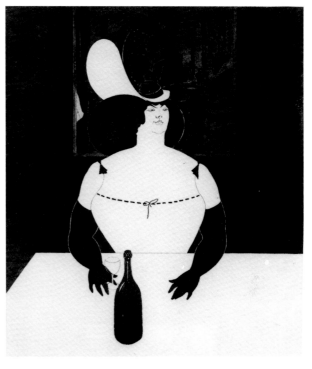

Fig. 4
Beardsley, *The fat woman*
1894, 0.18 x 0.16 m., Indian ink
The Tate Gallery, London

Fig. 5
Picasso, *Lady seated in a chair*
1900-1901, 0.40 x 0.52 m., conté crayon and pastel
Private collection

27

La femme au noeud rose: Jeanne Wenz

The woman with the pink bow:
Jeanne Wenz

1886

0.80, 0.58 m.; 31½, 22⅞ in.

Oil on canvas

Dortu, 1971: P.264

The Art Institute of Chicago

Jeanne Wenz was the sister of Frédéric (cat. no. 35), one of Lautrec's fellow students at Cormon's studio. Jeanne posed for Lautrec twice, first in 1886 for this portrait and again in 1888 when he used her as a model for a café subject illustrative of a dance-hall ballad (fig. 1). Lautrec's first picture of Jeanne, painted in 1886 according to Joyant, is so restrained and delicate, particularly in comparison with that of her brother, that it seems as if Lautrec was intent on expressing his model's gentle and unpretentious personality.

He limits his color scheme to the somber palette he preferred in this period, utilizing a close range of values in green, gray, blue and brown. The resulting quality of sober simplicity is reiterated by the starkness of background, the dignity of the profile pose, and the severe vertical accent of the ladder-back chair. Lautrec, always a master at balancing opposing forces in a picture, relieves the somber effect and avoids harshness, however, with a variety of carefully contrived details. The oblique baseboard, the table, and the corner of a canvas stacked against the wall add a faint note of studio informality and visual irregularity to the otherwise restrained portrait, just as the loose tendril of curling hair at the back of her head and the gaiety of the pink scarf soften the rigidity of Jeanne's pose and the sobriety of the colors.

Strictly profile portraits are unusual in urbane European art after the mid-fifteenth century. When later artists occasionally did profile portraits, most frequently they did so to imitate the dignity of antique portrait bust reliefs or to emphasize the sitter's simplicity and modesty as, for example, Chardin did. Lautrec's exposure to the stylistic anachronism came not only from his study of earlier paintings but also from Princeteau (cat. no. 6), who had an idiosyncratic preference for profiled renderings of animals. In addition, Lautrec's appreciation for the profile portrait must have deepened by his study of the occasional pictures of this type done by Renoir, in whose studio he reportedly spent many hours (Natanson, 1951, p. 15).

N.E.M. AND C.F.S.

Fig. 1
Toulouse-Lautrec, *The absinthe drinker (Jeanne Wenz)*
1888, 0.71 x 0.49 m., oil on canvas
From the Collection of Mr. and Mrs. Paul Mellon

28

La blanchisseuse

The laundress

1886-1887

0.93, 0.75 m.; 37, 30 in.

Oil on canvas

Dortu, 1971: P.346

Private collection

Although the model for this picture has sometimes been identified as Rosa, it seems apparent that she is really Carmen Gaudin, one of Lautrec's favorite models beginning in 1885. The mistaken identification must have arisen from a related painting of the same model wearing identical clothing, entitled *À Montrouge—Rosa la rouge* (Rosa the redhead) (fig. 1). This painting was dated to 1888 by Joyant, who also claimed (I, p. 98) that the title was derived not from the name of the model, but from a song of Aristide Bruant's, of which Lautrec's picture was an evocation.

Since Carmen had red hair, she was a perfect model for that painting and for Lautrec's use in general, as he had a passion for redheads. He discovered her in the street outside a restaurant where he had been dining with his friend Henri Rachou in 1885. Catching a glimpse of the simple working girl's russet hair and gamin face, Lautrec was overcome with enthusiastic admiration and, exclaiming to Rachou that she had a wonderful raw quality (Gauzi, p. 129), begged him to approach her and persuade her to become his model. He painted a series of moody, Henneresque portraits of her in 1885 (for example, figs. 2 and 3), but Joyant does not identify her as the model for any later paintings. In fact, given Joyant's dates, there are no other depictions of models in a studio setting during the entire period between 1885 and early 1888. Since both Gauzi (p. 130) and Rachou (Mack, p. 61) agree that Lautrec used Carmen regularly for a long time, this absence of pictures of her seems inexplicable.

The paintings Lautrec exhibited at Les XX in Brussels in 1888, which Joyant dates to that year, were actually executed in 1887 (Murray, pp. 180-181). Among these was *La rousse au caraco blanc* (see cat. no. 15, fig. 1), the model for which again appears identical in clothing, hair color and style, and facial features to the woman he posed for *A Montrouge, Rosa la rouge*, for *La blanchisseuse*, and for *Tête de femme rousse en caraco blanc* (fig. 4), the latter two of which were dated by Joyant to 1889. Given the extreme similarities between the model for these paintings and Lautrec's 1885 portraits of Carmen, it seems likely that she posed for them all, as well as for other works of a later date (see cat. no. 39 and P.352).

On the basis of the subdued color and mood, simplified compositions, and more densely modelled volumes, *À Montrouge, Rosa la rouge*, *Tête de femme rousse en caraco blanc*, and *La blanchisseuse* were all probably executed slightly before *La rousse au caraco blanc*. They relate in style, composition, palette, and atmosphere to works of 1886 or early 1887, such as the portrait of Jeanne Wenz (cat. no. 27) and *À Grenelle: L'attente* (cat. no. 29). All of these earlier paintings are subdued in color yet more subtle and refined than the somewhat crude, raw pictures of 1885. When Lautrec made his initial foray into the seamy world of Parisian lower classes, he wanted his subjects to embody all its coarseness and brutality (cat. no. 25). His exclamation on seeing Carmen for the first time was, "What an air of spoiled meat she

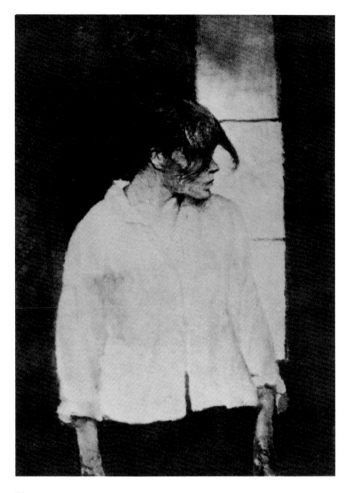

Fig. 1
Toulouse-Lautrec, *At Montrouge, Rosa the redhead*
1886-7, 0.70 x 0.47 m., oil on canvas
The Barnes Foundation, Merion
Photograph copyright (1979) by The Barnes Foundation

has" (Gauzi, p. 129). In the years that followed, however, as his sensibilities changed, he considerably modified the strident quality of the works he produced after his first contact with the Zolaesque *demi-monde*. His paintings became increasingly elegant and subtle in mood as he sought to endow even the tawdriest subjects with decorative qualities and make them expressive of his own developing psychological insight. *La blanchisseuse* and the other two related pictures most probably date from late 1886 or early 1887, because later in 1887 Lautrec's color became more brilliant and jewel-like and his figure style flatter and more delicately rendered (see cat. nos. 31, 32). The attribution of these pictures to this period therefore seems a reasonable solution to the mystery of Carmen's disappearance from Lautrec's repertoire during that year.

Gauzi commented that Lautrec portrayed Carmen as a laundress (p. 130), but Joyant identifies only one tiny study of her by this title (fig. 5). He dates it to 1885, but the model's wide white blouse is strikingly similar to the figure of *La blanchisseuse* and the study possibly represents Lautrec's original pictorial idea for the subject.

In our version, Lautrec posed Carmen in profile leaning on a table in the studio. Her simple, smock-like white blouse and the rumpled cloth on the table in front of her are the sole props Lautrec used to suggest that she represents a laundress. Unlike Degas, whose series of laundry pictures in 1882 depicted characteristic activities such as ironing, Lautrec preferred to treat the subject as a psychological study. Carmen leans forward to gaze pensively out of the window, her back sagging wearily as she transfers her weight to her arms. Eyes hidden by a straggling lock of hair, her serious expression and slumping pose create a sensation of fatigue and melancholy which is augmented by the somber colors. Her body, contrived as a great oblique triangle filling the canvas nearly to its edges, is locked into place by a few carefully disposed vertical and horizontal forms.

By the size of the figure and the extreme boldness and simplicity of the geometric composition with its powerful light-dark contrasts, Lautrec has endowed *La blanchisseuse* with a physical monumentality that intensifies her mood of somber reflection and recalls similar works by Vermeer. Body inclined toward the open window and face gently illuminated by its light, the figure of the laundress expresses a sense of quiet yearning. By abruptly cropping the window with its open view and by curtaining the model's eyes with her hair, Lautrec implies that her vision is directed not outside but inward. The masked eyes protect her from the prying gaze of the spectator as well, isolating her in introspection and suggesting how mysterious and hidden our real selves are from one another.

N.E.M.

Fig. 2
Toulouse-Lautrec, *Carmen*
1885, 0.53 x 0.41 m., oil on canvas
Sterling and Francine Clark Art Institute, Williamstown

Fig. 4
Toulouse-Lautrec, *Redheaded woman in a white blouse*
1886-7, 0.59 x 0.48 m., oil on canvas
Thyssen-Bornemisza Collection

Fig. 3
Toulouse-Lautrec, *Carmen, the redhead*
1885, 0.24 x 0.15 m., oil on panel
Musée d'Albi

Fig. 5
Toulouse-Lautrec, *The laundress*
1885, 0.24 x 0.16 m., oil on panel
Musée d'Albi

29

À Grenelle: L'attente

Waiting at Grenelle

c. 1887

0.56, 0.468 m.; 22, 18⁷⁄₁₆ in.

Oil on canvas

Dortu, 1971: P.328

Sterling and Francine Clark Art
Institute; Williamstown, Massachusetts

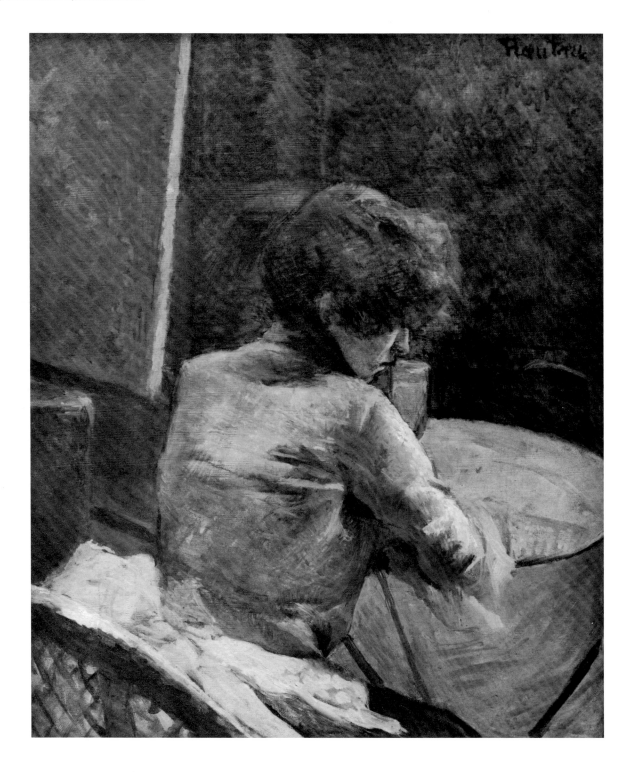

Lautrec must have painted this evocative picture of a woman drinking absinthe at a café table sometime during 1887, after producing *À Grenelle, buveuse d'absinthe* (cat. no. 26), the painting on permanent exhibition at Aristide Bruant's café Le Mirleton. Lautrec's student friend Gauzi apparently confused these two paintings when he wrote his memoirs almost fifty years later. Gauzi recalled that Lautrec reclaimed the picture from the Mirleton at the instigation of their friend Frédéric Wenz in order to submit it to an exhibition in Rheims, where it was purchased by Wenz's father. But *À Grenelle, buveuse d'absinthe* was sold with Bruant's estate in 1905, and it was *À Grenelle: L'attente,* a painting Gauzi never mentions, which was bought by Wenz. Perhaps when Frédéric suggested that Lautrec retrieve his Mirleton picture to send to Rheims, Lautrec, not wishing to annoy Bruant, simply sent another painting of the same theme and mood.

Gauzi's confusion is easy to understand, for the two paintings are very similar in both theme and title. He apparently conflated the two in his mind, because he describes the Mirleton absinthe drinker as seated at a round café table (*guéridon*) which Lautrec kept in his studio both as a prop for posing pictures and as utilitarian furniture for serving apéritifs (Gauzi, p. 45). But the Mirleton drinker actually sits at a rectangular table, and the setting in no way suggests Lautrec's studio, which he did not acquire until the summer of 1886. Prior to that he shared his friend Henri Rachou's, and his models from that period are posed against a limited, neutral setting. While Bruant's picture looks as if it were set in a café, the conspicuously stacked canvases in the background of *À Grenelle: L'àttente* call attention to the fact that the model was posed in the studio. Painted later than *À Grenelle, buveuse d'absinthe,* this work also utilizes the round table which Gauzi remembered from Lautrec's studio and which Lautrec incorporated into an 1888 picture of a solitary female drinker, *A la Bastille, Jeanne Wenz* (see cat. no. 27, fig. 1).

Lautrec's decision to pose a café subject amidst the clutter of his studio reveals his characteristic interest in exploring the multiple levels of fiction and reality that are involved in the process of creating art (see cat. nos. 23, 41). While many of his "naturalist" predecessors, most notably Degas (cat. no. 95, fig. 1) and Manet (fig. 1), had portrayed similar melancholy scenes, they maintained the

Fig. 1
Manet, *The plum*
c. 1877, 0.73 x 0.50 m., oil on canvas
National Gallery of Art, Washington
Collection of Mr. and Mrs. Paul Mellon

pretense of capturing an unposed subject in her actual milieu. This group sought unconventional poses and effects which, by appearing uncontrived, evoked a sense of immediacy and heightened realism. This deception created a paradoxical dilemma for artists pursuing truth, and Lautrec attempted to expose as much of the artifice involved as possible. His abiding concern was to convey the fullest possible expression of truth, and the realities he depicts are at once fuller and subtler than those of his older colleagues. Since his table functioned both as prop and personal furniture, the seated woman can be understood simultaneously as a model posed for a studio composition and a visiting friend having a drink. In a sense, Lautrec extended the reality of the café environment he frequented into his own studio when he chose to serve his friends at a table of this type. His painting perfectly expresses this unity of his art with his life and the mingling of artifice and truth which is as unavoidable an aspect of reality as it is of making pictures.

The nature of Lautrec's relationship to the generation of "naturalist" artists who preceded him is apparent in another aspect of this work. He probably adopted the unusual ¾ rear-facing view from his friend Renoir, who was already using it in the 1870s (fig. 2), and by 1887 many artists had incorporated into their work the motif of a hat concealing the model's eyes (fig. 3). But Lautrec had the capacity to transform these common devices into an evocation of poignant emotion that surpassed the decorative or "naturalist" intentions of his older colleagues. The hair which conceals his model's eyes seems less artificially contrived than Renoir's and Tissot's hats, and creates a softer, more intimate effect. And by slightly altering the disposition of small details of his figure's anatomy, by the angle of the barely hunched shoulder, the droop of the mouth, and the downward tilt of the head, Lautrec has suggested the despondency of this solitary drinker with a subtlety unmatched by any of his contemporaries.

N.E.M.

Fig. 2
Renoir, *Young girl with a bouquet of tulips*
1878-1879, 0.55 x 0.46 m., oil on canvas
Private collection, Paris

Fig. 3
Tissot, *The newspaper*
1883, pastel
Musée du Petit Palais, Paris

30

Poudre de riz

Rice powder

1887

0.65, 0.58 m.; 25⅝, 22⅞ in.

Peinture à l'essence on board

Dortu, 1971: P.348

Rijksmuseum Vincent van Gogh,
Amsterdam

As Murray (p. 80) realized, this painting, which Lautrec chose for his debut exhibit with Les XX in Brussels early in 1888, was completed the previous year. Although Joyant (I, p. 268) describes the jar on the table as a container of rice powder for makeup, the otherwise empty table suggests a café scene, similar to other pictures by Lautrec of unescorted women at tables (cat. nos. 26, 29). When Van Gogh wrote asking his brother whether "Lautrec finished his picture of a woman leaning on her elbows on a little table in a cafe?" (Van Gogh, II, p. 544), he may have been referring to this painting, since his brother bought it from Lautrec immediately. Writing from Arles, where he installed himself in February, 1888, Van Gogh suggested to his brother that a new painting (fig. 1) would be a fitting pendant to this Lautrec. "I do not think that my peasant would do any harm to the de Lautrec in your possession if they were hung side by side, and I am even bold enough to hope that the de Lautrec would appear even more distinguished by the mutual contrast, and that on the other hand my picture would gain by the odd juxtaposition, because that sun-steeped, sunburned quality, tan and air-swept, would show up still more effectively beside all that face powder and elegance" (Van Gogh, III, p. 6).

Van Gogh's portrait of the gardener Escalier does contrast vividly with Lautrec's in terms of color selection and theme. Yet the pictures have similar dimensions and both set a figure decoratively against a contrastingly toned background. In other words, despite the vast differences between them, the paintings share significant artistic premises. Most important, Van Gogh interpreted Lautrec's work as emblematic of artifice and urbanity in the way in which his own work was invested with wholesomeness, the soil and sun. The title of Lautrec's picture refers not to the model's activity but to her artificially pallid complexion, which Lautrec accentuated against the background mosaic of brushstrokes that enhalo her. Judging from these pictorial emphases, Lautrec was altogether aware that his genre scene could be interpreted as a symbol of modern urban values.

Lautrec's model leans forward on the table where she waits for someone to buy her a drink. Her posture and facial features express her resigned depression, which Lautrec attempted to complement with carefully invented pictorial details. For example, the model's slumped silhouette is extended by the line of her chair's back, and their joined forms suggest the collapsed weight she transfers to the table. Although the table is supported by slender, unobtrusive legs, Lautrec has positioned the extreme foremost corner of the tablecloth as if it rests on air, and as if its delicate white point supports the table and the sad woman whose face is powdered white like that of a mute clown.

C.F.S.

Fig. 1
Van Gogh, *Portrait of the gardener Patience Escalier*
1888, 0.69 x 0.56 m., oil on canvas
Stavros S. Niarchos Collection, London

31

Madame la Comtesse A. de Toulouse-Lautrec, mère de l'artiste

The Countess A. de Toulouse-Lautrec, mother of the artist

1887

0.54, 0.45 m.; 21¼, 17¾ in.

Oil on canvas

Dortu, 1971: P.277

Musée d'Albi

Lautrec painted this exquisite portrait of his mother reading in the summer of 1887 and was so pleased with it that he exhibited it the following year at Les XX in Brussels. Following a personal predilection he manifested throughout his career, he posed her seated in profile and set the image centrally in his composition. The central placement and profile pose endow the countess with the hieratic dignity of the early Renaissance portraits Lautrec so admired, a formal effect that is enhanced by her upright posture and straightbacked chair.

Lautrec has avoided any sense of grandeur or regality in this portrait, however, contriving instead to make every detail expressive of the countess' modest and gentle personality. Her simple hairstyle and sober, dark high-buttoned dress with its chaste white collar certainly contribute to this effect, as does Lautrec's muted palette. His flickering mixture of cool lilac-greys, violet-blues and greens is relieved from austerity by the dull rose masses of the drawing room furniture, which add warmth to the painting and echo the subdued curves of the countess' body and chair arms. But it was through his treatment of his mother's face that Lautrec achieved the most subtle aspects of his characterization. Once again he has represented her with downcast eyes (see cat. no. 12) to capture her introspective and quiet nature, and he offsets any hint of severity in her firmly pursed mouth by his delicate rendering of the slight double chin that softens her face. The setting, too, reinforces her air of unassuming tranquility. With its simple furniture and evenly placed vertical and horizontal accents, the room breathes a sense of quiet repose and unostentatious solidity.

It is quite possible that Lautrec modelled his mother's portrait after similar types of images formulated by his friend Renoir in the late 1870s (fig. 1). However, his older "Impressionist" colleague always pursued sensuous effects and his painting lacks the psychological characterization of Lautrec's. Renoir's image is more relaxed and purely decorative than Lautrec's, and far more simply structured. By using a cooler range of colors and firmer outlines, and by constructing a more complex spatial envelope with a geometric arrangement of vertical and horizontal elements in place of Renoir's shallow backdrop, Lautrec has given his portrait the meditative serenity of a Vermeer.

N.E.M.

Fig. 1
Renoir, *The reader*
1877, 0.63 x 0.53 m., oil on canvas
Private collection

32

Au Cirque Fernando, l'écuyère

At the Circus Fernando, the equestrienne

1887

0.98, 0.61 m.; 38¾, 36½ in.

Oil on canvas

Dortu, 1971: P.312

The Art Institute of Chicago

Joyant (I, p. 86) recalled that Lautrec sincerely wanted to accomplish large-scale decorations and undertook mural-scale canvases depicting scenes observed at the Cirque Fernando to satisfy that ambition. Two photographs of Lautrec's studio record his efforts. Lautrec is at work painting *Au Moulin Rouge, la danse* (p. 21, fig. 6) in one of them (fig. 1), which must therefore date from 1890. An approximately 8-foot tall picture is visible behind the rue Caulaincourt studio clutter, including the enormous portable stairs built to permit Lautrec to reach the upper portions of the mural. The cross-bracing for the stairs is visible in the background of Lautrec's portrait of Mr. Manuel, 1891 (P.377).

This oversized painting represents the Cirque Fernando: the background contains grandstands with spectators watching the ringmaster, Mr. Loyal, crack his whip to a galloping horse, only the hooves of which are visible in the photograph. In the immediate foreground a gigantically tall clown in a star-spangled costume faces the viewer. Two drawings give the best idea of how this figure would have been placed in the mural (D. 1.437 and D. 3.920). According to Gauzi (p. 119), the clown held out a hoop for an equestrienne to jump through. Another large figure in the foreground in front of the ringmaster is just partially visible. A second photograph, which can be dated to 1895 since it shows Lautrec and a friend admiring *Au salon* (cat. no. 75, fig. 1), faintly records part of the same figure and indicates that Lautrec had not yet destroyed the paintings and stairs by this date. Gauzi (p. 120), however, recalls that Lautrec allowed Maurice Guibert to continue with the picture during the 1890s before Lautrec unstretched and destroyed it. Had he preserved it, Lautrec's circus mural would have been his most ambitious work, comparable in scale only to the now badly damaged canvases for La Goulue's tent done in 1895 (p. 27, fig. 17, and cat. no. 25, fig. 2).

The half dozen paintings and the related drawings which Lautrec devoted to the circus theme in 1887 have a special interest, for they are either preparations for the envisioned mural, or they are condensed meditations done on a more manageable scale either during its execution or after its abandonment. A few paintings from 1893 (for example, P.448, P.489) indicate that Lautrec maintained interest in the theme. Several years later in 1899, when he was confined to a sanitorium, Lautrec decided that the most convincing demonstration of his mental health would be a series of master drawings. Working from his uncanny visual memory, he produced a large suite of circus drawings, a masterly reprise of his early mural project (fig. 2). These late works, which constitute one of Lautrec's highest achievements, comparable to the tragicomic graphic epics of Tiepolo, Goya, Picasso or Matisse, testify to the deep personal commitment he made to capturing human nature in the spectacle of the Cirque Fernando.

The Cirque Fernando (later renamed the Cirque Medrano) was among Lautrec's favorite Montmartre haunts. Princeteau frequently took Lautrec to the circus (Duret, p. 69), and Lautrec in turn habitually shepherded friends

Fig. 1
Photograph of Lautrec in his studio
c. 1890. Portions of his circus mural are visible at the left

Fig. 2
Toulouse-Lautrec, *At the circus*
1899, 0.22 x 0.31 m., crayon
The Art Institute of Chicago

there (Rothenstein, p. 65). He was surely aware that the colorful scenes had captivated some of his elder colleagues, for example the artists Renoir (see cat. no. 37, fig. 1), Degas and Tissot (fig. 3) and the writer E. de Goncourt. According to Gauzi (pp. 130-132), the idea came to Lautrec shortly after meeting Zandomenghi (1841-1917), an Italian painter closely associated with the "Impressionists" whose works he helped Lautrec come to appreciate. Zandomenghi had a special interest in figures partially cropped at the edge of the canvas, a device explored by many of his Impressionist colleagues and one Lautrec used repeatedly for his circus pictures.

Aware that Lautrec was in search of a model for his equestrienne, Zandomenghi introduced him to Suzanne Valadon, who apparently posed for that figure (P.322). Although Lautrec's two known portraits of Suzanne (P.249, P.250) are dated to 1885 by Joyant, judging from their style they, too, date from 1887. Lautrec depicted Suzanne side-saddle on a white horse, galloping around the arena perimeter towards a clown holding a hoop which the horse would pass below, while the rider dived through. That feat fascinated Lautrec, who represented it not only in the Art Institute painting, but in a large vertical format version (cat. no. 33), in a painted fan (fig. 4), and a crayon sketch (S.D. 30). He even decorated a tambourine (P.316) with the vignette drawn in sharply foreshortened perspective, so as to suggest that the frame of the tambourine is the hoop through which the equestrienne has just passed.

In all of these works the equestrienne is conducted by Mr. Loyal, the famous ringmaster at the Cirque Fernando of whom Lautrec also made a drawing (D. 3.057). Lautrec portrays him in *Au Cirque Fernando, l'écuyère* silhouetted against the white sand of the arena floor seen from above. His feet cropped by the frame, Loyal's figure seems to swoop forward following the gracefully bowed profile with which Lautrec drew him. The arc of his body and those of his whip, the grandstand tiers, and the clown's hoop repeat the essential structuring motif of Lautrec's decorative scheme, unifying it and charging it with centripetal momentum. The stylized flatness of the figure of Loyal placed against a solid contrasting ground suggests the influence of Japanese prints, as does the horse (D. 3.220) which can be compared with Hokusai's revered sketchbook illustrations (fig. 5).

Both the Art Institute picture and the destroyed mural include representations of onlookers at ringside. The inclusion of the audience is a crucial detail, for Lautrec persistently brought together observers and what they observe in his art in order to suggest the experience of being one spectator amongst many, and to express his conviction that the crowd possesses as much dramatic interest as the performers it gathers to watch.

Both *Au Cirque Fernando, l'écuyère* and a related smaller painting (fig. 6) were selected by Lautrec to be among those at his debut exhibition with Les XX in Brussels early in 1888, for the catalogue of which he prepared

Fig. 3
Tissot, *The ladies of the cars*
c. 1883, 1.43 x 1.00 m., oil on canvas
Museum of Art, Rhode Island School of Design

Fig. 4
Toulouse-Lautrec, *Circus scene*
c. 1888, 0.28 x 0.58 m., watercolor
Private collection

Fig. 6
Toulouse-Lautrec, *At the Fernando Circus, horsewoman on a white horse*
1888, 0.58 x 0.78 m., pastel gouache on board
The Norton Simon Foundation

Fig. 5
Hokusai, sheets no. 10 verso and 11 recto of *The sketches of Hokusai, Vol. 6*
1817, 0.16 x 0.23 m. (book), woodblock print
The Art Institute of Chicago
The Ryerson Collection

a circus drawing (D. 3034). Later that year the Art Institute of Chicago picture was purchased, along with *Au Moulin Rouge, la danse* (P.361), by Joseph Oller, one of the directors of the Moulin Rouge, who installed them both in the entranceway to the famous cabaret. Many artists admired them there: for example, Seurat's masterful *Le cirque* (fig. 7), a reprise of a theme he investigated earlier in the decade, is surely an appreciative response to Lautrec's extraordinary picture, and both Bonnard (fig. 8) and Picasso as well utilized Lautrec's imagery in circus works of their own.

C.F.S.

Fig. 7
Seurat, *The circus*
1890-1891, 1.85 x 1.50 m., oil on canvas
Musée du Louvre, Paris

Fig. 8
Bonnard, *Circus rider*
1894, 0.25 x 0.33 m., oil on panel
The Phillips Collection, Washington, D.C.

33

Au cirque: "Clown"

At the circus: Clown

1887-1888

1.15, 0.42 m.; 45⅜, 16⅝ in.

Oil on canvas

Dortu, 1971: P.314

Private collection

This wonderful painting groups together all the major elements Lautrec used for his large circus mural (see cat. no. 32) and, like *Au Cirque Fernando, l'écuyère,* it records a stage in Lautrec's exploration of his most ambitious project. Evidently Lautrec considered a variety of formats within which to arrange his cast of figures, and this tall, narrow painting investigates a stacked organization of details. Lautrec, who must have been fond of the vertical format used for Chinese scroll paintings, conceived several important works along similar proportions (for example, cat. nos. 46, 81).

In this picture, the clown and hoop are placed low in his composition, and are severely cropped by the corners in much the same way as the bizarre faces of later works were lodged in the foreground (see cat. no. 52). Apparently the acrobat and horse visible directly above the hoop have just completed their stunt, to the pleasure of the ringmaster and two clowns. The scribbled indication of a grandstand evokes the background blurring unavoidable when a spectator's gaze follows a moving object. The bold shorthand for the grandstand unites with the fluid silhouettes of the ringmaster and clowns to create the effect of movement, even within the restrictive confines of this narrow vertical composition.

C.F.S.

34

Au cirque: dans les coulisses

At the circus: behind the scenes

1887-1888

0.67, 0.60 m.; 26⅜, 23⅝ in.

Oil on canvas

Dortu, 1971: P.321

Collection of The Newark Museum

This painting and its preparatory drawing (D. 3.056) are part of Lautrec's concentrated investigation of circus themes begun in the mid 1880s. The two female figures likely represent the Guillas sisters, acrobat friends of Princeteau. When Duret (1920, p. 71) claimed that Lautrec posed the sisters for a circus scene, he must have been referring to the Newark picture, because it alone includes two female circus performers. It is of interest to note that Lautrec's composition is close to one used by Seurat around 1882-1883 for a conté crayon drawing of a similar theme—a horse flanked by clowns (fig. 1).

Like Lautrec's other circus pictures, this is carefully studied. The centrally placed horse's head is a compositional pivot in relationship to which the figures and background arches are disposed. A special feature of the Newark painting is the prominent pattern of long shadows in the foreground. Taken with the shadow of the horse in *Au Cirque Fernando, l'écuyère* (cat. no. 32), and the shadows of dancers in *Au Moulin Rouge, la danse* (p. 21, fig. 6), those in the Newark painting testify to Lautrec's brief but important interest in a special visual motif during the later 1880s.

C. F. S.

Fig. 1
Seurat, *Study for La parade*
c. 1882, 0.31 x 0.24 m., conté crayon drawing
The Phillips Collection, Washington, D.C.

35

Frédéric Wenz

1888

0.55, 0.46 m.; 21¾, 18⅛ in.

Oil on canvas

Dortu, 1971: P.329

Museum of Fine Arts, Houston; Gift of
Sarah Cambell Blaffer, Robert Lee
Blaffer Memorial Collection

Lautrec's painting of his fellow student from Cormon's atelier is among his most extraordinary portraits. Perhaps motivated by the powerful block-like anatomy of the sitter (see cat. no. 24), Lautrec painted him with a forceful directness uncommon in his other portraits or those painted by his contemporaries. Only Renoir had painted such condensed, sculptural portraits, for example that of *Victor Chocquet* (1876), but even Renoir's works lack the starkness of the portrait of Wenz. As is characteristic of Lautrec's work, the simplicity of pose and unpretentiousness of setting conceal the careful planning and arrangement which underlie the composition. Indeed, the complicated rectangular structure of Lautrec's portrait is comparable to one of Mondrian's 1920s abstractions. The repeated horizontals and verticals representative of the wall panelling and pictures in the background interlock with the blocky masses of Wenz's head and shoulders, accentuating their square lines and emphasizing their forceful character. The background structures coincide so repeatedly with the major lines of Wenz's anatomy that they act like a constraining barrier counteracting the power of the sitter's physique and the aggressive energy of his personality.

The only clue to the date of *Frédéric Wenz* lies in Gauzi's comment (p. 45) that Lautrec painted it shortly after *Artilleur et femme* (cat. no. 24), which Joyant placed in 1886. It was in that year that Lautrec first painted Wenz's sister as well (cat. no. 27). Despite these arguments, Dortu suggests a later date, *circa* 1888, which seems likely on stylistic grounds.

N. E. M. and C. F. S.

36

Madame Lili Grenier

1888

0.55, 0.46 m.; 21¾, 18⅛ in.

Oil on canvas

Dortu, 1971: P.303

Mr. Yasuo Suita

Lili Grenier was the wife of one of Lautrec's fellow students at Cormon's atelier. Lautrec shared lodgings with the couple in the mid-1880s and accompanied them on their vacations to Villiers-sur-Morin (cat. no. 22). According to Gauzi (p. 58n), Lili had been a model for Degas prior to her marriage, but she was reluctant to pose for Lautrec because his harsh portraits were often unflattering. She yielded to his requests on several occasions, however (D. 2.985 and P.302), and sat for two portraits in 1888. In both of them she wore a Japanese kimono, undoubtedly part of her cherished collection of costumes. Lautrec, Lili and her friends from the Comédie Française enjoyed dressing themselves in her costumes in order to be photographed (Gauzi, pp. 137-138).

This portrait, which belonged to Dr. Bourges (cat. no. 46), is both simple and direct. The composition consists of the triangular form of Lili's head and torso inscribed within the nearly square canvas. Lautrec elaborated his rather inert pictorial idea, however, by having her turn her head to the right. This subtly adjusted the figure's spatial disposition, for the angle at which her head is turned corresponds to the portrait's triangular composition and by implication restates the triangularity in another dimension.

If Lautrec chose an elementary composition, however, he apparently did so to provide a stable scaffold for his liquid brushwork. He indicated the embroidery on Lili's robe with creamy strokes of white, pink and red, and for the background wall he applied feathery strokes in confetti colors. These lively accents relieve Lili's serious facial expression. What might be called Lautrec's light-hearted brushwork, taken together with his humorless composition, creates a paradoxical mood. At once gay and meditative, Lili's portrait is characteristic of Lautrec's uncanny ability to evoke personality with a minimum of pictorial means.

C. F. S.

37

**Monsieur Samary, de la Comédie
Française**

Mr. Samary of the Comédie Française

1889

0.75, 0.25 m.; 29½, 20½ in.

Peinture à l'essence on board

Dortu, 1971: P.330

Musée du Louvre,
Galerie du Jeu de
Paume, Paris

With the exception of M. Loyal in *Au Cirque Fernando*, Lautrec's brilliant portrait of *M. Samary* taking the role of Raoul de Vaubert in Jules Sandeau's play *Mademoiselle de la Seiglière* is the first of his portraits of entertainment personalities on stage and off, a subject which fascinated him from 1891-1896. Already in *M. Samary* Lautrec had probed his favorite themes: the relationship between sincerity and pretense or reality and theater, and that between observer and observed, actor and spectator. As all eyes, including Lautrec's (presumably from his elevated viewing position in a theater box), are turned to the actor, he raises his monocle to return their gaze. In doing so, Samary sets his arms and legs at perpendicularly posed angles, creating a structural motif which Lautrec repeats and varies in all of the background details to give the picture its extraordinarily tight compositional unity.

Although portraits of famous players costumed in their well-known roles were a longstanding tradition in European painting and graphic arts, artists seldom exposed the fictional element of their subjects' pretense before coarsely painted scenery, or depicted them from a point of view which implied that they were seen on a stage from a theater seat. Lautrec did both, and the peculiarities point up his chosen role as a detached observer of his milieu, as well as revealing what types of works constituted his pictorial sources. These undoubtedly included paintings by Renoir (fig. 1), Degas (fig. 2), and Manet,

Fig. 1
Renoir, *Clown at the circus*
1868, 1.92 x 1.28 m., oil on canvas
Rijksmuseum Kröller-Müller, Otterlo

whose *Lola de Valence* (1862, Jeu de Paume), a special favorite of Lautrec's in the collection of his patron, Camondo (Natanson, 1951, p. 99), makes use of theater flats in the background. Perhaps a more important source of inspiration, however, were eighteenth- and nineteenth-century Japanese prints depicting popular Kabuki actors (fig. 3). Lautrec, a connoisseur of Japanese art, was almost certainly indebted to these prints for both the motif of the steeply tilted stage boards and the unusual and highly decorative color combination of purple and green.

Entirely his own, however, are Lautrec's wonderful sense of design, evident in the repeated angles and forms of the actor and the backdrop tree, and his flamboyant brushwork. The latter is most noticeable in the whipped froth of Samary's ruffled shirt and his distorted facial features, which anticipate the graphic daring of Francis Bacon.

C.F.S.

Fig. 2
Degas, *The star*
1878, 0.37 x 0.27 m., monotype and pastel
The Philadelphia Museum of Art

Fig. 3
Būnchō, *Arashi Hinaji as Yuga-gozen in*
"Ima-o-sakari Suehiro Genji"
1768, 0.31 x 0.15 m., woodblock print
The Art Institute of Chicago, The Clarence Buckingham
Collection of Japanese Prints

38

Au bal du Moulin de la Galette

The dance hall at the Moulin de la
Galette

1889

0.90, 1.00 m.; 35½, 39⅝ in.

Oil on canvas

Dortu, 1971: P.335

The Art Institute of Chicago: Mr .and
Mrs. L. L. Coburn Memorial Collection

Like *Au Cirque Fernando* (cat. no. 32), *Au Bal du Moulin de la Galette* is an ambitious composition which Lautrec created for public exhibition. In fact, after its debut at the Salon des Indépendents in 1889, Lautrec chose to exhibit it frequently, in 1890, 1891 and 1893. On these occasions he presumably had to borrow the painting from its owner, the artist Joseph Albert, whose profile portrait is prominent in the picture's right foreground (Joyant, I, p. 126).

Lautrec evidently did not plan to include Albert's portrait originally, for he is absent from the vertical-format painted study (fig. 1) which preceded the final work. The young woman in profile at the left, however, was important to Lautrec's first idea, and an exquisite painted study for her head exists in Moscow (P.351).

Since according to one account (Arsène Alexandre, cited by Cooper, p. 76) it was Albert who introduced Lautrec to his idol, Degas, *Au Moulin de la Galette* is

Fig. 1
Toulouse-Lautrec, *Study for Moulin de la Galette*
1889, 0.41 x 0.32 m., panel
Private collection, Paris

understandably reminiscent of Degas' early café scenes (fig. 2), as well as the slightly later ones by Manet (fig. 3). And Constantin Guys had also executed a number of dance-hall scenes whose format and vigorous sketch-like technique could have influenced the background of Lautrec's work (see cat. no. 25, fig. 1). Yet the sole witness account of the genesis of *Au Moulin de la Galette* (Gauzi, pp. 84-89) claims that Lautrec painted it to emulate Renoir's pictures of the same locale (figs. 4, 5). If so, Lautrec's response to Renoir's picture transforms its Sunday afternoon gaiety into an atmosphere of melancholy. With the exception of general highlights in red, yellow, and flesh tones, Lautrec's *Au Moulin de la Galette* utilizes a drab color scheme which isolates the faces of

Fig. 2
Degas, *Women in front of a café*
1877, 0.41 x 0.67 m., oil on canvas
Musée du Louvre, Paris

Fig. 3
Manet, *Café, Place du Théâtre Français*
1881, 0.32 x 1.04 m., oil and pastel on canvas
The Glascow Art Gallery, The Burrell Collection

Fig. 4
Renoir, *Le Moulin de la Galette*
1876, 1.31 x 1.75 m., oil on canvas
Musée du Louvre, Paris

onlookers observed in crowded solitude. The opposed profiled figures in the foreground and the similarly opposed diagonals of the bench back and floor boards create a compositional structure of balanced tensions (Cooper, p. 76). It is interesting to note that the bold use of diagonals and the curiously abrupt juxtaposition of large foreground figures watching small entwined forms further back in space seems to repeat the pictorial structure and mood of Gauguin's *The vision after the sermon* (fig. 6), which Lautrec could have seen at Théo Van Gogh's gallery in Paris.

The powerful, almost spiritual mood of Lautrec's picture is accentuated by the marvelous foreground still-life. The conspicuous pile of tipsily stacked saucers testifies

Fig. 5
Renoir, Illustration for Zola's *L'Assommoir*, Paris 1878

Fig. 6
Gauguin, *The vision after the sermon*
1888, 0.73 x 0.92 m., oil on canvas
The National Gallery of Scotland, Edinburgh

to the repeated glasses of mulled wine (the Moulin de la Galette's specialty) drunk by the occupant of the nearest table, who, although he sits outside the frame of the picture, must be Lautrec himself. The saucers suggest the hours spent by the artist, or by extension the viewer of the picture as well, in watching the dance hall spectacle.

If Lautrec was indebted to his older associates for aspects of his painting's theme and composition, the harsh, joyless leisure he captured in *Au Moulin de la Galette* had in its turn an enormous influence on the others of his circle. Within months Van Gogh (fig. 7) followed Lautrec's lead in pursuing the same subject, and slightly more than a decade later, when Picasso saw the work exhibited in 1902, the entire composition as well as individual figures within it haunted him and reappeared in his own art (fig. 8).

C.F.S.

Fig. 7
Van Gogh, *Ballroom at Arles*
1888, 0.65 x 0.81 m., oil on canvas
Musée du Louvre, Paris

Fig. 8
Picasso, *Le Moulin de la Galette*
1900, 0.86 x 0.14 m., oil on canvas
The Solomon R. Guggenheim Museum, New York

39

Femme rousse assise dans le jardin de M. Forest

Red-headed woman seated in the garden of Mr. Forest

1889

0.646, 0.537 m.; 25½, 20⅞ in.

Oil on canvas

Dortu, 1971: P.343

Private collection

This brilliant portrait was painted against the familiar backdrop of the foliage in the garden of M. Forest. It seems likely that the model, sometimes identified with that of *La blanchisseuse* (cat. no. 28) as Rosa, is actually Carmen Gaudin, for both have the same hair and features as the 1885 portraits of Carmen and the various versions of *La rousse au caraco blanc*. Since Lautrec reportedly used Carmen for a long time (Gauzi, p. 130) her appearance in 1889 is not unusual, especially as Rachou recalled that Lautrec painted Carmen in M. Forest's garden (Mack, p. 61) and only this picture and two related ones from the same date record this occurrence (fig. 1 and P.353).

The overwhelming beauty of this portrait lies in the sumptuosity of its color and exuberance of brushwork. Obviously influenced by the "Impressionist" profile por-

Fig. 1
Toulouse-Lautrec, *Red-headed woman in mauve*
1889, 0.71 x 0.58 m., oil on board
The Norton Simon Foundation, Los Angeles

traits posed in gardens by Manet (fig. 2) and Renoir (fig. 3), Lautrec has contrived a similar figure whose undulating contours are poised against a flat, decorative background in the manner of the early Renaissance portraits the artist loved. The curving arabesque of her body is echoed by the armchair, and both sinuous forms are played off against the angular fronds of spikey shrubbery. Lautrec was a consummate master at intensifying the essential quality of a form by juxtaposing it with forms of a contrasting nature. His characteristic use of this device sets his work apart from that of the Impressionists with their more homogeneous surfaces.

Lautrec extended this artistic idea to all other aspects of the picture as well. While the Impressionists' colors are rich and sensuous, Lautrec intensifies his even further by juxtaposing contrasting complementaries. The carefully orchestrated oppositions of orange and blue-violet, cerise and green, have a vibrancy that is reinforced by the bold, energetic facture. While Manet and Renoir tended to handle the picture surface fairly evenly, giving equal attention to both figure and ground, Lautrec concentrates attention more closely on his model by contrasting her densely painted form with the more thinly and sketchily treated peripheries of the canvas. Finally, whereas his older colleagues were preoccupied exclusively with the decorative effects of forms and colors seen in outdoor light, Lautrec reveals his abiding concern for capturing some quality of inner life in his subject. The single detail of the woman's eye gazing fixedly into the distance beyond the picture frame suggests idle meditation, an essential human activity that the Impressionists seldom sought to portray.

After 1889 Carmen disappeared from Lautrec's repertoire. She was by all accounts an excellent model, punctual, reliable, and capable of immobility (Gauzi, p. 158), and had been a fruitful source of inspiration for Lautrec for a number of years. Gauzi reports that the beautiful red hair which first attracted Lautrec to her in 1885 (cat. no. 28) owed something of its color to dyes, but that the artist, frequently preferring the artificial to the real, did not mind this at all (p. 158). Gauzi also remembers Lautrec telling him that he lost interest in her abruptly one day when, after a lapse of six months during which she had not sat for him, Carmen reappeared at his studio with brown hair (Gauzi, p. 159). It is possible that this event signalled the end of their working relationship.

N.E.M.

Fig. 2
Manet, *Portrait of Mrs. Manet at Bellevue*
1880, 0.82 x 0.65 m., oil on canvas
Private collection, New York

Fig. 3
Renoir, *Marie-Thérèse Durand-Ruel sewing*
1882, 0.64 x 0.54 m., oil on canvas
The Sterling and Francine Clark Art Institute, Williamstown

40

Tête de femme dans le jardin de M. Forest

Woman in the garden of Mr. Forest

1889

0.55, 0.46 m.; 21¾, 18⅛ in.

Oil on canvas

Dortu, 1971: P.344

The Metropolitan Museum of Art, New York

During 1889, Lautrec often posed his models in the garden of Mr. Forest (see cat. no. 39). He found it a particularly satisfying setting because the brilliant green shades of the foliage acted as the perfect decorative foil for his models' hair and clothing. Lautrec sought out red-headed models throughout his career because he found the russet tones immensely provocative and beautiful, and here he has played them off with great subtlety against the rich green background and the deep pink of his model's blouse.

With characteristic flair, Lautrec has established a gentle irony in the contrast between his model's face and torso. Not conventionally attractive with her thick lips, heavy chin, and turned-up nose, the woman's plain features are offset by the seductiveness of her body. Lautrec has intensified the allure of her swelling bosom by painting her blouse in washes so thin and transparent as to reveal the outlines of her chemise. This gauzy flimsiness and the tilted thrust of her chest alter the effect of her coarse, blunt visage and stiffly held head, giving her an unexpected appeal.

N.E.M.

41

La femme au chapeau noir, Berthe la sourde

Woman in a black hat, Berthe the deaf

1890

0.62, 0.45 m.; 24½, 17¾ in.

Peinture à l'essence on board

Dortu, 1971: P.373

Private Collection

Nothing is known about Berthe la sourde (the deaf), a model whom, according to Joyant, Lautrec used in 1890. Lautrec painted two portraits of her, in both of which she is primly dressed and holds an umbrella across her lap. But the settings and consequently the color schemes of the works are entirely different: for one she wore a light dress and sat in Forest's garden (fig. 1); for the other she wore black and posed in Lautrec's studio.

Like several earlier works posed in his studio, this portrait of Berthe la sourde is a wry mixture of candor and contrivance. The cluttered wicker chairs and canvases in the background are foils for the model's coloring and her orderly, pyramidal figure. Their casual informality serves to emphasize the stiff self-consciousness of her pose and her look of wide-eyed attention. Although indoors, she neither removes her hat nor relinquishes the umbrella, which became an important prop in Lautrec's composition of interlocking triangular forms. Looking altogether out of place, the model seems to have a merely formal role as if she were above all a strong, dark triangular shape used for pictorial purposes. But it is this contrast between Berthe's image and Lautrec's studio which in the end draws attention to her and arouses curiosity about her quiet thoughts as she sits for the artist on the edge of her chair. Consequently, Lautrec managed to heighten his characterization of his sitter by placing her in a foreign context. As so often in his art, artifice and reality reciprocate with absurd intensity.

C.F.S.

Fig. 1
Lautrec painting Berthe la sourde in the garden of Mr. Forest
1890

42

Mademoiselle Dihau au piano

Miss Dihau at the piano

1890

0.63, 0.48 m.; 24⅞, 19 in.

Peinture à l'essence on board

Dortu, 1971: P.358

Musée d'Albi

Marie Dihau, whose portrait Lautrec executed early in 1890, lived with her brothers (cat. nos. 43, 44) at 6 rue Frochot, where Marie gave piano and singing lessons. The musical Dihau family had been friendly with Degas since the 1860s, at which time he had painted their portraits. Lautrec idolized these paintings and sometimes shepherded friends to see them (Vuillard, p. 141). It was Marie Dihau who first introduced Lautrec to Degas, whose portraits of the Dihaus overshadowed Lautrec's by his own estimate (Joyant, I, p. 130).

Degas had painted Marie at the piano in one of his portraits of her (fig. 1), and Lautrec thought it appropriate to include this picture in his own. It is visible on the wall, immediately above the music stand. However, the Degas portrait of Marie which Lautrec allegedly praised as "primitive" (Joyant, I, p. 130) must be the one in profile, today in the Metropolitan Museum, New York.

As was the case with his *Absinthe drinker* (cat. no. 26) Lautrec's portrait of Marie Dihau at a keyboard reiterated a genre theme that originated in the seventeenth century. In the 1860s and 1870s such avant-garde artists as

Fig. 1
Degas, *Portrait of Miss Dihau*
1869-1872, 0.39 x 0.32 m., oil on canvas
Musée du Louvre, Paris

Whistler, Manet, Degas, Renoir (fig. 2) and Tissot (fig. 3) took up the theme as a result of their renewed interest in modern life subjects. Lautrec and other artists of his generation were always aware of the example of their much admired older colleagues. When between 1886 and 1890 Emile Bernard and Van Gogh, fellow students of Lautrec's with Cormon, and Lautrec himself executed piano portraits (figs. 4, 5), their similarities to one another and to the sources of their mutual inspiration were striking.

Painted in strict profile, Lautrec's portrait of Marie captures her intense concentration as she accompanies her musical partner, whose presence outside the frame of the picture is implied by the music stand in the foreground. This device functions here, as elsewhere in Lautrec's work, to strengthen the picture's sense of lively immediacy by transforming the spectator into a participant in the music-making. It was common for the artists of Lautrec's circle to talk about the musicality of painting and to seek ways of establishing visual correspondences to musical forms and effects. Lautrec's complicated composition, with its repetitions and interlockings of triangular and rectangular forms evokes the disciplined structure of musical passages. Its quality of mathematical precision is then enlivened and enriched with a shimmer of delicate color harmonies and virtuoso brushwork.

Satisfied with his portrait, Lautrec exhibited it frequently, beginning at the Salon des Indépendents in the spring of 1890. It was possibly included in a show later that year at the Cercle Volney (Corr., p. 122n2), and perhaps once again with Les XX in Brussels in 1892 (Dortu, Grillaert and Adhemar, p. 30). In 1895 Lautrec repeated the principal elements in a second picture of a woman at the piano (P.579), painting further variations in 1896 (P.630), 1897 (cat. no. 93) and 1898 (P.658), when he again portrayed Marie Dihau, now accompanying a singer.

C.F.S.

Fig. 3
Tissot, *Lady at piano*
c. 1881, 0.41 x 0.33 m., watercolor
The Museum of Art, Rhode Island School of Design

Fig. 2
Renoir, *Lady at the piano*
1875, 0.94 x 0.74 m., oil on canvas
The Art Institute of Chicago, The Mr. and Mrs. Martin
A. Ryerson Collection

Fig. 4
Bernard, *Portrait of the artist's mother*
1888, 0.73 x 0.79 m., oil on canvas
Private collection, France

Fig. 5
Van Gogh, *Miss Gachet at the piano*
1890, 0.10 x 0.50 m., oil on canvas
Kunstmuseum, Basel

43
Le jovial M. Dihau
Jolly Mr. Dihau
1890
0.42, 0.303 m.; 16⅝, 12 in.
Peinture à l'essence on board
Dortu, 1971: P.381
Musée d'Albi

This portrait of the third member of the Dihau family was painted during the same general period in 1890 as those of his brother and sister (cat. nos. 42, 44), and utilizes a similar green-purple system of complementary colors. Lautrec exhibited it twice during 1891, first at the Cercle Volney in February, and again with the portrait of Henri's brother Désiré at the Salon des Indépendents in March. The whimsical title *Le jovial M. Dihau* perfectly suits Lautrec's evocation of his patient, mildly amused friend braced somewhat stiffly on his cane. But the same sense of visual disparity between figure and setting evident in the portrait of Désiré permeates the picture of Henri as well. Lautrec's choice of a somewhat distant profile pose seems to relate less to his other paintings of intimate friends than to his portrayals of actors on the stage, and the odd detail of the tipped hat creates a striking resemblance to his earlier portrait of M. Samary (cat. no. 37). Lautrec's equipment shack in M. Forest's garden, only lightly indicated to the right, seems to have no more substance here than a stage set; indeed Dihau's formally posed figure looks as if it belongs against a backdrop of theater flats.

N. E. M. & C. F. S.

44

M. Désiré Dihau, Basson de l'Opéra

Mr. Désiré Dihau, bassoonist of the
Opéra

1890

0.56, 0.45 m.; 22⅛, 17¾ in.

Dortu, 1971: P.379

Musée d'Albi

According to Joyant, Lautrec painted his portraits of the Dihau brothers (cat. no. 43) in 1891, in his favorite outdoor setting of M. Forest's garden. But Joyant and others also list both pictures as having been exhibited early in the year, first in February at the Cercle Volney and again at the Salon des Indépendants the following month.

The backdrop of foliage in both pictures indicates either that Lautrec executed them the previous summer or fall, before the leaves fell, or that he painted the setting from memory during the winter months of 1890 or January of 1891. It seems far more likely that he posed the pictures earlier in 1890 than that he contrived a fictitious outdoor setting in the winter, especially since the portraits of male friends he was working on at the beginning of 1891 (Corr., p. 129) were all executed against a studio backdrop (cat. nos. 46, 47). The portrait of Marie Dihau (cat. no. 42) had been exhibited in the Salon des Indépendants early in 1890, and it seems probable that Lautrec would have painted her brothers soon afterwards.

In both of these portraits there seems to be an odd discrepancy between the informality of the garden setting and the attire and poses of the Dihaus. Désiré Dihau was a bassoonist at the Paris opera, and he and Lautrec enjoyed a long, collaborative friendship beginning in the late 1880s. For example, in 1895 Lautrec designed fourteen lithographic illustrations for Dihau's musical compositions. He was already familiar with Degas' portrait of Désiré in the orchestra pit of the Opéra (fig. 1), a work he deeply admired and must have been conscious of when

Fig. 1
Degas, *Orchestra of the Opéra*
1868, 0.53 x 0.45 m., oil on canvas
Musée du Louvre, Paris

formulating both a lithograph of Dihau (fig. 2) and his painted portrait. Beginning in 1888 and continuing sporadically through the 1890s, Lautrec occasionally employed the unusual device of posing portrait subjects from a ¾ rear-facing view. Since this pose exposes very little of the sitter's features, it may be surmised that the artist's motive in selecting it was to achieve formal decorative effects with the interplay of shapes against the background setting. In the case of this picture, however, the use of this particular angle as well as Dihau's pose astride a stiff indoor chair, seem to be droll allusions to his friend's profession and to Degas' portrait. Lautrec portrayed Désiré in evening clothes at an angle from which one might view him seated in the orchestra pit. The newspaper, a conspicuous prop which Lautrec used in no other picture, becomes analogous to the sheet music which would always appear before him, and the odd detail of the lower half of a statue on a pedestal which fills the lefthand background is suggestive of the musician's habitual view of figures on the stage above him. Lautrec has transformed Degas' theatrical representation into a witty and unusual evocation of character type by removing Désiré from his customary setting.

Both the ¾ rear-facing pose and other aspects of this painting reveal the influence of the "Impressionists" whose work he greatly admired. The pose had been used by Renoir since 1879 (fig. 3), and both Monet and Renoir had developed the compositional device of a garden path running vertically up the side of a picture to unify foreground and background. That Lautrec was consciously utilizing this structural motif can be seen from its repetition in another portrait painted in the setting of M. Forest's garden that year, *Le pierreuse* or *Casque d'or* (cat. no. 46). Common to both pictures also is the shimmering color scheme of purples and greens, harmonious complementaries used frequently by Monet and Renoir in landscape paintings of the late 1880s and 1890s, and appearing in many Japanese prints as well.

N.E.M.

Fig. 2
Toulouse-Lautrec, *For you!*
1893, 0.27 x 0.20 m., lithograph
The Art Institute of Chicago

Fig. 3
Renoir, *Young woman reading an illustrated journal*
c. 1877, 0.46 x 0.55 m., oil on canvas
The Museum of Art, Rhode Island School of Design

45

La pierreuse ou Casque d'or

The pierreuse or Golden helmet

1890

0.647, 0.53 m.; 25½, 21 in.

Peinture à l'essence on board

Dortu, 1971: P.407

Walter H. Annenberg

Casque d'or (Golden helmet) was a prostitute who enjoyed a popularity of legendary proportions during the 1880s and 1890s. She achieved her first notoriety (Huisman and Dortu, p. 64) as the mistress of Liaboeuf, an anarchist assassin of policemen, and later became the sub-mistress of a brothel in the rue des Rosiers (Schaub-Koch, p. 186). Her allure was so immense that crowds of bullies allegedly beat each other up in the streets over her favors. Frequently knives and revolvers were brought into play with such abandon that in addition to two men killing each other because of her, stray bullets sometimes hit imprudently curious bystanders (Gauzi, p. 84).

According to Joyant, Lautrec posed her in the spring or summer of 1891 in his favorite outdoor setting of M. Forest's garden, but the similarity of the picture to the portrait of Désiré Dihau (cat. no. 44) makes it likely that it was executed in 1890. He painted her seated, facing the spectator with an expression of direct and good-humored frankness. Garbed in a tight-fitting mandarin jacket which eliminates any suggestion of the model's reputed provocative sexuality, crowned with a topknot in the style popularized by La Goulue (Huisman and Dortu, p. 92), Casque d'or with her wistful smile recalls Watteau's images of pierrots in gardens. It was typical of Lautrec's sympathy and insight that he has characterized the notorious prostitute by an expression of such appealing candor, and portrayed her in a tranquil natural setting so at odds with her flamboyant reputation.

As was frequently his habit in portraits, Lautrec painted Casque d'or's face and hair more densely than her body or the background, which are blocked in loosely with vigorous strokes. The contrast between these areas serves to focus even greater attention on the model's head and makes her open gaze all the more compelling. Lautrec's color scheme and composition are ones he obviously found satisfying, as he used the same palette of purples and blue-greens and the same garden path running vertically up the right side of the picture in his portrait of Désiré Dihau. Of course Casque d'or is dominated by the wonderful helmet of orange hair shadowed with violet that gives the work its title, and which Lautrec artfully intensified by its juxtaposition with the vivid blue-green foliage behind her.

N.E.M.

46

M. le docteur Bourges

Dr. Bourges

1891

0.79, 0.50 m.; 31⅛, 20 in.

Peinture à l'essence on board

Dortu, 1971: P.376

Museum of Art, Carnegie Institute;
Pittsburgh, Pennsylvania

In February 1891 Lautrec wrote to his mother that he was busy with three portraits, which were among the pictures he exhibited beginning on March 20th at the Salon des Indépendents (Corr., p. 124). The letter identifies the subjects of the portraits, all friends of the artist, as Gaston Bonnefoy, Louis Pascal (cat. no. 47), and Dr. Henri Bourges, with which last Lautrec had shared lodgings since 1887. Lautrec posed each of them standing near a double wooden door in the corner of his rue Caulaincourt studio. The tawny planked wood floor and doors and the pale blue studio walls provided Lautrec with a subdued, almost neutral backdrop against which the dark formal attire of his models stands out in sharp silhouette. In all of the portraits, the figures' dandified elegance is set against a casual decorative interplay of rectangles and diagonals, opened doors and stacked frames. In terms of color scheme and composition, each painting amounts to a variation upon a set theme, one first attempted by Lautrec in 1888 when he painted the portrait of François Gauzi (P.297). Gauzi (p. 150) recalled that Lautrec wanted to stress verticality, a preference sustained in all the subsequent works in the group.

The Gauzi portrait, the group done early in 1891, and the four similar works Lautrec painted afterwards (cat. no. 85; P.377, P.383, P.659) all honor an important tradition of modern portraiture—that of the isolated, elegantly attired standing figure set against a neutral or

Fig. 1
Whistler, *Arrangement in flesh color and black: portrait of Duret*
c. 1882-1884, 0.19 x 0.90 m., oil on canvas
The Metropolitan Museum of Art, New York

decoratively embellished background. Degas, Manet, Whistler (fig. 1), Tissot (fig. 2), Caillebotte (fig. 3), and others (fig. 4) undertook the genre, which had a popularized counterpart in the satiric illustrations done by Bertall or Daumier, for example, or Pellegrini (*Vanity Fair's* "Ape").

Unlike the other artists, Lautrec exhibited three similar portraits jointly, as if they were a short series. Although no one had exhibited compositional variations of portraits together, Degas and Monet had popularized and developed serial exhibitions starting in the late 1870s.

The portrait of Dr. Bourges, painted on a toned cardboard support, is studiously composed. His tall shape is echoed by the door to the left and the Chinese scroll painting on the wall at the right. It is as if Lautrec included the scroll in this and related portraits (P.383) to draw attention to the relationship between his own compositional taste and Oriental design principles. To counter the repeated verticals, Lautrec employed a clutter of canvases propped in the lower right foreground, and inclined Bourges' head slightly downwards. Bourges seems to be casually appreciating some of Lautrec's works while pulling on his glove, a golden accent exactly at the center of the composition.

C.F.S.

Fig. 2
Tissot, *Portrait of Eugène Coppens de Fontenay*
1867, 0.69 x 0.39 m., oil on canvas
The Philadelphia Museum of Art
The W. P. Wilstach Collection

Fig. 3
Caillebotte, *Paul Hugot*
1878, 2.04 x 0.92 m., oil on canvas
Private collection

Fig. 4
Roll, *Portrait of Mr. Alphand*
1888, 1.56 x 1.30 m., oil on canvas
Musée du Petit Palais, Paris

47
Monsieur Louis Pascal
1891
0.77, 0.53 m.; 30⅜, 20⅞ in.
Peinture à l'essence on board
Dortu, 1971: P.467
Musée d'Albi

Louis Pascal, brother of Juliette (P.279), was a cousin of Lautrec's with whom he attended school and cooperated on youthful publications and puppet shows. Lautrec's portrait of Pascal is a monument to their friendship which continued until Lautrec's death. Although Coquiot (1921, p. 208) listed the portrait as one exhibited at the Salon des Indépendents in March 1891 (see cat. no. 46), Joyant dated it two years afterwards. A letter (Corr., p. 124) written in February 1891 confirms Coquiot's information. Since Lautrec frequently reworked earlier pictures, however, Joyant may be right as well. Judging from extant pen (fig. 1) and oil sketches (P.446), Lautrec's first pictorial idea for the portrait was to pose Pascal standing with his back turned, hands in his pockets and cane held with rehearsed elegance. The pose is a variant of Lautrec's portraits of Dr. Bourges (cat. no. 46) and Gaston Bonnefoy (P.410), which were painted at the same time against the background of a corner in the rue Caulaincourt studio.

But Lautrec ultimately preferred to reposition Pascal in profile, head turned slightly, and to crop his body below the hips. From this new angle, the cane slants across the painting and repeats the almost completely hidden diagonal of the baseboard and the slanted picture frames piled against the wall. These subtle diagonal accents enliven an otherwise simple composition of repeated broad vertical bands (doors, figure, and wall), as do a series of small aligned details of golden color: the doorknob, cane head, glove and moustache. Lautrec's stylistic understatement characterizes Pascal's presence as debonair. Equally as important as subtleties of design, however, are Lautrec's exquisitely descriptive painting of the head and the delicate play of colored shadows, for example in the vertical gray-green and yellow hatchings on the door.

C.F.S.

Fig. 1
Toulouse-Lautrec, *Monsieur Louis Pascal*
c. 1893, 0.18 x 0.11 m., pen
Private collection

48

M. Lemerle

1891

0.80, 0.63 m.; 31½, 24⅞ in.

Oil on canvas

Dortu, 1971: P.382

Columbus Museum of Art, Ohio
(Howald Fund Purchase)

The curious inscription on this portrait indicates that Lautrec was befriended by the Lemerles, who apparently owned an inn called "Cassoir," where Lautrec vacationed. His queer signature—"H. Quatre"—is undoubtedly an allusion to the founder of the Bourbon dynasty after whose descendents Lautrec was named. Perhaps the artist and Mr. Lemerle shared an interest in Lautrec's distinguished geneology.

Apparently left incomplete, the portrait is based upon a peculiar composition. Three stark accents—two trees and a bench—enframe the sitter. He is dressed in a dark blue workingman's smock and a pale gray cap. Taken from the sitter's back, Lemerle's portrait shares the drollness of Lautrec's portrait of Désiré Dihau (cat. no. 44).

C.F.S.

49

Femme rousse assise

Seated red-headed woman

1891

0.64, 0.52 m.; 25¼, 20½ in.

Peinture à l'essence on board

Dortu, 1971: P.610

Musée du Louvre, Galérie du Jeu de
Paume, Paris

According to Joyant, this painting is called *La toilette*, dates from 1896 and relates closely to two other pictures depicting seated nude or semi-nude women seen from the back (fig. 1 and P.609). Although the pictures bear a strong superficial resemblance to one another, there are both documentary and stylistic reasons for believing that this painting was executed in 1891.

In a letter to an art dealer which has been tentatively dated to 1890 (Corr., p. 117), Lautrec mentioned two pictures which he said had been exhibited earlier in the year at Les XX in Brussels, one of which was "a red-haired woman seated on the floor, seen from the back, nude." There is no picture placed by Joyant in 1889 or the early 1890s that even remotely corresponds to Lautrec's description of this seated, red-headed nude.

The list of the contents of the 1890 exhibition of Les XX includes only the vague titles *Rousse* and *Étude*, but that for Les XX of 1892 mentions a *Femme rousse assise* which could very well have been this painting. Since the exhibitions of Les XX were held at the beginning of the year, the pictures submitted to them were usually painted during the previous year. In 1889 Lautrec executed no paintings of nudes or semi-dressed women engaged in boudoir activities. During the early 1890s, however, he became preoccupied with rear views (see cat. nos. 44, 48, 53, 54), and in 1891 he did a series of pictures of women

Fig. 1
Toulouse-Lautrec, *Model resting*
1896, 0.63 x 0.48 m., oil on board
Private collection

in loose wraps combing their hair (fig. 2, P.389, P.391). Two of these depict the women seated on patterned rugs, partially silhouetted against a piece of rumpled white drapery with studio clutter set obliquely in the background.

Although the model in the so-called *La toilette (Femme rousse assise)* is not combing her hair, these paintings seem related both compositionally and in terms of style. The earlier pictures are more tightly painted than those from 1896, more complicated in their careful arrangements of background paraphernalia, and more sharply colored. *La toilette* glows with complementary oppositions of creamy yellow and blue-violet, the brilliant red-gold of the model's hair balanced by the green highlights scattered throughout the composition. The related pictures from 1896 and 1897 appear less studiously posed. Greatly simplified in setting and gentler in outline, they utilize pastel palettes of more homogeneous and subdued tones and create an effect of poetic reverie. It therefore is likely that *La toilette* belongs with the group of paintings from 1891, and that Lautrec's letter to the dealer was written in 1892.

The pose of *Femme rousse assise* seems to have been influenced by Degas, who in 1881 painted a nude model seated on a cushion on the floor in a position very similar to Lautrec's (fig. 3). But Lautrec transformed Degas' pose into a work of greater compositional complexity and dissimilar mood. His model's compact body lacks the fleshy sensuality of Degas', and Lautrec has composed her so as to create a subtle balance between the flat planes and angles of her back, arm and leg and the rounded contours of hips and buttocks. He set the model on a rumpled cloth whose angular folds repeat and emphasize the almost geometric structure of her form, an effect very different from that sought by Degas when he placed his figure on a large curved pillow to accentuate her voluptuousness. The crispness of Lautrec's modeling and the draping of the woman's hips further de-emphasize the sensuality ordinarily implied by the combination of nudity and dark stockings.

Finally, Lautrec expanded the minimal, neutral setting common to his "naturalist" predecessors into a spacious environment contrived to balance and echo his figure. The diagonal floorboards run perpendicularly to the oblique angle on which the model and rug are placed, creating a zigzag movement that leads the eye back through the composition. In the background Lautrec arranged a semicircle of objects to complement the circle of the woman's fallen peignoir, and their combined round shapes and straight lines reiterate the structure of her body, just as their yellow and blue tonalities repeat her colors. In this beautifully integrated and exquisitely painted picture Lautrec achieved one of his most unusual and powerful images, an inspiration to the younger generation of artists who viewed it in the Musée du Luxembourg (fig. 4).

N.E.M.

Fig. 2
Toulouse-Lautrec, *Woman combing her hair*
1891, 0.43 x 0.30 m., oil on board
Musée du Louvre, Paris

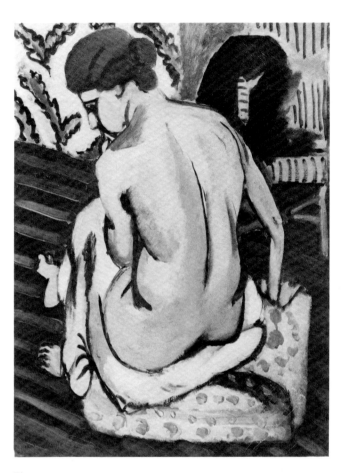

Fig. 4
Matisse, *Seated nude*
1918, 0.61 x 0.45 m., oil on canvas
The Philadelphia Museum of Art, Whitte Collection

Fig. 3
Degas, *Woman combing her hair*
1881, 0.74 x 0.61 m., oil on canvas
Private collection

50

Jane Avril sortant du Moulin Rouge

Jane Avril leaving the Moulin Rouge

1892

0.84, 0.63 m.; 33¼, 25 in.

Peinture à l'essence on board

Dortu, 1971: P.414

Wadsworth Atheneum, Hartford;
Bequest of George A. Gay

The portraits Lautrec painted of Jane Avril (1868-1943) in 1892 are the culmination of just less than a decade's study of cabaret life. The mixed chords of gaiety and despair which predominate in these subjects better suited this celebrated dancer than any of Lautrec's previous models. Her pallid, rice-powdered face peeping from a heavy midnight-blue coat is as fragile as the little pink which accents her matching hat. Dressed as if in mourning, her hands pocketed, the dancer takes a short, funereal step like that of a somnambulist. Her private melancholy is all the more poignant set against the glittering walls and pavement at the entrance to the Moulin Rouge.

It was there that Jane Avril made her debut in 1889, after enduring a childhood of deprivation and indignity. Something of her past flavored her self-taught style of dance, which was less boisterous than that of such associates as La Goulue (cat. no. 51). In fact, Jane Avril was most greatly admired for her solo dances. The legendary expressive range of her dancing is perhaps suggested by her reputedly wide literary tastes and the extraordinary circle of artistic friends she kept, including Lautrec (Mack, pp. 147-154).

Lautrec did not invent the theme of an unescorted woman lost in the implacable geometry of street fronts and corners. His older colleagues, for example, Sargent (fig. 1), had already developed similar poignant images of urban life from the example of nineteenth-century Japanese master prints (fig. 2). Dwarfed, at least in emotional terms, by the stark settings, and isolated from figures who share the de-Chiricoesque cityscapes, these women are emblematic of melancholy. Lautrec, who had already explored compositions designed to concentrate attention on single figures abandoned in the midst of otherwise carefree crowds (P.331), invented moving new details for this portrait. For example, the other figures, one of whom is Jane's friend Edouard Dujardin (cat. no. 52), move away from her with backs turned. Presumably Lautrec hoped to suggest that under different circumstances these people would applaud Jane's gay dances in the Moulin-Rouge. Outcast from that artificial setting to the reality of the streets, however, performer and spectators ignore one another.

The flickered brushwork, which Lautrec seems to have borrowed from his associates among the Indépendents, in particular the deceased Van Gogh, is bright and gay, and Lautrec may have chosen the idiom on this rare occasion to evoke the glitter of the famous dance hall. In addition, the confetti-like background suggests twinkling gas lights and perhaps even the spotted reflections of a rain-dampened sidewalk at night.

If Lautrec represented an evening scene, however, he accumulated its darkness in the dancer's overcoat, which plays a dirge at a carnival.

C.F.S.

Fig. 1
Sargent, *Street in Venice*
1882, 0.45 x 0.54 m., oil on panel
National Gallery of Art, Washington, D.C.,
Gift of the Avalon Foundation

Fig. 2
Hiroshige, *Ōdenma-chō street*
1858, 0.36 x 0.23 m., woodblock print
The Art Institute of Chicago, The Clarence Buckingham
Collection of Japanese Prints

51

La Goulue entrant au Moulin Rouge

La Goulue entering the Moulin Rouge

1891

0.80, 0.60 m.; 32, 23⅝ in.

Peinture à l'essence on board

Dortu, 1971: P.423

The Museum of Modern Art;
New York, Gift of Mrs. David M. Levy

Lautrec had admired La Goulue, the celebrated cabaret dancer, since as early as 1886, but she was unwilling to pose for him at first (Mack, p. 142). During 1891 and 1892, however, Lautrec devoted an important group of works to her. Both this picture, in which she is presented *en face,* and another (P.423) depicting her from the rear record her nightly tour of state through the Moulin Rouge where she was a star. In this painting, the cabaret's name is indicated in reverse on the window in the background. The attractive La Goulue, busty and wasp-waisted, set fashion trends (Yvette Guilbert, cited by Huisman and Dortu, p. 92) with her elegant hair style and bold dress, despite her coarse personality and unwholesome reputation. Lautrec understood and accentuated her proud, disdainful swagger, and transformed her into an idol of elegance. Linked arm in arm with her sister (to the left) and a friend, La Goulue snarls blankly at her admirers, a hardened counterpart to the alluring queens of high-class fashion such as Tissot painted (fig. 1).

Lautrec's picture quite possibly relies upon Japanese and Renaissance models. For example, a formally attired courtesan flanked by attendants was a traditional

Fig. 1
Tissot, *The reception*
c. 1883-1884, 1.42 x 1.01 m., oil on canvas
Albright-Knox Art Gallery, Buffalo, gift of
Mr. William M. Chase, 1909

subject for Japanese graphic artists (fig. 2). If their prints supplied a pre-existing genre of portraiture, however, Lautrec's intertwined figures echo the mannered poses of his favorite Renaissance masters, such as Botticelli (fig. 3) and Benozzo Gozzoli (Joyant, I, p. 150). As a result, Lautrec has elevated a Montmartre strumpet to the rank of goddess.

Adopting a hallmark of "Impressionist" art, Lautrec cropped his figures at the bottom and sides of his picture. La Goulue's sister was insulted by this artistic license, which exaggerated her corpulence (Gauzi, p. 42). Only partially indicated figures and faces were nonetheless a source of pictorial energy and humor for Lautrec. In addition, cropping the lower parts of the body was a device Lautrec had used since as early as 1889 to indicate both movement (Johnson, p. 15) and immediacy. The cropping, like Lautrec's simplified drawing and broad modeling, are comparable, of course, to works by one of his favorites, Manet (fig. 4).

Lautrec was particularly proud of this work, which he exhibited on at least four separate occasions, despite needing to borrow it from Charles Zidler, the director of the Moulin Rouge, who owned it and displayed it in the entrance corridor of the popular night resort.

C.F.S.

Fig. 2
Koryūsai, *The courtesan Kaoru of Shin Kana-ya*
c. 1777, 0.39 x 0.26 m., woodblock print
The Art Institute of Chicago, The Clarence Buckingham
Collection of Japanese Prints

Fig. 3
Botticelli, *Allegory: fresco from the Villa Lemmi,* detail
c. 1480, fresco
Musée du Louvre, Paris

Fig. 4
Manet, *Skating*
1877, 0.92 x 0.72 m., oil on canvas
Courtesy of the Fogg Art Museum, Harvard University
Bequest—Collection of Maurice Wertheim, Class of 1906

52

Au Moulin Rouge

At the Moulin Rouge

1892-1895

1.235, 1.41 m.; 48½, 55⅜ in.

Oil on canvas

Dortu, 1971: P.427

The Art Institute of Chicago

The l
succe
it pr
La C
and
at th
perm
Rouş
Laut
a tal
(fror
Guil
(see
hims
the
fron

A
189
ray,
the
L-sl
(fig
ord
and
and
Au
eni

Fig. 1
Toulouse-Lautrec, *At the Moulin Rouge,* original version
1892, oil on canvas
Photo from *Le Figaro Illustré*, April 1902

mask-like faces beginning no earlier than 1895 (cat. nos. 81, 99), this final version of our picture was apparently not undertaken until then. As the added figure of May Milton is nearly identical in coiffure, hat, dress, and facial features to the portrait Lautrec painted of her in 1895 (cat. no. 77), this seems a reasonable date for the completion of this new version. In its finished state, *Au Moulin Rouge* vividly parallels a description of the cabaret written by the Belgian painter Henry Evenpöel to his father in 1893: "Heads pass by in the crowd. Oh, heads green, red, yellow, orange, violet. Vice up for auction. One could put on the door front, People, abandon all modesty here" (Sutton, 1956, p. 72).

Lautrec's original painting was clearly a modern recapitulation of rowdy sixteenth- and seventeenth-century banquet scenes, many of which Lautrec knew from museums whose collections he had studied, such as the Louvre and the Musée Royal in Brussels (fig. 2). As the earlier artists had, Lautrec grouped a series of penetrating portraits closely together in the foreground, beyond which smaller vignettes punctuate a complicated background space. At the center of his picture Lautrec portrayed himself as a passer-by, unobserved and apparently inattentive to the table of friends. Yet *Au Moulin Rouge* is a compendium of exactly observed and masterfully executed details, such as Dujardin's posture as he leans forward clutching his cane, La Macarona's dimpled smirk, and Jane Avril's delicately poised pinky (which is absent in the preparatory sketch for her: P.458).

There is space enough here to mention only a small fraction of the picture's rich details. Several, however, should be discussed together since they all deal with mirrored resemblances. For example, Dujardin's bulk at the left is reflected in a narrow glass partition, through which the walls and lights of the adjacent room are visible. These latter continue uninterrupted to the right of the partition, whereas Dujardin's reflection is dramatically cropped. Lautrec included a similar detail at the upper right, where La Goulue preens herself in a mirror which reflects her gesture from the hips upward, but which, observed from this point of view, does not reflect her companion. Lautrec's head, although spatially removed from those of his friends around the table, is aligned with the heads of Guibert and Sescau, both of whom are portrayed here as baffling look-alikes to Lautrec. It has been suggested (Dortu, Grillaert, Adhémar, p. 30) that Lautrec exhibited his vibrant record of night-life in Brussels in 1892 with the title "Nocturne." If so, Lautrec emulated Whistler's musical titles for this picture which is charged with visual counterpoint and unexpected harmonies.

The dramatic additions Lautrec undertook about 1895 required no changes in his original picture other than the overpainting of part of Guibert's body with the shoulder of the added figure. Her physical immediacy and the accelerated thrust of the diagonal railing extended in the bottom left of the addition contribute powerfully to the final version's increased visual energy and the enhanced effect of the cabaret's highly charged atmosphere. Lautrec may have reconsidered his original picture with any number of contemporary works in mind, particularly ones by Renoir, Gauguin and Munch. All of these artists had used similarly looming figures in foreground corners as well as exaggerated diagonals to achieve heightened emotional impact in their pictures.

The existence of prototypes, however, hardly diminishes Lautrec's achievement. His barbarously disfigured image of May Milton, with her blue-green skin, deep, skeletal eye sockets, and hat seemingly metamorphosed into antennae, is among the most haunting images in the entire history of art. The impact of *Au Moulin Rouge* on early twentieth-century artists was extraordinary, judging from the numerous works apparently done after its example, from Picasso's moody cabarets to Boccioni's visions of gaudy lust (fig. 3).

N.E.M. & C.F.S.

Fig. 2
Hemessen, *The prodigal son*
1536, 1.40 x 1.98 m., panel
Musées Royaux des Beaux-Arts de Belgique, Brussels

Fig. 3
Boccioni, *The laugh*
1911, 1.10 x 1.45 m., oil on canvas
The Museum of Modern Art, New York

53

Femme rousse vue de dos

Red-headed woman viewed from the
rear

1892

0.78, 0.597 m.; 30¾, 23½ in.

Peinture à l'essence on board

Dortu, 1971: P.404

Musée d'Albi

Between 1890 and 1892 Lautrec was intrigued by figures seen from the rear, which he explored in a number of studies (P.401, P.403, P.405) and incorporated into many paintings (for example, cat. nos. 44, 48, and 49). This particular study was executed in preparation for the large foreground figure in *Le Nouveau Cirque: La clownesse aux cinq plastrons* (cat. no. 54). Despite the absence of a chair in our study, the general configuration of pose is the same and the details of hat, hairstyle, fur collar and puffy sleeves are identical. Although the woman in the final version sits upright, in the study Lautrec explored the possibility of posing her leaning forward to rest her arm on the low parapet of her box. The figure of the dancer she watches on the stage below is sketchily indicated here, and perhaps Lautrec altered her posture for the final painting to leave more room for the background scene of performer and distant spectator.

Lautrec's extreme facility in drawing technique is evident in this rapidly executed sketch. Always more preoccupied with heads than with clothing, he has concentrated the densest amount of detail in the model's hair and hat. In fact, Lautrec has made the hat here the dominant accent of the study by blocking it in with light strokes that contrast sharply with the dark lines of the rest of the figure. The hat's swooping contour increases the lively sense of movement implicit in the figure's pose, and attests to Lautrec's perpetual fascination with amusing headgear.

N.E.M.

54

Au Nouveau Cirque, la clownesse aux cinq plastrons

At the Nouveau Cirque, the clowness before five shirtfronts

1892

1.68, 0.86 m.; 46, 34 in.

Peinture à l'essence on board

Dortu, 1971: P.406

The Philadelphia Museum of Art: Purchased for the John D. McIlhenny Collection

A group of painted studies and drawings (P.430, P.431, P.434, P.515 and D. 4.556) attest that Lautrec envisioned an important work based on the ballet, *Papa Chrysanthème,* which was staged at the popular Nouveau Cirque in November 1892 (Mack, pp. 217-18). The ballet's simple plot is a forerunner of *The King and I:* an Oriental prince brings a Western bride back to his native country. To evoke the locale, the center of the stage arena was flooded to form a water lily garden, and the major production numbers took advantage of the extraordinary set.

In several of his sketches, including this completed preliminary study, Lautrec recorded the Western bride's dance for her new acquaintances at the Oriental court. Her hair and gown gracefully tossed in broad pastel arabesques, she flutters over water lily pads floating on the garden pond.

For this work, Lautrec adopted a thematic convention popularized by Daumier and other illustrators by the 1850s and elaborated by a host of artists in the 1870s and 1880s, including Renoir, Degas (fig. 1), and Seurat (fig. 2). That convention was developed to represent spectators watching theatrical performances, to juxtapose the fiction of theater with the reality of contemporary audiences, and to diagram the interaction between observing and being observed. Aware that people dressed for the theater in order to parade in public and came to observe one another as much as to see a performance, artists traded upon the

Fig. 1
Degas, *Dancer with a bouquet*
1878, 0.40 x 0.50 m., pastel
The Museum of Art, Rhode Island School of Design,
Gift of Mrs. Murray S. Danforth

193

paradoxical levels of reality and artifice inherent in the double spectacle. The condensed spatial dialogue between fellow spectators and a more distant performance suggested unexpected compositional opportunities, odd angles of vision and dramatic shifts in scale, for all of which there were exciting compositional prototypes in recent Japanese graphics.

Lautrec's interest in the convention began as early as 1881 (P.121) and continued throughout the 1880s (cat. no. 37). During the 1890s, images of spectators at a theater became a staple of Lautrec's thematic repertoire (cat. nos. 57, 87), especially in his graphic work. For example, *La clownesse aux cinq plastrons* is closely related to Lautrec's well-known *Divan Japonais* poster of 1892 (fig. 3). Indeed, the model for that poster, Jane Avril, is probably also the model for the spectator watching *Papa Chrysanthème.*

Judging from the limited color scheme of just six tones, Lautrec intended to develop it as a poster and was aware from the outset of that medium's technical restrictions. But this work was apparently commissioned as a design for a stained-glass window by Louis Comfort Tiffany, who produced a suite of nine related windows for the Salon of the Société Nationale des Beaux-Arts in 1895. In addition to Lautrec, Bonnard, Denis, Roussel, Vallotton and Vuillard were among the artists who collaborated with Tiffany. The complicated group commission for the windows was evidently organized by Samuel Bing, who exhibited them as a group later in 1895 at his famous *Maison de l'Art Nouveau.* Indeed, the organic, snaking lines orchestrated throughout Lautrec's picture distinguish it as one of his most stylized *art nouveau* images, as do the decoratively interrelated areas of color. Based largely on Japanese pictorial formulae, the conventions of *art nouveau* were well suited for Lautrec's image from *Papa Chrysanthème,* whose plot celebrates the meeting of East and West.

Lautrec spoofed the message of cultural exchange with a wonderful background detail. The "five shirt fronts" referred to in the design's title are the comical row of identical male spectators seated on the far side of the arena. Her opera glasses lowered, the female spectator in the foreground seems to have just scrutinized her distant counterparts (see cat. no. 57). Upon doing so, however, she must have discovered that they have foreign physiognomies and top-knots, and are not Parisian gentlemen at all, but members of the Oriental court. These figures, spectators actually called for as part of the ballet's cast, are a witty *double-entendre.* Both players and members of the audience, the "five shirt fronts" straddle the dividing line between audience and performance which so interested Lautrec.

C.F.S.

Fig. 2
Seurat, *At the "Concert Européen"*
1887-1888, 0.31 x 0.23 m., conté crayon
The Museum of Modern Art, New York
Lilli P. Bliss Collection

Fig. 3
Toulouse-Lautrec, *Le Divan Japonais*
1893, 0.79 x 0.59 m., lithograph
The Art Institute of Chicago

55

Charles Conder

c. 1892

0.47, 0.355 m.; 18⅝, 14 in.

Peinture à l'essence on board

Dortu, 1971: P.462

Courtesy Aberdeen Art Gallery;
Aberdeen, Great Britain

The English neo-rococo artist Charles Conder (1868-1909) caroused with Lautrec at Montmartre cabarets in the early 1890s. Lautrec posed him for several works, including *Aux Ambassadeurs: Gens Chic* (fig. 1 and D. 3442) which was commissioned as an illustration for *Le Figaro Illustré* (July 1893).

Lautrec often posed models apart from the eventual contexts in which he envisioned using them. (Gauzi, pp. 151-153). For Conder's portrait he was stringently economical, recording only those details he would need for a carefully preconceived picture. For Conder's body Lautrec used just a few elegant outlines, already rhythmically adjusted to integrate with details to be added in the final composition. The line of the lapel and cummerbund, for example, are calculated to rhyme with those for the carafe. Otherwise Lautrec merely "filled in" the contours with hatching. He took pains, however, to note every highlight and shadow on Conder's face, which is set to characterize debonair urbanity.

C.F.S.

Fig. 1
Toulouse-Lautrec, *At "Les Ambassadeurs" (Gens chics)*
1893, 0.85 x 0.65 m., gouache on oil paper
From the Collection of Mr. and Mrs. Paul Mellon

56

**Au bal masqué—Les fêtes parisiennes—
Nouveau confetti**

At the masked ball

1893

0.39, 0.54 m.; 15½, 21½ in.

Mixed media

To appear in a supplement to Dortu

From the collection of Steven Straw
Company, Inc., Newburyport,
Massachusetts

The masked ball was an event which periodically punctuated the hectic night-life of the Montmarte cabarets. It was an occasion on which dance-hall entertainers and their devoted audiences mingled in an intoxicated frenzy of revelry, their habitually eccentric costumes and exotic hair-dos rendered even more intriguing by the bizarre grotesquerie of masks. At these riotous parties wine flowed freely and the dancers abandoned themselves to the wildest and most indecorous gyrations.

Lautrec always delighted in "dressing up" and throughout his life was enthralled by costumes and disguises. His fascination with the bawdiness and depravities of the cabarets must have been intensified by the glittering spectacle of the masked ball. He depicted these revels on a variety of occasions beginning in 1889 and continuing throughout the 1890s (see cat. no. 99 and P.331, P.478, P.628). Some of these scenes focus on the staid figures of conventionally dressed gentlemen spectators who view, somewhat dispassionately and from a safe distance, the giddy dissipations of masked dancers in the backgrounds. Other versions of the theme move in closely on the participants, however, and this picture is one in which Lautrec has captured the flow of movement on the thronged staircase of the Opéra.

The diagonal composition is dominated by the central figures of two women descending the steep stairs with linked arms, one reeling intoxicatedly while her companion doffs her mask to reveal an expression of gloating pleasure. The grossly misshapen mask of the figure ascending from corner right adds an aspect of brutish abandon to the scene as it leers up at the women above. Reminiscent of the gigantic mask-like face of May Milton looming up from the corner of *Au Moulin Rouge* (cat. no. 52), the bizarre face is artfully balanced by another masked head on the upper left side of the composition. This reveler ogles the women sharply with popeyed gaze, his enormous false nose thrusting out from the ruffles of a polka-dotted domino. Smiling slyly, the left-hand woman casually lifts her elbow to knock his nose askew, while her companion, avid in her haste to return to the ball, remains oblivious of the lecherous glances enframing them on either side.

Although this humorously suggestive painted lithograph is not listed in the Dortu catalogue, a very similar study for it is (P.433). Cruder and blunter in its forms and composition, it lacks many of our picture's most successful details. The huge dark corner mask was originally merely the black glove of the woman's extended arm, in our version now bent to hold her flame-shaped mask. This mask itself was at first a long, undulating paper streamer descending from the hand of the gentleman higher up the stairs. For this finished print, Lautrec filled the background with a rhythmic grid composed of the rippling curves of the upper loge across the room, and the gently spiralling paper streamers wafting down to the floor below.

The two women in this work have never been identified, but it is interesting to note that, despite the obviously caricatured exaggeration of the features, the left-hand figure looks remarkably like Cha-U-Kao, the lesbian clowness from the Moulin Rouge whom Lautrec was to paint repeatedly in 1895 (see cat. no. 80). In addition to the similarities of their broad shoulders and unusual, towering white wigs, the presence of a brunette lover might indicate that this was the first step in Lautrec's preoccupation with this mysterious and elusive character.

N.E.M.

57

La loge au mascaron doré

Study for Theater box with golden mask

1893

0.408, 0.324 m.; 16⅛, 12⅞ in.

Oil on canvas

Dortu, 1971: P.470

Musée d'Albi

According to Joyant, this extraordinary work served as a preliminary study for Lautrec's well-known lithograph, *La loge au mascaron doré* (fig. 1). The final work, probably based upon a composition by Degas, was composed as a programme for Luguet's play *Le Missionaire*. Joyant's proposal seems accurate, judging from such similarities between the programme and this study as the figure of a woman looking through opera glasses. The starkly divided composition, the empty bottom of which represents the front of a theater box observed from across the house, was evidently invented to leave room for the lettering which would need to be added at a later stage. In addition, the intensely dramatic colors in this study—the velvety purple background broadly studded with raw strokes of green, cream, red and brown—are more in keeping with Lautrec's lithographic works than with his paintings at this time. Nonetheless, it is interesting to note that small pictures with comparable light rectangular zones at the bottom of their compositions (such as P.284) are included in the backgrounds of two earlier portraits (cat. no. 15, fig. 1 and P.336). They indicate that the present composition was not a completely new departure for Lautrec.

The woman's opera glasses, her companion's glance to the right and her escort's monocle together leave no doubt about Lautrec's theme—spectators observed (cat. nos. 38, 54). The confronted spectator could be called a "cropped theme," since the object of his attention is necessarily left out of the picture. Looking at a picture of someone looking unavoidably stimulates imaginative participation, as if the figures in the picture were returning the scrutiny of the painting's viewer. Lautrec's interest in this thematic conceit reflects the wide popularity of theater spectators as subject matter for art during the second half of the nineteenth century. He and other artists, including Guys, Manet, Degas, and Renoir explored several variations of the theme (see cat. nos. 32, 37, 87), including scenes which portray only spectators who look back out of the picture (fig. 2) and consequently seem to be interested in the observers at galleries and exhibitions who have paused before them. As all of the artists were aware, spectators at a theater were often as much a spectacle as the play. The lurid shadows and unexpected highlights in Lautrec's study transform theater spectators into a compelling pictorial drama.

C.F.S.

Fig. 1
Toulouse-Lautrec, *Theater box with golden mask*
1893, 0.30 x 0.24 m., lithograph
The Art Institute of Chicago, Gift of Mrs. Gilbert
Chapman in memory of Charles B. Goodspeed

Fig. 2
Renoir, *The theater box*
1874, 0.81 x 0.65 m., oil on canvas
The Courtauld Institute of Art, London

58

Caudieux

1893

1.14, 0.88 m.; 45, 34¾ in.

Peinture à l'essence on paper

Dortu, 1971: P.474

Musée d'Albi

Lautrec was in great demand as an illustrator in 1893, when two magazines, *Echo de Paris* and *Le Figaro Illustré*, ran features about cabaret performers and Parisian nightlife to which he contributed. For each issue Lautrec depicted Caudieux, a rotund cabaret singer, first doing a jig (fig. 1) then powdering his face in a dressing room (fig. 2).

In addition to the illustrations, Lautrec was commissioned to make a poster for Caudieux during the same year. This picture, based upon rapid sketches (D 3.369 and D 3.453), is a preparatory study for the poster (fig. 3), which was subsequently reproduced in an article in *Le Monde moderne* praising modern poster art.

For the poster, Lautrec relied upon a favorite device which he had adapted from Manet and others beginning in 1888: cropping the lower extremities of a standing figure to evoke gliding movement (Johnson, p. 15). Caudieux jaunts offstage on his disproportionately tiny legs, a detail Lautrec sought to express during the execution of this study. He only roughly indicated the background he was to develop for the poster: a diagonal at the left indicates the stage floor seen from above; rapid strokes at the right mark the prompter in his box. The study testifies to Lautrec's gifts as a portraitist, and, taken together with a drawing (D. 3.324) and the poster, records the subtle adjustments which Lautrec invented to find the lively arabesques characteristic of his best poster designs.

C.F.S.

Fig. 1
Toulouse-Lautrec, *Caudieux (the little Casino)*
1893, 0.27 x 0.21 m., lithograph
The Art Institute of Chicago, Gift of Mr. and Mrs. Carter Harrison

Fig. 2
Toulouse-Lautrec, *Mr. Caudieux, actor at the café concert*
1893, 0.68 x 0.48 m., oil on board
Private collection

Fig. 3
Toulouse-Lautrec, *Caudieux*
1893, 1.30 x 0.95 m., lithograph
The Art Institute of Chicago

59

La Macarona en jockey

The Macarona as a jockey

1893

0.52, 0.39 m.; 20⅜, 15¼ in.

Peinture à l'essence on board

Dortu, 1971: P.476

The Art Institute of Chicago

La Macarona was a Spanish dancer in the Montmartre cabarets, a habituée of the same exotic milieu frequented by La Goulue, Jane Avril, and the other performers Lautrec adored. Her world-weary face is a prominent feature in his magnificent *Au Moulin Rouge* (cat. no. 52), where she shares the central table with the other regulars at the dance-hall. Lautrec later chose to paint her once again in this unusual characterization as a jockey.

Lautrec produced this tracing mounted on board to use as an illustration for Gustave Geffroy's article "The Balls and the Carnival," which he wrote for the February, 1894 issue of *Le Figaro Illustré* as part of their series on the pleasures of Paris. The theme of the article explains the oddity of La Macarona's attire, since many of the dance-hall entertainers loved to appear in costume and the masked ball was a highlight of their hectic night life. But La Macarona's choice of a masculine costume, especially one used for riding and associated with boots and whips, suggests that her fancy-dress was the outward symbol of a dominating personality. Her tough, aggressive pose thrusts hips and pelvis into prominent display, creating a sexual invitation accentuated by the tight jodhpurs with their swelling contours. But the real power of this portrait lies in the startling disparity between the mannish garb of outdoor sport and La Macarona's white-painted, sagging face. Lips twisted cynically and eyes circled with deep shadows, the aging dancer epitomizes the artifice and corruption of the Parisian demi-monde. It is indicative of Lautrec's penetrating insight and penchant for irony that he has chosen to illustrate an article on the gaieties of Parisian entertainments with such a sad and disillusioned image.

N.E.M.

60

Jane Avril dansant

Jane Avril dancing

1893

1.01, 0.75 m.; 39¾, 29 in.

Peinture à l'essence on board

Dortu, 1971: P.482

Stavros S. Niarchos Collection

Many of the entertainers at the Moulin Rouge were invited during the early 1890s to perform at the more fashionable Jardin de Paris on the Champs-Elysées. To celebrate Jane Avril's (cat. no. 50) debut there, Lautrec designed a suggestively ribald poster which has become one of his best-loved images (fig. 1). In this poster the dancer lifts her black stockinged leg to reveal a flounce of petticoats, as if to tantalize the orchestra's rather grotesque bass viol player, whose instrument's neck erectly salutes her flirtation.

Although for the medium of lithography Lautrec was limited to broad areas of color, the striking painted study for her figure records the rippling colors of her skirt and under garments with cascades of rapid strokes in pink, blue, yellow, white and vermillion. The unearthly shadows which transform her face and bright orange hair, which had to be sacrificed for the poster, suggest the dancer's popular sobriquets "La Folle" (the mad woman) and "La Mélinite" (an explosive) (Rothenstein, p. 63; and Mack, p. 149). Indeed, without this extraordinary study it would be difficult to appreciate Joyant's apt comparison of the dancer to a "delirious orchid."

Acording to Joyant (I, 84), Jane chose the color of her dress to correspond with the moods of each particular dance she performed. Orange-vermillion, which she wears for the poster, was the color for the "Scottish."

C.F.S.

Fig. 1
Toulouse-Lautrec, *Jane Avril at the Jardin de Paris*
1893, 1.30 x 0.95 m., lithograph
The Art Institute of Chicago

61

Monsieur, madame, et le chien

Man, woman and dog

1893

0.48, 0.60 m.; 19, 23⅝ in.

Oil on canvas

Dortu, 1971: P.494

Musée d'Albi

This picture is closely related to the portraits of *M. Delaporte* (P.464) and *M. Boileau* (P.465) done in the same year. For each of them, Lautrec seated an isolated male model in a crowded milieu which he observes as he himself comes under the scrutiny of passersby. The portly model for *Monsieur, Madame et le Chien* was one Lautrec had used the previous year in an ambitious cabaret scene (fig. 1). Now Lautrec has him politely awaiting the whore of his choice in a brothel parlor. His bowler hat perched on the arm of the overstuffed red sofa, he sits quietly, hands drooping in his lap. The hands are a particularly telling detail: a ring indicates the client is married, while the cigarette held between his fingers dangles suggestively at his crotch, a droll emblem of his expectations.

This is the most Daumieresque of all Lautrec's paintings and distinctly recalls various versions of the *Third class carriage* (fig. 2). Like Daumier's, Lautrec's figures pay no heed to the others crowded around them in a public place. To suggest a crowd Lautrec used a mirror backdrop which doubles the heads of the major figures. Lautrec conveys a subtle commentary here on the remoteness of people from one another in urban life. Waiting in idle boredom to participate in an act of sexual intimacy, the customer remains aloof from any social contact with the madame seated beside him. A matched pair in their stodgy corpulence, their resemblance to a bourgeois married couple makes their psychological isolation even more pointed. While the woman gestures toward someone outside the picture, her little lap dog yaps irritably at the stranger, who remains expressionless. His attention is no

Fig. 1
Toulouse-Lautrec, *A corner of the Moulin de la Galette*
1892, 0.98 x 0.88 m., oil on board
National Gallery of Art, Washington, D.C.
Chester Dale Collection

Fig. 2
Daumier, *Third class compartment*
1856-1858, 0.26 x 0.34 m., panel
Private collection

doubt riveted on the woman in red whose presence in front of him is revealed by her reflection in the mirrored background. Lautrec's painting is in fact a compendium of unacknowledged glances cast in different directions. The implications of these glances enliven the ponderous stillness and create a suspense which is brought to a pitch by the repeated juxtapositions of clashing color complementaries. Perhaps in accordance with Seurat's widely known theories, Lautrec has balanced and tempered these intense color contrasts with the broad expanse of the figure's white clothing.

Pictures which qualify simultaneously as portraits and genre scenes, in that one carefully rendered figure dominates a crowded milieu, had been a staple in the repertoires of Degas, Manet (fig. 3) and Caillebotte, to take obvious examples. Lautrec surely had their works in mind when he undertook this painting, but he expanded the convention daringly by choosing to depict, as Picasso later would (fig. 4), a brothel waiting room instead of the more typical café. He probably envisioned this scene as one of a series of related paintings, each describing a pedestrian aspect of brothel routine. In addition to this representation of a waiting client, he began other pictures of prostitutes mounting the stairs (P.459-P.497), remaking their beds (P.498 and P.503), sharing mealtime interludes (P.497), and fixing their hair and make-up (P.506 and P.551-553). His other vignettes of brothel life represented the delivery of fresh laundry (cat. no. 68) and women whiling away their time playing cards or simply seated in blank resignation waiting for clients (P.500, P.502, and cat. no. 75). Lautrec never completely realized this series, which preoccupied him from 1892 until 1895. The most impressive achievements connected with the undertaking, however, are his depictions of waiting: candidly observed and masterfully contrived evocations of dulled consciousness.

C.F.S.

Fig. 3
Manet, *At the café*
1878, 0.46 x 0.38 m., oil on canvas
Walters Art Gallery, Baltimore

Fig. 4
Picasso, *The poor violinist*
c. 1900, 0.21 x 0.23 m., oil on canvas
Private collection

62

Femme à sa fenêtre

Woman at her window

1893

0.585, 0.466 m.; 23, 18⅜ in.

Peinture à l'essence on board

Dortu, 1971: P.507

Musée d'Albi

Judging from its date and setting, Lautrec might have executed this picture as a part of his series depicting the routine daily life of brothels. In these paintings he repeatedly concentrated on capturing with utmost candor the often depressing realities of this aspect of modern life, yet he was equally concerned with transforming his subjects into ravishing decorative effects of color and form.

Whether one interprets the woman at the window here as a prostitute or simply as a model, Lautrec has transmuted a simple moment of unadorned inactivity into a poem of subtle color and design. By concealing most of the model's face he de-emphasizes her individuality and concentrates the spectator's attention on the sumptuous cascade of her red-gold hair and on her graceful silhouette. The room is flooded with violet light which binds figure and background inextricably together in a shimmer of delicate colors. The softly mingled pink, rose and apricot accents scattered throughout the composition are intensified by contrasting tones of muted green, blue, and purple to create a magical effect of *féerique*, an evocation of unearthly beauty wrought from ordinary, prosaic things.

Lautrec's composition is as subtle and artfully contrived as his exquisite color harmonies. The model's curving form is locked into a contrasting geometric structure contrived from the rectangular elements of setting and furniture, then unified with this framework through the repeated rounded accents of the bucket, pitcher and basin. These homely implements set around the model echo her essential shapes: for example, the pitcher repeats the form of her head, its handle jutting out like her fringe of hair and nose. The woman's loose hair and simple white garment are in keeping with the intimate accessories of her boudoir, and together they evoke a sense of repose and tranquility, a freshness and wholesomeness touched with poetry.

N.E.M.

63

Gants noirs d'Yvette Guilbert

Yvette Guilbert's black gloves

1894

0.628, 0.37 m.; 24¾, 14⅝ in.

Peinture à l'essence on board

Dortu, 1971: P.518

Musée d'Albi

After her "discovery" in 1890, Yvette Guilbert reigned as one of Montmartre's foremost entertainers. Lautrec immediately became a devoted fan and began in 1892 to include likenesses of her in posters and lithographs. Two years later, the artist and singer entered into negotiations for a poster which was never realized (P.519), and for a deluxe, limited edition book with lithographs by Lautrec and a text by the prominent socialist art critic, Gustave Geffroy. The book, which appeared in 1894, was in many respects a milestone in the history of publishing. It was the earliest elaborate album devoted to the then unusual subject of an entertainment celebrity. Both the songstress and the artist were pleased with the book, although judging from their recorded comments, they teased and spoofed each other recklessly (Wick, unpag.).

This painting is Lautrec's study for the book's cover (fig. 1)—a brilliant evocation of the subject reduced simply to her long black gloves (a Guilbert trademark) and a powder puff, all thrown carelessly on her dressing table. Evidently Lautrec experimented with the proportions of his format: after completing his sketch he extended it with additions at the top and bottom, but he subsequently returned to his original dimensions. Although Lautrec indicated the dressing table clearly in his study, for the book he simplified its form to a few bold diagonal lines. Of course, the gloves magically retain their expressive gestural character even after Guilbert has removed them, cradling the names of Geffroy and Lautrec which have not yet been added to the study. Lautrec's uncanny selection of expressive detail recalls his alleged retort to her: "My dear, don't you understand that I do not 'detail' you, I totalize you" (Wick, unpag.).

C.F.S.

Fig. 1
Toulouse-Lautrec, Album cover: *Yvette Guilbert*
1894, 0.26 x 0.18 m., lithograph
The Art Institute of Chicago

64

Yvette Guilbert Saluant

Yvette Guilbert taking a bow

1894

0.43, 0.235 m.; 17, 9¼ in.

Black crayon heightened with
watercolor

Dortu, 1971: A.214

Museum of Art, Rhode Island School of
Design, Providence, Rhode Island; Gift
of Mrs. Murray S. Danforth

This study was preliminary to the concluding illustration of the book Geffroy and Lautrec devoted to Yvette Guilbert (cat. no. 63). Lautrec had been an enthusiastic admirer of Yvette since her debut in 1890, when her unique vocal stylisations and unexpectedly elegant costume earned her the sobriquet "La diseuse fin de siècle" (Wicks, unpag.). For the final page of the book Lautrec depicted her taking a bow as she reappeared from behind the stage curtain. When Lautrec made a second series of illustrations for an English editor of the book in 1898, he again chose her bow as the last illustration for the suite (fig. 1). Yvette's long gloves and simple V-necked dress with butterfly bows at the shoulders were stage trademarks.

Taken from unexpected, often unflattering angles Lautrec's droll likenesses of entertainers seem caricatured, sometimes grotesquely so. Although Lautrec's primary objective was to record and express the performers' stage appearances under artificial lighting conditions, he was frequently accused of making unfair distortions for expressive purposes. It is difficult, however, to judge whether Yvette found Lautrec's depictions of her to be affectionate or not. She evidently complained that Lautrec drew her uglier than she was (Joyant, I, pp. 145-6), but on another occasion she herself claimed to be worthy only of "caricature" (Natanson, 1967, p. 188). Since she was an admirer of Beardsley's work (Weintraub, p. 186) it is unlikely that she was wounded by Lautrec's artistic license, no matter how extreme.

C.F.S.

Fig. 1
Toulouse-Lautrec, *Yvette Guilbert taking a bow*
1898, 0.30 x 0.24 m., lithograph
The Art Institute of Chicago

65

Femme à l'entrée d'une loge de théâtre

Woman at the entrance of a theater box

1894

0.81, 0.515 m.; 31½, 20½ in.

Oil

Dortu, 1971: P.523

Musée d'Albi

Lautrec frequently explored the genre episodes observed in the boxes and corridors of theaters. This expressionist vignette painted in 1894 is the most extraordinary of the group. At the center he placed a female figure with piled orange-red hair, wearing a yellow sheath dress, a short white cap, blue stockings and vivid yellow high heeled shoes. Her fragile elbows and ankles are exposed, although she is observed from the rear and consequently expressionless except for her bowed head. Still, Lautrec has so tellingly constructed the details of the setting that her turned-away figure becomes the protagonist in a suspenseful drama. The woman is poised on the threshold of the box as if ready to leave. Taken from an oblique angle, the sides of the door frame isolate her and break the composition into disjointed vertical bands. The leftmost of these includes part of an empty chair and a mirror which reflects the woman's escort, who stands facing her from the opposite side of the box. The velvety purples and reds of the dimly illuminated box interior symbolize emotional tension. Captured as she hesitates before departing, the proximity of the woman to her lover's reflection only intensifies the gap between them. These explicitly narrative details, the clashing accents of color and the fragmented composition are expressive of emotional rupture, such as that endured by characters in Zolaesque novels.

C.F.S.

66

Babylone d'Allemagne

1894

0.58, 0.39 m.; 22⅞, 15⅜ in.

Peinture à l'essence on board

Dortu, 1971: P.533

The Phillips Family Collection

Babylone d'Allemagne is the title of a novel written by Victor Joze, a Pole whose real name was Dobrski. It was third in a projected series of five novels which he called *La Ménagerie Sociale*. The second of the series was *Queen of Joy; morals of the demi-monde* for which Lautrec produced a well-known bookshop poster in 1892 (L.D.342).

Babylone d'Allemagne (The Babylon of Germany), subtitled "Berlin Morals," is a biting, satirical account of cosmopolitan German life. The novel follows the social adventures of amorous gentlemen, army officers and their women, which often take place in the cabarets and brothels of Berlin. The first line of the preface warns that, "It is probable that our 'friends' beyond the Rhine will not be happy reading this volume." (p. 7) In fact, *Babylone d'Allemagne* is such an insulting condemnation of the behavior and character of the German people that their ambassador to Paris strongly protested its publication in 1894 (Joyant, II, p. 106). *Babylone d'Allemagne* condemned German militarism, social corruption and morals by its portrayal of the Berlin equivalents of the environments and people so often encountered in Lautrec's art.

It is therefore all the more surprising that in this year which featured some of his greatest brothel paintings, Lautrec chose the scene of a military parade to illustrate this book. But he was a great lover of horses, and in chapter eight, two debauched officers who are principal characters take part in a grand military parade reviewed by Kaiser Wilhelm II. They are described as being "superbly mounted at the head of their squadrons." Their proud display provided Lautrec with the scene which he would use in the six works related to the *Babylone d'Allemagne* project.

This painting represents the first stage of the composition which was being designed for an advertising poster and book jacket (L.D.351 and L.D.76). The scene is structured by an evenly balanced X-shaped composition in which a group of cavalry on parade forms one diagonal while a sentry and a pedestrian couple stand at opposite corners to produce the other. The principally diagonal movement is begun by the massive head, arched neck and shoulder of the horse which enters the picture at the bottom right, an image for which Lautrec made a detailed drawing that should be dated to 1894 (D. 3.755). These studies and the central image of the white horse confidently express the artist's mastery of equine form.

E.M.M.

67

Babylone d'Allemagne

1894

1.362 x 0.956 m.; 54½ x 38¼ in.

Paper pasted on cardboard

Dortu, 1971: P.532

Estate of Germain Seligman

The overall balance of the first compositional study for *Babylone d'Allemagne* (cat. no. 66) lacked a dynamism that Lautrec finally achieved by removing the front horse and enlarging the image of the officer mounted on a white charger. The visual domination of the scene by this horse and rider, which were probably based on a life study (D. 3.563), was very economically worked out by Lautrec in a preliminary crayon sketch (D. 3.663).

Having arrived at a satisfactory composition, Lautrec then produced this large scale painting which sets the details and establishes the characters of the stolid, dull sentry, the dashingly arrogant cavalry officer and the flirtatious young woman whose head is turned by this vision of masculine bravado. Lautrec's masterful draftsmanship is seen to great advantage in this work, which contains some of his best large scale drawing.

In the final version of the poster (fig. 1), horse and rider have merged to create one large, impressive figure whose diagonal motion is emphasized by the sharp angles of the street which compress the movement towards the upper left corner. This sense of movement is increased by the contrast with the pedestrians who walk in the opposite direction, and by a repeated use of compositional diagonals extending from lower left to upper right. Lautrec would later refine this complicated dynamic structure in his portrait of Tristan Bernard (cat. no. 76), whose solidly planted figure with black hat and jutting beard resembles that of the sentry.

E.M.M.

Fig. 1
Toulouse-Lautrec, *Babylone d'Allemagne*
1894, 1.30 x 0.95 m., poster
The Art Institute of Chicago

68

Le blanchisseur de la maison

The brothel's launderer

1894

0.578, 0.462 m.; 22¾, 18¼ in.

Peinture à l'essence on board

Dortu, 1971: P.544

Musée d'Albi

During his artistic campaign at brothels from 1892 until 1895, Lautrec explored a wide range of subjects representative of the daily routine, as if the pictures were an episodic series. Lautrec's mood varied greatly from picture to picture. Whereas some of the series are stately or tragic, others are droll, and this picture is impish, salacious, even Jarryesque. The subject is the delivery of laundry to the brothel, where one of the employees checks the bill. The delivery man is a grotesque character taken from real life. Lautrec, who believed the man to be tubercular, evidently posed him in his rue Caulaincourt studio (Joudain and Adhémar, p. 41). Two drawings of the man (D. 3.687-3.688) record Lautrec's progressive exaggeration of his facial features into a grotesque satyr-like mask.

Lautrec's characterization of the model sets the tone of this painting. The delivery man's cold eyes stare lecherously at the prostitute, who stands oblivious of his voyeurism. Lautrec has shaped and positioned the laundry sack to resemble a huge penis, which the delivery man exerts himself to heave towards the woman. Lautrec frequently found it amusing to suggest penises through obvious counterparts (see cat. no. 61), usually canes (fig. 1). Here his visual punning was inspired by comical grotesque figures popular in Oriental pornographic prints

Fig. 1
Toulouse-Lautrec, *Gaston Bonnefoy*
1891, 0.71 x 0.37 m., oil on board
Thyssen-Bornemisza Collection, Lugano

and in priapic art from classical antiquity, as, for example, those on lamps uncovered at Pompeii (fig. 2). In many of his possible sources, the dwarves used halters to support their oversized members, and Lautrec has converted the halter ties into the knot of the laundry sack. He was not alone in his interest in ancient pornography. Aubrey Beardsley's controversial *Lysistrata* illustrations (1896) obviously testify to a similar connoisseurship of classical pornography and an equal enjoyment in the ribald re-application of its conventions.

Characteristically, Lautrec used juxtaposed complementary colors throughout his painting in order to achieve maximum vibrancy. The block of intense red beneath the delivery man's legs, for example, is all the more potent in contrast with the greens of the laundry bag and his coat.

C.F.S.

Fig. 2
Anonymous, *Grotesque*
first century A.D., 0.22 m., bronze
National Museum of Naples

Fig. 3
Beardsley, *The Spartan ambassadors*, from *Lysistrata*
1896

69

Femme de maison

Prostitute

1894

0.56, 0.41 m.; 22⅛, 16¼ in.

Peinture à l'essence on board

Dortu, 1971: S.P.5

Private collection, New York

At the beginning of 1894, the noted naturalist author Edmond de Goncourt, who had himself sought to bring uncensored realism to the novel, complained that Lautrec's new and direct style was abusive: "One has no right to push the cult of the ugly so far" (cited by Sutton, p. 71n). Yet the brutal frankness of this portrait of a prostitute, painted later in the year, outstrips any of Lautrec's prior works in terms of untempered, even exaggerated, candor. It is as if Lautrec intended to parody his own typically delicate and emotionally indirect idiom of profile portraiture with this unflattering and imperious likeness.

The naïve and decorative characteristics generally associated with profiles fascinated Lautrec from the outset of his career. This obsession intensified in 1892, when he received a commission to decorate the grand salon of the brothel on the rue d'Amboise. For that project he created pictures to imitate eighteenth-century panelling inset with medallion-shaped portraits (many in strict profile) of the prostitutes available at the brothel (P.440-457). The project stimulated Lautrec's artistic interest in brothel subject matter, and during the following two years he continued sporadically to do somewhat formal and elegant bust portraits of the whores (fig. 1 and P.509, P.539, P.540, P.542).

Although related to this short series of prostitute portraits, which were similar to those produced earlier by Japanese graphic artists (for example, Utamaro), this picture was executed in an altogether different mode. According to Joyant (II, p. 66), Lautrec began to paint in a summary style on cardboard early in the 1890s, after admiring lively oil sketches by Raffaëlli. Like him, Lautrec often used the buff tone of his cardboard support to "represent" a local color in his pictures. Here, for example, the buff corresponds to the flesh tones of her jowls and shoulders, which are covered with a transparent chemise. Apparently Lautrec drew indications of her features with coarse brush strokes in several tones and then added areas of dense color to her hair, upper face and lips, delineating the background wall with closely hatched, bold strokes of crimson. The intensity of the red heightens the ghostly effect of the whitened facial features immediately juxtaposed against the background wall. As a result, the area of his model's upper face is dramatically isolated and mask-like.

Accounts of Lautrec's work with prostitute models vary; presumably he painted them both in the brothel and posed in his studio, and occasionally, according to Gauzi (p. 139), he painted them from memory. Although Lautrec made several pencil drawings of this model (D. 3.480, D. 4.043, D. 4.049), and may have based the final work on them, this particular portrait recalls an anecdote recounted by Romain Coolus, the writer friend who sometimes accompanied Lautrec at work in the brothels. Teasing a potential model, Lautrec admitted, "What interests me is the gargoyle," insinuating that her face was monstrous. "Very well, Count, excuse me," she replied, "here's my 'gargoyle.' Full face or profile?" (Georges-Michel, p. 17).

C.F.S.

Fig. 1
Toulouse-Lautrec, *Prostitute*
1894, 0.225 x 0.16 m., oil on board
Musée d'Albi

70

Maison de la rue des Moulins—Rolande

Brothel in the rue des Moulins—Rolande

1894

0.51, 0.70 m.; 20⅛, 27½ in.

Peinture à l'essence on board

Dortu, 1971: P.545

Maître Maxime Blum

In 1894 Lautrec installed himself at a newly opened brothel at 24 rue des Moulins, which would soon gain a reputation throughout Europe as one of the most luxurious and well equipped establishments of its kind. This house and its inhabitants were to provide the artist with the themes, settings and models which would dominate his work for the duration of the year.

One of his favorite models at the rue des Moulins was a prostitute named Rolande whom Lautrec featured in at least thirteen paintings and drawings, ten of which have been previously unidentified. These works can be divided into two thematic series: that of the most intimate moments of lesbian sexuality, of which this painting is a part, and that of prostitutes lounging in the reception room of the rue des Moulins brothel. Like many of Lautrec's favorite models, Rolande had red hair which the artist rendered in a variety of shades from blondish-red to orange. The other prominent features which make Rolande recognizable are a long, pert nose that points upward at an unusual angle, and a thin jutting chin which acts as an elegant foil to her nose.

The first of this series on lesbian lovemaking shows Rolande seated on the edge of a bed with one foot on the floor and the other leg extended on the bed. In her lap she cradles the head of her dark haired lover (fig. 1). In the painting shown here Rolande has shifted her position so that her relaxed and yielding body lies on the bed. Her chemise is lifted to her breasts, revealing the ample yet sensuous curves of her abdomen. Rolande's legs are open to welcome her lover's kisses in what must surely be one of the most explicit depictions of lesbian sex in the art of the period. The third painting in the series is *Au lit* (cat. no. 71) which shows the same scene from the corner of the bed rather than from the side.

Rolande is also the model Lautrec used for the woman seated on the right in the two studies for the foreground of *Au salon de la rue des Moulins* (cat. no. 73). The artist seems to have been so fond of her as a model that he also posed her as the woman in profile seated on a stuffed couch in the rear of the salon, and it is in this pose that Rolande makes her appearance in the finished work (cat. nos. 74, 75, P.560). Lautrec also made several exquisite portrait drawings of Rolande that study her unique features in full-face as well as profile (D. 3.729, D. 3.739, D. 3.745).

E.M.M.

Fig. 1
Toulouse-Lautrec, *The divan—Rolande*
1894, 0.52 x 0.57 m., oil on board
Musée d'Albi

71
Au lit
In bed
1894
0.52, 0.673 m.; 20½, 26½ in.
Oil on board
Dortu, 1971: P.547
Musée d'Albi

Among Lautrec's earliest brothel pictures are a series of lesbian couples under the covers of a bed (P.436-439). Two years later he returned to the theme with less success in works which experiment with a rococo abundance of pillows, bolsters, and bed linens (cat. no. 70 and P.546).

This is certainly the most effective of the group, largely because of the original composition which Lautrec plotted in a preparatory drawing (D. 3.741). The armless chair with its sharp shadow is cropped in the lower right foreground, an accent of emptiness and uprightness balanced perfectly against the rich tumble of figures in bed. Their intimacy is warmed by lights filtering in through curtains on to the wall.

The lovers are barely indicated. The figure on the left is difficult to locate precisely, since she lies in the random abandonment of sleep. However, Lautrec's favorite model Rolande is identifiable by her distinctive nose, here seen from below and indicated by a few quick strokes. Her head is thrown back onto a pillow, eyes lost in a mass of disheveled hair and shadow. This raw, unalluring face, somewhat shocking in a scene of intimacy, rivals the distorted anatomies invented by Bacon and deKooning.

C.F.S.

72

**Deux femmes demi-nues de dos—
maison de la rue des Moulins**

Two semi-nude women viewed from
the rear—brothel on the rue des Moulins

1894

0.54, 0.39 m.; 21¼, 15⅜ in.

Peinture à l'essence on board

Dortu, 1971: P.556

Musée d'Albi

This painted sketch is one of four which record the evolution of *Deux femmes de la maison* (fig. 1), one of the most important of Lautrec's brothel series. For the final painting, which depicts two prostitutes waiting in line for one of the obligatory medical inspections to which they were submitted periodically, Lautrec posed his figures in profile. This study, however, indicates that he had considered showing them from the rear, while another study (fig. 2) explores a three-quarters frontal pose. Evidently Lautrec experimented with several options in order to find the one most expressive of the resignation with which the women faced this degrading routine.

Lautrec's depiction of the controversial theme is steeped in pathos evoked by his choice of color and certain carefully observed details: the sad facial expressions, the superfluous gesture of hiking the scanty chemise, and the vulnerable pallor of the exposed haunches. The option of posing his models from the back, which he explored in this moving study, was rejected possibly because it was too impersonal. But Lautrec did make use of it for the sharply cropped figure he depicted in the extreme right of *Au Salon* (cat. no. 75). Finally, it is of interest to note that all of the paintings connected with Lautrec's portrayal of the medical examination may reflect his admiration for Rembrandt's well-known portrait of Saskia (fig. 3), which depicts her hitching up her skirt to wade.

C.F.S.

Fig. 2
Toulouse-Lautrec, *Blond prostitute*
1894, 0.68 x 0.48 m., peinture à l'essence on board
Musée du Louvre, Paris

Fig. 1
Toulouse-Lautrec, *Two prostitutes*
1894, 0.84 x 0.61 m., peinture à l'essence on board
National Gallery of Art, Washington, D.C., Chester Dale Collection

Fig. 3
Rembrandt, *Woman bathing in a stream*
1655, 0.62 x 0.47 m., oil on panel
National Gallery, London

73

Les deux amies

The two friends

1894

0.475, 0.34 m.; 18⅞, 13⅜ in.

Peinture à l'essence on board

Dortu, 1971: P.550

Musée d'Albi

This is the larger and apparently the more developed of two oil studies for the central foreground figures in *Au salon* (cat. no. 75). In the first (fig. 1) Lautrec posed Mireille, the darker haired woman, slid down on the plush brothel divan, while her companion leans toward her with a caress. Both the outline of the conjoined figures and the awkward warmth expressed by their gestures and features were altered for this second sketch. Now Mireille, curled on the couch, snuggles responsively to her companion's petting. The overall outline of the grouping undulates, whereas in the first version it had been more jagged. Lautrec also added another female figure (dramatically cropped) in the right background, witness to the public setting for the couple's tenderness.

For *Au salon* Lautrec changed these figures once again. Eliminating all sexual overtones, he separated the women with a cushion across which they are barely turned to one another in silent understanding. The cropped figure at the right is finally characterized more fully as an equal participant in the general numbness.

C.F.S.

Fig. 1
Toulouse-Lautrec, *The two friends*
1894, 0.48 x 0.34 m., peinture à l'essence on board
The Tate Gallery, London

74

Au salon de la rue des Moulins

In the parlour of la rue des Moulins

1894

0.60, 0.40 m.; 23⅝, 15⅞ in.

Oil on canvas

Dortu, 1971: P.558

The Armand Hammer Collection

The Belgian modernist connoisseur Octave Maus bought this vivid study of the poses and color chords for the left section of *Au Salon* (cat. no. 75) from Lautrec. As was the case for the studies of the central figures (cat. no. 73), Lautrec at first arranged these women in relatively stiff poses. Indeed, the leftmost figure of Lautrec's favorite model Rolande boasts one of Lautrec's most hieratic, even Egyptian, silhouettes. The relaxed rolls of flesh evident under her chemise are indicated largely by modelling in shades of vibrant pink. Lautrec's ability to "draw" with color was, of course, what Matisse (pp. 237, 314) considered to be Lautrec's fundamental achievement. Clearly, from the outset he wanted to orchestrate bold areas in a rich range of red tones for *Au salon,* and in this study he pitched the pink chemise against a deep saturated orange in the tufted divan—a daring juxtaposition of large color fields. Only the blue and green tones of the right-hand figure's dress and the greens in the background mirror, relatively small accents within the overall composition, relieve and balance the dominant reds with their charged emotional connotations.

Lautrec chose to alter the left figure's costume for *Au salon.* In that painting she wears a deeper toned dress with a dark bodice, the lines of which create graceful arabesques lacking both the rigidity and the boldness of the study. He made only minor adjustments to the right-hand figure, whose left arm cradles a velvet pillow in the final work. The modifications of color and pose harmonize this important figural grouping within the studiously refined and stately *Au salon.*

C.F.S.

75

Au salon de la rue des Moulins

Interior in the rue des Moulins

1894

1.115, 1.32 m.; 44, 52¼ in.

Oil on canvas

Dortu, 1971: P.559

Musée d'Albi

Au salon, which represents the interior of one of the brothels Lautrec frequented, is the culmination of his efforts to paint pictures of brothel life, a project he began by 1892. He studied this subject matter over a long period of time at first hand to attain absolute authenticity of atmosphere and characterization. Like Balzac and Zola, the great "naturalist" authors whom he deeply admired, Lautrec systematically compiled notes before undertaking the actual painting. These took the form of pencil sketches (D. 3556, D. 3558 and D. 3657) and rapid oil studies. For example, two oil sketches (see cat. no. 74) study the pair of figures ultimately included at the left of *Au salon,* while the figure at the far right is based on a major painting (see cat. no. 72, fig. 1) for which Lautrec made no fewer than three studies. His preoccupation with every detail led him to complain that he could not capture the quality of light peculiar to the brothel if he worked at his studio, and to wonder if he could continue with the project (Gauzi, 1954, p. 139).

According to Gauzi (p. 14), Lautrec responded to a friend's warning that *Au Salon* would be difficult to exhibit by saying, "I don't intend to ever let the picture go out; I made it because it amuses me." However, there are other indications that later he may have changed his mind and exhibited it at the beginning of 1896 in his first one-person exhibition. On that occasion Lautrec decorated a separate room with green and red striped wall coverings where he hung his brothel pictures. Access to this room was strictly limited by the artist to a select number of personal friends. Although no catalogue records exactly which paintings Lautrec showed there, and although contemporary critics avoided specific references to these "licentious" works, a ribald photograph (fig. 1) taken in Lautrec's studio shows *Au salon* displayed in an elegantly

Fig. 1
Photograph of Lautrec and model in his studio
c. 1895. Note circus mural at far left background

simple frame which he had chosen for it. Presumably he would not have troubled to have the frame made if he had not considered exhibiting the picture.

Lautrec's zeal for expressing the reality of his own milieu and period was in no way at variance with his intense appreciation for the masterpieces of art produced by other civilizations. He was aware that the truths of human nature which were his subject matter were universal truths, and he considered *Au salon* a monumental modern-day contribution to a rich and long tradition of brothel art. Joyant correctly suggested (I, p. 154) that *Au salon* was indebted to Japanese wood block prints made by Utamaro among others, which recorded life in Tokyo's pleasurable Edo district (fig. 2). Lautrec was a collector and connoisseur of these prints. He was also surely aware that some of his favorite French artists, in particular Constantin Guys (fig. 3) and Degas (fig. 4) had made extraordinary works based on the same theme, though always in small-format pieces which were not for public exhibition. Such images were, of course, the pictorial counterparts of the rich literature on brothels produced, for example, by Balzac, the Goncourt brothers, Maupassant and Huysmans.

The most important visual prototype for *Au salon*, however, is Carpaccio's well-known painting of *Two courtesans* (fig. 5), a reproduction of which Lautrec displayed in his studio (Huisman and Dortu, p. 87). In *Au salon* Lautrec repeated in his own mode all the significant features of his great sixteenth-century predecessor's work. Carpaccio's influence is evident in the figural groupings, body postures, and silhouettes of the prostitutes, as well as in their blank or resigned expressions.

The most masterful aspects of Lautrec's picture are his portrayals of the individual women, some of whom can be identified (for example, Rolande, and Gauzi, p. 141, claims the woman in the immediate foreground is Lautrec's favorite, Mireille). Nonetheless, Lautrec has organized the exotic interior of the brothel with consummate skill. The circular divans repeat and emphasize the voluptuous curves of the women's bodies, and a profound tension is achieved by the discrepancy between the opulence of the setting and the bleak faces of the prostitutes. Lautrec evoked the charged sexual atmosphere of the brothel through his orchestration of color as well. His delicate pinks, oranges and crimsons are intensified by the complementary green-toned reflections in the wall mirrors. In accordance with Symbolist color theory in the 1880s and 1890s, Lautrec's contemporaries Van Gogh and Gauguin felt that the color combination of red and green evoked the sensation of passion, and Lautrec has given this idea full pictorial expression.

In the history of modern French painting *Au salon* has a central position between the exotic sensuality of Ingres' *Le bain turc* of 1863 (Louvre) and the abstract power of Picasso's *Les demoiselles d'Avignon* of 1907, which itself evolved from his earlier Lautrec-like brothel pictures. The impact of *Au salon* on other artists was immediate. Edouard Munch, for example, was inspired by Lautrec's work when he revisited Paris from 1896 to 1897 (fig. 6).

Lautrec made a large pastel replica of *Au salon,* (Mack, p. 255), which today also belongs to the Musée d'Albi.

C.F.S.

Fig. 2
Choki, *View in a green house*
1796, each set of triptych 0.31 x 0.17 m., woodblock print
The Art Institute of Chicago
The Clarence Buckingham Collection of Japanese Prints

Fig. 3
Steel engraving after Guys, *Interior in a bordello*
c. 1860
New York Public Library

Fig. 4
Degas, *Resting*
1879, 0.16 x 0.21 m., monotype
The Estate of Pablo Picasso

Fig. 5
Carpaccio, *Two courtesans*
c. 1495-1500, 1.64 x 0.94 m., oil on panel
Museo Correr, Venice

Fig. 6
Munch, *Brothel scene*
c. 1895, oil on canvas
Oslo Kommunes Kunstsamlinger Munch-Museet

76

Tristan Bernard au vélodrome Buffalo

Tristan Bernard at the bicycle racetrack
"Buffalo"

1895

0.645, 0.81 m.; 25½, 31½ in.

Oil on canvas

Dortu, 1971: P.571

Private collection

Paul "Tristan" Bernard (1866-1947) and Lautrec adored one another (Coquiot, p. 41). Bernard's caustic sarcasm and acerbic wit peppered his articles, poems, plays, short stories and novels, many of which appeared in *La Revue Blanche* and its humoristic supplements, for which he was an editor. Lautrec supplied illustrations and book covers for some of Bernard's works, but their friendship was based largely on a mutual enthusiasm for the recently introduced sport of bicycling. Bernard, who edited *Le Journal des Vélocipédistes,* was the sports director for two bicycle racetracks, and Lautrec joined him on Sundays at the "Buffalo."

In 1895 Lautrec began to explore horizontal format pictures of the racetrack (D. 4.104 and LD. 146 and 147), apparently for the commissioned lithographs to advertise sporting goods manufacturers (L.D. 359 and 360). Each of these compositions depicts the racetrack's banked curve and the sweeping straightaways leading into and away from it. The motif seems to have fascinated Lautrec, who used it for this remarkable portrait of Bernard, a haunting character study set within a delicately calculated composition.

The pentimenti in the foreground, especially along the foremost border of the infield, indicate that Lautrec adjusted the angle of the track's curve for what were possibly a variety of pictorial reasons, the most evident of which was to suggest velocity. Although the curve as represented in Bernard's portrait is inaccurately sharp, the pinched reversal of the track's direction from left to right suggests daredevil speeds. Since Bernard's figure masks the far corner of the turn, the infield seems to have a triangular rather than a rounded shape. Indeed, Lautrec's composition is a medley of related triangular forms disposed in opposing directions to suggest rapid movement around the track. The apex of the infield curve, for example, draws the eye left, whereas the apex of Bernard's beard seen in profile reverses the field. The form of his beard and that of the grandstand across the track maintain a back and forth dialogue which suggests the approach and then recession of cyclists speeding along the course. In addition, the coloristic intensity of the grandstand perceived in relationship to the neutral color of Bernard's tweeds energizes a back and forth oscillation between foreground and distance.

The calmly rooted figure of Bernard counters the extraordinary suggestion of movement. It is as if Lautrec designed the background for the portrait to emphasize his friend's authoritative professional role as racetrack director. His form is positioned at the apex of an imaginary triangle, the other apeces of which are marked with poles whose rigid forms reiterate Bernard's dominating presence. Even so, Bernard's dominion is petty. The vivid grandstand is conspicuously vacant, and consequently Bernard seems enraptured by the hollow echoes of departed spectators. The ironic interplays of presence and absence, movement and repose, charge Lautrec's portrait of Bernard with melancholy poetry.

The technical virtuosity of the portrait extends beyond its evocative composition. The strokes of green and brown hatched loosely over the canvas represent respectively the delicate textures of grass and tweed. Finally, the reduced scheme of four large color areas is among the most elegant and simple Lautrec ever achieved.

E.M.M. & C.F.S.

77

Miss May Milton

1895

0.65, 0.48 m.; 25½, 19 in.

Peinture à l'essence on board

Dortu, 1971: P.572

The Art Institute of Chicago

According to Joyant, Lautrec met May Milton, an English dancer, in 1895. May, for whom Lautrec executed his well-known poster that same year, was reportedly unattractive: "Her pale almost clownish face, rather suggestive of a bull-dog, had nothing with which to rivet attention" (Joyant I, p. 198). Even so, Lautrec's portrait of her was considered to be brutally disfiguring by the artist's early biographer, Coquiot (p. 155), who saw the picture in Théodore Duret's collection: ". . . May Milton with a swollen face, with a heavy jaw, whitish yellow in color, as if retaining a magma of pus turned to yellow and pale green below a bladderous envelope. This painting is a hideous terror. This polished red mouth falls; it opens like a vulva; it has no further defense; it has no further toughness; it opens, it lets everything enter."

Although Coquiot's response appears dangerously unobjective, Lautrec seemingly painted this portrait of May prior to adding her grotesquely distorted face to his *Au Moulin Rouge* (cat. no. 52). The coiffure, hat and dress in the portrait are identical to those of the figure in *Au Moulin Rouge,* which Joyant (I, p. 288) incorrectly identified as "Mlle. Nelly C." Since May was a particularly intimate friend of Jane Avril's, it was fitting that Lautrec juxtapose their portraits in his large masterpiece.

The fact that this portrait has an unfinished appearance did not prevent Lautrec from exhibiting it in 1898 in London, where the dancer would have been recognized as a popular entertainer. Lautrec did several portraits which similarly contrast a face rendered densely and in detail with torsos and accessories sketched loosely over the cardboard support, a technique borrowed from Raffaëlli (Joyant, II, p. 66).

C.F.S.

78

Lucien Guitry et Jeanne Granier (Dans "Amants" de M. Maurice Donnay)

Lucien Guitry and Jeanne Granier in "The Lovers" by Maurice Donnay

1895

0.65, 0.52 m.; 25⅝, 20½ in.

Peinture à l'essence on board

Dortu, 1971: P.577

Mr. Alain Delon, Paris, France

Lautrec's interest in theatrical subjects intensified towards the end of 1893, when the newspaper *L'Escarmouche* employed him to prepare illustrations of current stage successes. At the same time he began to collaborate with acquaintances at the avant-garde Théâtre Libre, for whom he designed programs and occasionally worked on sets (P.534). The success of these projects undoubtedly contributed to several important commissions during the next years when Lautrec specialized in theatrical subjects. For example, in 1894 he produced an album devoted to Yvette Guilbert (cat. nos. 63, 64). The following year he began a similar series of prints depicting May Belfort and then in 1895 a series of thirteen lithographic portraits of celebrated stage personalities (L.D.150-L.D.162). These included Sarah Bernhardt, as well as Lucien Guitry (1860-1925) and Jeanne Granier (1852-1939), who played opposite one another in Maurice Donnay's *Les Amants* at the end of 1895. Lautrec studied this performance in two oil sketches (P.576) and a watercolor (A.227), although none of the preliminary works was ever carried to completion or eventually published.

The Delon picture, an extraordinary example of Lautrec's economical methods of characterization, explores the poses and costumes of Guitry and Granier in the roles of Georges Vétheuil and Claudine Rosay respectively. It is impossible to associate Lautrec's study with any specific scene in Donnay's comedy, since the development of its plot depends almost entirely upon intimate conversations between these urbane characters. *Les Amants* was a sophisticated version of a common theme: the frustrations of adulterous passions. Both veteran flirts, Vétheuil and Rosay go through all the motions of an affair, and finally agree for the sake of convenience to be merely friends. The paradox of passion coupled to detachment is the innovative humor of Donnay's play, which must have had a special appeal for Lautrec, himself a cynical observer of the rites of seduction.

C.F.S.

79

L'abandon, ou les deux amies

Abandon, or the two friends

1895

0.45, 0.67 m.; 17¾, 26⅜ in.

Peinture à l'essence on board

Dortu, 1971: P.598

Dr. Peter Nathan

L'abandon's quality of graceful repose makes it the most "classic" of the lesbian paintings which Lautrec first undertook about 1892, presumably at the same time he was commissioned to decorate the salon of a brothel in the rue d'Amboise. Natanson obviously sensed this quality when he compared *L'abandon,* whose background consists largely of the surface of the golden sofa, to a bas-relief (Natanson, 1951, p. 84).

The unmistakable grandeur of Lautrec's *L'abandon* calls into question the motive generally attributed to Lautrec's decision to paint prostitute pictures. According to most accounts, Lautrec actually lived in brothels for months, sometimes with his writer companion Romain Coolus. Coolus himself claimed that he and Lautrec lived in his studio nearby in the rue Caulaincourt and not in brothels (Georges-Michel, p. 16). His claim is substantiated by Jules Renard, who visited the studio in December 1894 (Renard, p. 65) when Lautrec had two women models posed together on a bed. There is no doubt, however, that Lautrec spent an extraordinary amount of time in the brothel at all hours of the night and day. The object of this intense personal scrutiny was to observe absolute, unaffected candor of appearance, behavior, and gesture. Models, Lautrec explained, are stiff and lifeless (*empaillé*), whereas the brothel residents "are altogether without pretensions" (Natanson, 1951, p. 71). Lautrec even possessed a treasured photograph of two women embracing, which he showed to his friend Charles Maurin with the peremptory assertion, "This is superior to all else. Nothing could rival such guilelessness" (Schaub-Koch, p. 169).

Pictures of lesbians, if not commonplace, were attempted by several nineteenth-century painters, most notably Courbet (fig. 1). But the direct sources of Lautrec's inspiration for *L'abandon* were erotic Japanese Shunga prints of the eighteenth and nineteenth centuries, of which Lautrec had his own collection (Leclercq, p. 60). Although generally portraying heterosexual couples, the stylized conventions of Shunga prints differentiate male and female forms only in slight details, so that to Western viewers the figures often seem to be the same sex. Consequently, many Shunga prints, for examples the frontispiece (fig. 2) to Utamaro's *Uta-makora* evoke Lautrec's pictures.

Fig. 1
Courbet, *Sleep*
1866, 1.35 x 2.0 m., oil on canvas
Musée du Petit Palais, Paris

Fig. 2
Utamaro, *Uta-makora* (Lovers—from *Poems of the Pillow*)
1788, 0.25 x 0.38 m., woodblock print
Mann Collection, Highland Park, Illinois

Lautrec, who could allude to several disparate visual sources in one work, also seems to have absorbed the influence of the great *Rokeby Venus* (fig. 3) by Velasquez, an artist whose achievement caused Lautrec to doubt his own abilities (Natanson, 1951, p. 289). He would have seen the *Rokeby Venus* in the National Gallery most recently while in London in June 1894. Although Lautrec uses two figures, the reclining woman viewed from the rear, the pose of the bent elbow, and the mirror-like relationship of faces all suggest that he had Velasquez in mind.

Literary as well as visual sources undoubtedly stimulated Lautrec, since Balzac, the Goncourt brothers, Maupassant and Huysmans, among others, all wrote about the daily routine of brothels. In the case of *L'abandon*, however, it seems likely that Lautrec recalled "Les femmes damnées" from Baudelaire's *Les Fleurs du Mal*, since sometime after their meeting in 1890, Lautrec confided to Arthur Symons that the poem inspired some paintings (Symons pp. 51-52). "Les femmes damnées" describes the post-coital adoration and conversation between lesbians lounged on enormous cushions.

At some point in the production of *L'abandon* Lautrec adjusted its dimensions by adding two new strips of canvas, a broader piece at the left and an extremely narrow one at the right. Lautrec made additions of this sort to several important pictures (for example cat. nos. 52, 63), for what were probably a variety of reasons. In *L'abandon*, as in the portraits of Paul Sescau (P.383) and Georges-Henri Manuel (P.377), both from 1891, Lautrec's additions appear to readjust the relationship of an anatomical extremity, a foot or an elbow, to the edge of the canvas. It is as if he first wanted the extremities to coincide with edges, but later decided that more space was necessary to improve his composition and develop its mood. Certainly *L'abandon* is enhanced by the left-hand addition, which expands the space and intensifies the quality of langour. The right-hand addition, oddly, is so narrow as to have no significant effect on the picture's appearance. Taken together, however, the additions result in a canvas in which the ratio of height to width is approximately that of the "golden ratio." Since that proportion does not usually appear in his works, Lautrec most likely arrived at the pleasing proportions through intuition, or through the necessity of fitting his picture to an available frame.

Although there is no clear evidence that Lautrec exhibited the picture publicly, close associates admired it (Symons, p. 61), presumably at Lautrec's studio. It is probable that when Lautrec's friend Bonnard (fig. 5) produced his illustrations for Verlaine's *Parallèlement*, a book of poems about lesbians published in 1900, he did so under the influence of *L'abandon* or Lautrec's other related works.

Since he undertook three closely related paintings at the same time as *L'abandon* (fig. 4; P.597 and P.602), and since he often created works in a series and sometimes exhibited these related works together, possibly Lautrec envisioned exhibiting *L'abandon* with the others, following a practice originated during the 1860s and exploited most successfully during the following years by Degas and Monet.

N.E.M. & C.F.S.

Fig. 3
Velasquez, *Rokeby Venus*
c. 1644-1648, 1.23 x 1.77 m., oil on canvas
National Gallery, London

Fig. 4
Toulouse-Lautrec, *The sofa*
1895, 0.63 x 0.80 m., oil on board
The Metropolitan Museum of Art, New York

ÉTÉ.

Et l'enfant répondit, pâmée
Sous la fourmillante caresse
De sa pantelante maîtresse :
« Je me meurs, ô ma bien-aimée!

« Je me meurs : ta gorge enflammée
Et lourde me soûle & m'oppresse;
Ta forte chair d'où sort l'ivresse
Est étrangement parfumée;

17

Fig. 5
Bonnard, Illustration for Verlaine's *Parallèlement*, Paris
1900
The Art Institute of Chicago

80

Femme mettant son corset

Woman putting on her corset

1896

0.842, 0.60 m.; 33⅛, 23¾ in.

Peinture à l'essence on board

Dortu, 1971: P.618

Musée d'Albi

Lautrec produced this bravura oil sketch as a preliminary study for the tenth plate of his lithographic album *Elles*. In it he reveals his consummate mastery of drawing technique, for the entire complex figure of a woman adjusting her corset has been suggested with the barest number of rapid, expressive strokes of color. Using a minimal palette of primaries, Lautrec balanced the delicate warmth of mustard yellow with bold accents in red and blue. The image he achieved is at once powerful and fragile, for the woman's massive bulk is rendered ethereal by the incandescence of the color and the sheer economy of means.

Elles consists of a series of eleven plates depicting partially dressed or robed women engaged in a variety of boudoir activities. Rendered with the same candor as his brothel paintings of the preceding years, these images have generally been assumed to portray prostitutes in a *maison close*. The lithograph for which this picture is a study (fig. 1) represents an expanded scene in which a figure in evening clothes and top hat watches the woman dressing herself. Joyant and others have identified this figure as Charles Conder, an English painter who came to Paris to finish his education and became Lautrec's friend in the early 1890s. But Joyant elsewhere recalled (I, p. 174) that Conder returned to London in 1894 and that Lautrec spent time with him there on subsequent visits, so it is doubtful that this work from 1896 depicts him. The misidentification could have come from the similarity of Conder's puffy-shouldered jacket and blond hair in *Aux Ambassadeurs—Gens chics* (see cat. no. 55, fig. 1) to that of the figure in *Elles*.

Natanson, who was very close with Lautrec during this period, asserts (1951, p. 52) that Lautrec's inspiration for the series *Elles* came from his observation of "the two

Fig. 1
Toulouse-Lautrec, *Elles—woman putting on her corset*
1896, 0.52 x 0.40 m., lithograph
The Art Institute of Chicago

bodies of a lesbian couple." The theme of lesbian lovers was one that had fascinated Lautrec since the early 1890s and in the intervening years he had devoted a great number of paintings to the subject (see cat. nos. 70, 71, 79 and P-436-P.439). As was made explicit in all Lautrec's brothel and lesbian pictures, prostitutes frequently had female lovers and, far from being mutually exclusive, the two worlds were mingled inextricably. This interpretation of *Elles* seems to be born out by several features of the series. The first page of the album is a portrait of a dancer at the Moulin Rouge and Nouveau Cirque named Cha-U-Kao, a known lesbian (Perruchot, p. 239) who habitually dressed as a clowness. Lautrec depicted her here in her pantalooned costume, seated mannishly with widespread legs. All the other plates in the album portray what appear to be the same two women, one blond and the other brunette, usually represented singly but on two pages posed together (plates 3 and 9).

There has been a general problem in identifying the models for *Elles*. With the exception of Cha-U-Kao's portrait, only two of the plates have been associated with specific people. Plates 3 (fig. 3) and 9 are described by Joyant as representing Madame Baron and her daughter Paulette ("Popo"), whom Adhémar tells us was being kept by Paul Guibert (Adhémar, no. 202). But the images hardly seem in keeping with this identification, for the facial expressions of the two women indicate some sensual involvement that in mother and daughter would border on incest, and with the exception of one plate, *Elles* seems to represent two women living in considerable intimacy.

The same two women, one fair and one dark-haired, appear throughout the album, and when one compares the blond to Lautrec's portraits of Cha-U-Kao, the similarities are vivid. Her features are almost identical with those of the massive woman serving breakfast in bed, particularly in the characteristic slight raising of the eyebrows and the mouth lifted at the corner. Even the flounced collar of the woman's dressing gown recalls the clowness' ruff. The contradiction between this woman's sagging bulk and the nipped waist and uplifted breasts of Cha-U-Kao's painted portraits can be resolved by remembering the corset, that essential transformative accountrement of female dress in the late nineteenth century. The resemblance between the woman washing herself in plate 6 (fig. 4), and a portrait Lautrec did of Cha-U-Kao in 1895 (fig. 5) is unmistakable, however, and permits the supposition that *Elles* was based on the private life of the notorious clowness. If so, Joyant's identification of Madame Baron must be mistaken. Given Lautrec's fascination with Cha-U-Kao and the frequency with which he depicted her during 1895, it is easy to believe the subtly suggestive *Elles* was inspired by this mistress of disguise.

The only aspect of *Elles* that appears at first not to bear out this interpretation is the presence of a man's top hat tossed on a chair in Lautrec's lithographed cover, and the

Fig. 2
Toulouse-Lautrec, *Elles—the seated clowness, Cha-U-Kao*
1896, 0.52 x 0.40 m., colored lithograph
The Art Institute of Chicago

Fig. 3
Toulouse-Lautrec, *Elles—woman with a tray*
1896, 0.40 x 0.52 m., colored lithograph
The Art Institute of Chicago

Fig. 4
Toulouse-Lautrec, *Elles—woman washing herself*
1896, 0.52 x 0.40 m., colored lithograph
The Art Institute of Chicago

Fig. 5
Toulouse-Lautrec *The clowness*
1895, 0.57 x 0.42 m., oil on board
Musée du Louvre, Paris

single scene for which our painting was the study and which seems to represent a gentleman spectator. But before Lautrec executed this lithograph he painted a large oil version (fig. 2), and in this picture the onlooker gazing pensively at the woman appears to be female as well, her bosom conspicuous under her jacket. Lautrec habitually frequented the lesbian bar La Souris, to which many women came in men's clothing, and in this same year he did a lithograph (L.D.175) of another lesbian Mary Hamilton, wearing tails and starched shirt. The "gentleman" in evening dress and the top hat in *Elles* could therefore be understood as Lautrec's subtle allusions to lesbian male-female role playing, as well as a witty spoof on the popular "naturalist" theme of gentlemen ogling courtesans at their toilette, of which Manet's 1877 painting of Zola's *Nana* is the best example (fig. 7).

Lautrec could have had an excellent reason for altering his painted study for the album and making the ambiguous figure of the spectator more superficially male in the final lithograph. In 1892 he had contributed a painting of lesbians (P. 436) to the Symbolist exhibition at La Barc de Boutteville's gallery, and police forced the dealer to remove it from the display window (Perruchot, pp. 180-181). It is reasonable to assume that in such a climate of public distaste Lautrec would yield to pressure to modify the most overt lesbian allusions of an album meant for publication.

N.E.M.

Fig. 6
Toulouse-Lautrec, *Woman putting on her corset*
1896, 1.03 x 0.65 m., oil on canvas
Musée des Augustins, Toulouse

Fig. 7
Manet, *Nana*
1877, 1.50 x 1.16 m., oil on canvas
Kunsthalle, Hamburg

81
Danseuse
Dancer
1896
2.00, 0.72 m.; 79, 28⅝ in.
Oil on canvas
Dortu, 1971: P.612
Private collection

The grand *Dancer*, certainly one of Lautrec's very greatest works, was never publicly exhibited during his lifetime. The engraver Adolphe Albert, who had been a fellow student with Lautrec under Cormon, bought it. Given its tall and narrow dimensions, perhaps Albert set the painting in some decorative scheme. Albert may even have suggested the subject, since except for this masterpiece, Lautrec avoided ballet pictures after 1890. His decision to do so must have been in part out of deference to his idol Degas, who had made the theme of ballerinas virtually his own (fig. 1). Of course, Lautrec had explored the theme while he was a student with Albert (fig. 2 and cat. nos. 22, 23) but the raw style he used at that time was unsuited to the delicacy of the theme and his reliance upon Degas' achievement was all too obvious. Whatever the reasons for undertaking this unique late work, Lautrec approached the ballet theme with bold originality. It was the acquired skill and strength of ballerinas that led him to refer to them in general as "a deluxe animal." (Natanson, 1951, p. 228). The extent to which he succeeded in expressing his admiration for them and his own artistic powers was best summed up by the distinguished critic Duret, who lingered before the *Dancer* when it was exhibited in 1925: "Look at this picture and then think about Degas' Ballerinas. It is so simple, and all I can do is to repeat; here genius, there talent" (Jedlicka, p. 207).

The *Dancer* was painted on a narrow vertical wooden panel. Its format was one which sporadically intrigued the artist (cat. no. 33), perhaps as a result of his admiration for Chinese painted scrolls (cat. no. 46). The wooden support provided him with a gray-brown toned base which deepens his pale colors and unifies them. Evidently he sketched the form of the dancer and theater flats loosely on the panel and then added washes of color: gray-green for the flats, its complementary pink for the figure's tights. Since the color corresponds imprecisely to outlined areas, the figure and setting both seem to flutter between color and form. Only the ballerina retains a flexed stability in a world of painted scenery and artificial light. Her body and tutu are shot with pale bluish shadows, which, taken with her orange hair and red mouth, constitute what French painters and writers generally called a quality of "féerique," or mirage-like visual fantasy.

If Lautrec did not pay careful attention to the set repertoire of ballet positions, he invented a bold composition, weighted to the lower right. The illusion of space is dependent almost solely upon his organization of color and the pale indistinct background. The set behind her continues far above the figure as if to express her potential to spring upwards and at the same time to magnify her erect stateliness.

C.F.S.

Fig. 1
Degas, *Two dancers*
c. 1890, 0.70 x 0.44 m., pastel on paper
The Art Institute of Chicago
The Amy McCormick Memorial Collection

Fig. 2
Toulouse-Lautrec, *Dancer*
1885, 0.80 x 0.65 m., oil on canvas
Private collection

82

M. Cyprien "Cipa" Godebski
1896
0.52, 0.40 m.; 20½, 15¾ in.
Peinture à l'essence on board
Dortu, 1971: P.625
Stavros S. Niarchos Collection

Cyprien "Cipa" Godebski, a Polish writer and sculptor, was among the guests at the Natanson summer home in Villeneuve-sur-Yonne. The hostess, Misia Natanson (cat. nos. 92, 93) was his half-sister. While enjoying their hospitality during the summer of 1896, Lautrec painted this robust portrait of Cipa, with whom he anticipated co-authoring a never realized collection of epigrams (Leclercq, p. 73).

Lautrec frequently depicted portrait subjects in garden settings. Most often he painted his sitters' heads more densely than other areas, which he scumbled with lively brushwork. The casual pose here, which Lautrec had investigated in a much earlier portrait (cat. no. 8), is nonetheless somewhat atypical. Lautrec preferred his models seated in profile or full-face. The head turned over the shoulder is reminiscent of seventeenth-century portraits, and even more of Cézanne's self-portraits. It is conceivable that Lautrec saw the first important Cézanne exhibition at Vollard's in 1895, which contained at least one portrait of this type. Perhaps Cipa's bearded face, rustic hat and pipe reminded Lautrec or the other guests of Cézanne's work, and suggested the composition most appropriate for this extraordinary portrait.

C.F.S.

83

Madame E. Tapié de Céleyran

1896

0.24, 0.165 m.; 9½, 6½ in.

Oil on panel

Dortu, 1971: P.613

Mr. and Mrs. Leigh B. Block, Chicago

Judging from Lautrec's correspondence, if he visited his family during 1896, it must have been after mid-September. In any event, family photographic records indicate that he painted this exquisite portrait of his cousin's wife that year. Lautrec posed her in a garden in front of the chapel on the Tapié de Céleyran estate, called Bosc (fig. 1).

Painted on a wooden panel, this profile portrait has the quality of a fifteenth-century Netherlandish miniature. Lautrec had painted many portraits in a garden setting, beginning in 1882 with one of his mother seated on a slatted bench (cat. no. 12). Originally inspired perhaps by similar portraits produced in the 1870s by Monet and Renoir, by 1896 Lautrec had made the genre wholly his own. Coloristically this picture retains a close relationship to these artists' works, however. Indeed, the delicate tones of white, pinkish cream, and yellow applied with careful stabs of his brush recall their "Impressionist" style. And the mauve ruffled collar worn by Lautrec's sitter recalls Renoir's particular fondness for that neo-baroque fashion.

Small wooden panels were one of Lautrec's favorite supports for portraits, beginning as early as 1879 (P.22-P.24). In the latter 1890s he chose to paint several intimate portraits of family members on these toned backgrounds (cat. no. 84).

C.F.S.

Fig. 1
Photograph of Lautrec at work
1896

84

Mademoiselle Béatrice Tapié de Céleyran

Miss Béatrice Tapié de Céleyran

1897

0.23, 0.16 m.; 9½, 6½ in.

Oil on panel

Dortu, 1971: P.640

Private collection, New York

"Kiki" Béatrice Tapié de Céleyran (1875-1913) was Lautrec's first cousin and goddaughter, whose portrait he painted twice (P.656) during a visit with his relatives in 1897. As in the portrait of the wife of his cousin painted the year before (cat. no. 83) Lautrec used a small wooden panel for a toned support. He painted his cousin at bust length, with sympathetic if scrupulous honesty. Her plain appearance is enriched by the loose virtuosity with which he described her pale dress and the softly complementary and decorative background. Her features are framed amidst the delicacy of these subordinate areas of the picture. Unpretentious in composition and direct in observation, this intimate picture, like so many of Lautrec's diminutive panels, is a nineteenth-century counterpart to fifteenth-century Netherlandish portraits.

C.F.S.

85

M. Henry Nocq

1897

0.64, 0.49 m.; 25¼, 19¼ in.

Peinture à l'essence on board

Dortu, 1971: P.639

The Alex Hillman Family Foundation

This is the last of the group of portraits of dandies (cat. nos. 46, 47) painted by Lautrec in his rue Caulaincourt studio, from which he moved in May 1897. Nocq was a Belgian craftsman known especially for his jewelry and medals. Unlike Lautrec's other "dandy" portraits, this includes an identifiable picture on a platform equipped with casters: *Marcelle Lender dans Chilpéric* (fig. 1), which he had painted the previous year. Turned to the left, arms on hips under a long dark cape, Nocq's pose echoes that of Mlle. Lender's partner in the earlier painting, as if Lautrec once again wished to draw a parallel between theatrical costume and pose and those rehearsed for daily contemporary life.

A painted study (P.639) for Nocq's portrait indicates that at first Lautrec posed him *en face,* hat removed, and chose a narrower format. In the final version, Lautrec decided to extend Nocq's silhouette by having him pose with arms jutting out behind him under his cape, distorting the shape and size of Nocq's body. The pictorially strong, but nonetheless unflattering line of Nocq's back suggests that he is stooped and that his head is oddly small. Nocq himself evidently found his portrait "spiteful in the extreme" (Perruchot, p. 254).

C.F.S.

Fig. 1
Toulouse-Lautrec, *Marcelle Lender in "Chilpéric"*
1896, 1.45 x 1.50 m., oil on canvas
Collection of Mr. and Mrs. John Hay Whitney

86

M. Paul Leclercq

1897

0.54, 0.64 m.; 21¼, 25¼ in.

Peinture à l'essence on board

Dortu, 1971: P.645

Musée du Louvre, Galerie du Jeu de
Paume, Paris

Paul Leclercq was a poet and a writer who participated in the founding of *La Revue Blanche* and became a close friend of Lautrec's during the 1890s. Lautrec wrote his mother that he considered him a "man of the world" (Corr., p. 193) and posed his portrait in such a way as to capture this quality. Indeed, Natanson, who claimed that Lautrec was infatuated with Leclercq (1951, p. 93), described the picture as "evoking the little Louis XIV marquis that Lautrec wished to make of him." (p. 14).

Leclercq is seated centrally in a reduced setting, the self-assurance of his commanding gaze and informally crossed legs somewhat undermined by the hands clenched protectively in his lap and the tension produced by the sole of his shoe pushing against the edge of the canvas. The expression on Leclercq's elegant face constitutes one of Lautrec's subtlest and most accomplished characterizations, and he has focused attention on it by contrasting its delicately painted details with the solid mass of the sitter's dark attire. One finely drawn eyebrow lifted, the corner of his mouth quirked slightly upwards under the pencil-thin moustache, his direct glance conveys an effect of penetrating awareness.

Leclercq's figure is silhouetted against a sketchily indicated studio background, the blue-green tones of which balance the yellow wicker chair in a subdued harmony. Lautrec has placed only one dominant accent in this setting: the large painting on an easel positioned directly behind Leclercq (fig. 1). It is the study of a woman putting on her corset which Lautrec produced in the previous year, preparatory to executing it as a lithograph for his famous album *Elles* (see cat. no. 80). The image is barely indicated here, brushed in with only a few rapid strokes of paint, but it would have been recognizable to a public familiar with this notorious work.

At the right side of this picture, a figure in evening clothes and top hat is seated in a pose similar to Leclercq's, head tilted on the same angle. It appears to be a gentleman watching moodily while his buxom companion performs this intimate act at her dressing table, but a closer glance reveals that the "gentleman" is a woman, her ample bosom visibly swelling her shirtfront and jacket. By juxtaposing this picture closely with Leclercq's head, Lautrec has incorporated into his portrait a subtle and witty reminder of his friend's worldly character.

N.E.M.

Fig. 1
Toulouse-Lautrec, *Woman putting on her corset*
1896, 1.03 x 0.65 m., oil on canvas
Musée des Augustins, Toulouse

87
La grande loge
The large theater box
1897
0.538, 0.462 m.; 21¼, 18¼ in.
Peinture à l'essence on board
Dortu, 1971: P.651
Private collection

The popular theme of spectators in theater boxes appealed to Lautrec's Balzacian interest in the human comedy, since spectators observed are dramas in themselves (cat. nos. 54, 57). The painting's composition is inventive and wrily humorous. The dominant color chord of softly shadowed red velvet is accented by the brighter trim which marks off each separate box. Seen obliquely, the boxes' trim provides a bold and syncopated compositional framework. The immediate foreground is divided symmetrically by the vaguely heart-shaped wedge of trim at the box's foremost corner. The deeply curved partitions between boxes are rendered as parallel asymmetrical red accents, each of which intersects the head of one of the figures and draws attention to it.

The silhouette of the stout male figure in evening dress fills his box with middle-aged bachelorhood. His availability is, of course, worthy of the consideration of two unescorted women, and in compositional terms the bachelor's mass is balanced by the empty chairs in the women's box. The subject of middle-aged flirtations had since the 1880s supplied artists with variations on a widespread pictorial theme. For example, in Mary Cassatt's *At the Opéra* (fig. 1) the woman in the foreground who is dressed in mourning is inspected by the preying eyes of a silver-haired Romeo across the house.

But in Lautrec's picture the little drama is "acted" by acquaintances whom he has impishly miscast. The man is Tom, a coachman for the Rothschilds, whom Lautrec knew from a bar they both frequented. Dressed like his master here, Tom is a caricature of the upper class gentleman. The woman in profile is Armande Brazier, the one-eyed former prostitute who at that time was the proprietress of *Le Hanneton*, a tough lesbian bar. The seductive glance of the mannishly-dressed Armande's coquettish companion divulges the irony with which Lautrec has handled his theme. Correctly perceived, the subject matter is brilliantly interrelated with Lautrec's composition, since the patterns of trim on the box cradle the women together, while separating them physically from Tom (Cooper, p. 134; Perruchot, pp. 253-254).

Although this picture may have been executed preparatory to the lithographs Lautrec based upon it (L.D., no. 204), it is equally possible that he was so delighted with the painting that he wanted to reproduce it in another medium.

C.F.S.

Fig. 1
Cassatt, *At the opera*
1879, 0.80 x 0.64 m., oil on canvas
Museum of Fine Arts, Boston

88

**Bouboule: Bulldog de Mme Palmyre,
à La Souris**

Bouboule: Bulldog of Mrs. Palmyre,
at La Souris

1897

0.61, 0.435 m.; 24⅛, 17¼ in.

Peinture à l'essence on board

Dortu, 1971: P.646

Musée d'Albi

Lautrec executed this extraordinary painted sketch preparatory to a lithographed menu for Palmyre, the proprietress of La Souris, a famous lesbian restaurant in the rue Breda (today the rue Henry Monnier). Bouboule was her pet, to which, according to Leclercq, she bore an uncanny resemblance: "a buxom woman with the ferocious appearance of a bulldog who, though in reality exceedingly kind-hearted, always seemed to be on the point of biting." Coquiot (p. 162) was much amused by the dog's gluttonous, concupiscent personality, and, considering his mistress's clientele, by his unfortunate dislike of women. As soon as they took their eyes off the dog, it sneaked under the table and forced itself, sometimes with effort, to urinate on their dresses.

Always fond of bulldogs, Lautrec must have been delighted by Bouboule. As Rivoire (Dec., 1901, p. 397) recalled: ". . . animals became persons for him, as (they do) in fables. Just as much as their form, more than their form, it is their character, it is actually their soul which he sought to grasp and express. He made portraits of animals just as he made portraits of men." Indeed, Lautrec's "portrait" captures the dense, querulous head and intense alertness of the dog, whose ears tremble and whose fat quivers. Lautrec achieved this extraordinary sense of verisimilitude with rapid, imprecise lines, defining every outline repeatedly and dotting the figure with bold highlights. His inventive graphic techniques preserve one of the most celebrated pets of fin-de-siècle night-life. Like Coquiot p. 162), we presume that Bouboule is now "in doggy heaven."

C.F.S.

89

L'Image—Marthe Mellot debout de
profil

L'Image—Marthe Mellot standing in
profile

1897

0.33, 0.24 m.; 13, 9½ in.

Gouache, India ink and pencil on board

Dortu, 1971: P.654

Private collection, New York

Lautrec's interest in the theater was a broad one that brought him into contact with the avant-garde of Parisian drama. This association was most active around 1897 when Lautrec produced graphic works for the Théâtre Antoine and the Théâtre de l'Oeuvre, two of the leading proponents of the Symbolist-oriented groups which were so strongly influenced by the work of Ibsen. Among the stage artists who performed in the plays of this new wave were the multi-talented Lugné-Poë and Marthe Mellot. The latter was married to Alfred Natanson of *La Revue Blanche* and, along with her sister-in-law Misia, was one of the most brilliant women of this milieu.

Mellot was a highly accomplished actress who received critical acclaim for her performances and had a reputation for great charm and a melodious voice (Jasper, p. 48). She often appeared with Lugné-Poë, as in Edouard Dujardin's *Le chevalier du passé* of 1892, when the author praised the skill and understanding of these two artists who helped create their roles (Jasper, p. 75).

In April of 1891 Mellot played in Dujardin's *Antonia,* the first of a trilogy entitled *La Légende d'Antonia* whose general theme involved the suffering male victim and the woman who ultimately betrays him. A Lautrec drawing, which Joyant dates eight years after the presentation (D. 4.562), is inscribed "Fin d'Antonia" and shows a female profile at the bottom of the sheet with the name "Mello" to its right. This must be a previously unrecognized portrait of Marthe Mellot, who originated the role of Antonia.

That Lautrec had a continuing interest in Mellot is proved by a later series of six drawings from 1900, which depict her on stage in Jean Richepin's play *La Gitane* at the Théâtre Antoine (S. 4.659-663, D. 4.672). These present the actress in a series of profile studies that capture her sharp features and the convincing bravado of her gypsy pose, and were done in preparation for Lautrec's last poster which appeared January 22, 1900 (L.D., no. 368).

The standing profile portrait that Lautrec painted of Mellot was intended to illustrate a cover for the October 1897 (no. 11) issue of the literary and artistic review *L'Image*. Although it is impossible to identify a specific role in Lautrec's depiction, the image has a quality of bleakness and isolation which is reminiscent of contemporary Scandinavian Symbolist drama. We know that on the previous September 30th, Mellot starred in the title role of Brieux's comedy *Blanchette* at André Antoine's Théâtre Antoine. She also had the lead in de Curel's *Le repas du lion*, which was later produced by Antoine as well. It was Antoine who gave the first French performances of Ibsen and Strindberg, and both he and the two previously mentioned playwrights were known for the marked influence these Northern writers had on their work. It therefore seems likely that Lautrec's portrait was meant to evoke this type of role.

Mellot's blue-black, high-collared dress and rich, dark hair accentuate the detached elegance of her whitened face, which stares into the wings to avoid confronting the viewer. The subtle tension this evokes is heightened by the half-curled, almost skeletal hand that is poised at her side. Mellot's attractive yet menacing presence suggests the role of the dangerously seductive female so important to French avant-garde theater at the turn of the century.

E.M.M.

90

Madame Berthe Bady

1897

0.703, 0.60 m.; 27⅝, 23⅝ in.

Peinture à l'essence on board

Dortu, 1971: P.647

Musée d'Albi

Berthe Bady was a Belgian actress who was active in avant-garde Parisian theater during the 1890s. She performed at the Théâtre de l'Oeuvre with Lugné-Poë and others during the same period and in the same types of Symbolist plays as Marthe Mellot (cat. no. 89), and Lautrec depicted her a number of times over the years in lithographs associated with her dramatic roles. In 1894 he produced two of these: one portraying her with Lugné-Poë in Beaubourg's *L'Image* (L.D.57), the other with Deblève in Bjoernson's *Au-dessus des forces humaines* (L.D.55). In 1896 he executed a last lithograph advertising her in Bataille's *La Lépreuse* (L.D.196).

In all of Lautrec's graphic illustrations, he represented Madame Bady in poses so extreme that they suggest caricature or melodrama. Although his painted portrait captures her seated informally with crossed legs, off-stage, Lautrec has used a variety of means to suggest the theatrical, self-dramatizing nature of an actress' personality. The flamboyant art nouveau chair, the large swooping curl on her forehead, and the self-consciously "casual" pose of chin in hand all attest to Madame Bady's profession, as does Lautrec's glowing palette of purple and green—a color combination he used for his 1889 depiction of the actor M. Samary on stage (cat. no. 37). This powerful portrait includes some of Lautrec's most bravura brushwork, comparable in its virtuosity to similar passages in the mature work of Rembrandt and Velasquez. With a few vigorous scrawls of white paint he has suggested the lace yoke of Madame Bady's gown and added an amusing visual note which, in combination with his sitter's friendly smile, lightens the dramatic overtones of his characterization.

N.E.M.

91

Femme rousse nue accroupie

Red-headed nude crouching

1897

0.47, 0.60 m.; 18¼, 23⅝ in.

Peinture à l'essence on board

Dortu, 1971: P.649

Baldwin M. Baldwin Foundation
Collection

Lautrec devoted much of the 1890s to studying and painting nude or partially clothed women, first in his brothel pictures and, in 1896, in his album *Elles*. In 1897 he turned aside from suites of this type, producing only occasional paintings of isolated nudes. All of these (P.637, P.648, P.650) lack the anecdotal character and brutal frankness of his previous series, and seem instead to celebrate the female form in subtle variations of pose and color harmonies. Lautrec's artistic powers were far too advanced by this time for these delicate pictures to be considered exercises. With their muted tones and fluid grace they more accurately recall Whistler's "nocturnes" or Degas' pastels.

This particular work could very well have been influenced by Degas, who in 1883 did a pastel-monotype of a similarly posed woman on an unkempt bed (fig. 1). As he so often did, however, Lautrec has stripped away the "naturalist" pretense of capturing a model in the midst of some candid activity. Degas' model crouches to play with a little dog whose presence legitimizes her posture, and by avoiding this type of "genre" accessory Lautrec emphasizes that his model is frankly posing.

Degas and Lautrec reveal different interests and sensibilities in the placement of their models as well. The hunched back and widely spread knees of Degas' nude create an ungainly effect suggestive of "natural," uncontrived action. Lautrec has chosen to position his model with back arched in a long, fluid curve that accentuates her outthrust buttocks, but with his characteristically subtle sensibility, he has softened the provocative element of the picture. His low-keyed palette of homogeneous pastel tones weaves figure and setting into a scene of dreamy, almost ethereal beauty. By averting his model's face and washing the surface with a hazy veil of pale, opalescent shades of pink and cream, salmon and blue, brown and violet, he has contrived a subdued and tranquil image reminiscent of the pictures he was to paint a few years later of Madame Poupoule (see cat. nos. 97, 108).

N.E.M.

Fig. 1
Degas, *Woman with dog on bed*
c. 1883, 0.26 x 0.31 m., pastel on monotype
Private collection

92

Madame Misia Natanson

1897

0.56, 0.46 m.; 22⅛, 18⅛ in.

Peinture à l'essence on board

Dortu, 1971: P.641

Mrs. Paul Sampliner

While visiting with his friends the Natansons at Ville-neuve-sur-Yonne in the summer of 1897, Lautrec painted this exquisite portrait of Misia reading in the garden. He painted her several other times (cat. nos. 93, 94) but Misia claimed that this picture was her favorite (Sert, p. 62). In her memoirs, she recalled that during this holiday she and Lautrec spent hours in the garden indulging in a favorite pastime. Misia would sit in the grass with her back against a tree, reading or pretending to read while Lautrec tickled the soles of her bare feet with a paintbrush, discovering "imaginary landscapes" (Sert, p. 51).

Although Misia is not seated on the ground here, the setting and pose are reminiscent of this idyllic game. Lautrec had painted numerous portraits over the years of women sitting in profile against a garden background (see cat. no. 39), but his picture of Misia has a freedom and energy that sets it apart from all others. As was frequently his habit, he painted her face and hair more densely than the rest of the surface to make them stand out as the dominant accents. Her head, rendered with extreme delicacy, is poised like a graceful flower over the mass of vigorous, loose brushwork with which Lautrec blocked in the ruffled yoke of her dress, her lower body and chair. His powerful, abstract strokes create an even greater contrast with her face, accentuating its refinement and serious expression.

Misia's gently inclined head continues the sinuous curve of the chair seat which is balanced and stabilized by the slashing, angled lines of its legs. With great sensitivity Lautrec avoided overloading the composition and distracting attention from Misia's face by leaving the surface of the background behind her head relatively smooth and even. Only in the bottom half of the picture do his strokes pick up velocity, the boldly dashed-in blades of grass enlarging rapidly to fuse with the long streaks of Misia's gown and chair. Skillfully balancing the dynamic forcefulness of his brushwork with a palette of delicately shaded tones in hazy green, pinks and white, Lautrec has created a poetic evocation not only of Misia's beauty, but of the airy summer days of their holiday together.

N.E.M.

93

Madame Misia Natanson

1897

0.80, 0.95 m.; 31½, 37½ in.

Cardboard glued to wood panel

Dortu, 1971: P.642

Kunstmuseum; Bern, Switzerland,
Donation Mrs. Hilde Thannhauser
from the Collection Justin Thannhauser

Lautrec adored the company of Misia Natanson, the impetuous, precocious, aristocratic child-bride of Thadée Natanson, who directed the influential *La Revue Blanche*. Her salons, which included Vuillard, Bonnard, Mallarmé, Verlaine, Debussy and Ravel, were the most brilliant of the waning nineteenth century, and Lautrec played an active role at them, especially between 1895 and 1897.

Misia's musical talents were nurtured from the age of six by Gabriel Fauré, with whom she shared an unbounded admiration for Beethoven (Sert, p. 24). When at the age of fifteen she wed Thadée, Fauré burst into tears because it would jeopardize her future as a pianist (Sert, p. 31). If Misia never fulfilled Fauré's expectations, she did continue with her music. Her admirer Mallarmé inscribed a fan to her:

Aile que du papier reploie

Bats toute si t'initia

Naguère à l'orage et la joie

De son piano Misia

(Cited by Wagner, p. 7)

In her memoirs, written years afterwards, Misia apparently misremembered an important sequence of events connected with Lautrec's most ambitious portraits of her (cat. no. 92 and D. 3.844). She recalled that this portrait was the first of them and that it was painted in the grief-laden solitude following the funeral of her friend Mallarmé, when she stayed at Villeneuve-sur-Yonne with Vuillard and Lautrec. In fact, Mallarmé died in September 1898, and Lautrec had already exhibited this portrait the previous May. Nevertheless, Lautrec frequently returned to works, sometimes after an interval of years (Rivoire, 1902, p. 260). He may therefore have soothed Misia's grief by reworking her portrait late in 1898. In any event, Lautrec's stately portrait is highly reminiscent of Manet's portrait of his wife at the piano (fig. 1) and Mallarmé was devoted to Manet's memory. Consequently, Lautrec's portrait of Misia would have fulfilled Mallarmé's idea of her. Lautrec knew Manet's portrait because his widow had given it to Joyant in 1894.

The picture is composed of broad areas of contrasted colors: the white of the dress versus the black piano, the rust of the stool versus the greenish blue of the art nouveau wallpaper. The curvilinear decorative accents certainly suggest the phrased arabesques of Misia's performance.

Evidently she is playing Saint-Saëns' piano transcription of Beethoven's *Ruins of Athens*, a piece Lautrec loved to hear, "insisting that it inspired him" (Sert, pp. 50-51). Misia recalled Lautrec entreating her, "Ah, the beautiful ruins, the wonderful ruins, once more the ruins, Misia." His supplication was, however, wasted on this occasion. Misia admitted that she was an "insufferable" model, who constantly peeked at Lautrec's progress and complained of too short a neck, too large a nose, and too small eyes (Sert, pp. 50-51). Her dogged surveillance guided Lautrec to one of his most flattering portraits; the artist, however, took "revenge" (cat. no. 94).

C.F.S.

Fig. 1
Manet, *The artist's wife at the piano*
1867-1868, 0.38 x 0.46 m., oil on canvas
Musée du Louvre, Paris

94

À table chez Monsieur et Madame Thadée Natanson

Dinner at the home of Mr. and Mrs. Thadée Natanson

1898

0.60, 0.80 m.; 23⅝, 31½ in.

Peinture à l'essence on board

Dortu, 1971: P.567

Museum of Fine Arts; Houston (John A. and Audrey Jones Beck Collection)

During his vacations at Villeneuve-sur-Yonne at the Natanson's country home, Lautrec produced several important portraits (cat nos. 82, 92) and this more anecdotal record of a dinner party. Seated from left to right are Vuillard, Misia Natanson, the painter Vallotton and Thadée Natanson, whose back is turned. All of them contributed to the brilliant intellectual climate sustained by Thadée's *La Revue Blanche*.

According to Misia (Sert, p. 51), Lautrec painted a "caricature" of a dinner party in which he characterized her as a procuress. He did so to take "revenge" for her unbearable behavior while she sat for a formal portrait in the autumn of 1898 (cat. no. 93). Her overbearing interference, no matter how charming in itself, must have reminded Lautrec of the domineering control he associated with the madame of a brothel. Lautrec portrayed her wearing rather heavy make-up, accentuated by garish ribbons and bows. He exaggerated the size of her upper body to matronly proportions which dwarf the meek artists seated to either side of her and the younger waitress (or prostitute?) in the background. Only Thadée's bulk matches that of his wife. Since Misia was her husband's junior by decades, the comparison Lautrec drew must have been insulting.

Lautrec was experienced at painting women of ill repute seated at tables, and in 1893 he did an important picture of a meal at a brothel (P.499). Furthermore, judging from anecdotes and hearsay, he took delight in insinuating that well-bred women were no better than whores. When on another occasion a host asked Lautrec if he were enjoying himself, the artist replied that he was, since he felt as if he were in a brothel, a comment which offended a duchess and a countess who were present (Schaub-Koch, p. 44).

C.F.S.

95

Au café: le consommateur et la
caissière chlorotique

At the cafe: the drinker and the
chlorotic cashier

1898

0.815, 0.60 m.; 32⅛, 23⅝ in.

Peinture à l'essence on board

Dortu, 1971: P.657

Kunsthaus, Zurich, Switzerland

Natanson (1950, p. 81) testified that Lautrec enjoyed evoking the styles and idiosyncracies of other artists' work in his own. Here he "quoted" the placement of figures in Degas' *L'absinthe* (fig. 1), and also the rhythmic alignment of heads and their reflections seen in a background mirror. Lautrec's contemporaries, for example, Courbet and Manet, had popularized the theme of a barmaid or cashier seen immediately behind a counter, as if to suggest that the spectator played an active role in a painting's fiction. Like theater box scenes, pictures of cashiers might be called "cropped," since they represent an activity the object of which is suggested to be outside of the picture.

Lautrec took an active interest in "cropped" pictorial subjects as early as the mid-1880s (cat. no. 30). It seems as if such subjects permitted a heightened immediacy, since the figures necessarily confront a spectator from the

Fig. 1
Degas, *The absinthe drinker*
1876, 0.92 x 0.68 m., oil on canvas
Musée du Louvre, Paris

most proximate foreground. In addition, since a spectator can imagine the possibility of his actual presence across a table (fig. 2) or counter from a represented scene, a heightened variety of "illusionism" comes into play. The picture not only describes a specific spatial situation but implies as well as a plausible role for the spectator. If in real life a spectator is almost always a participant, "realistic" paintings in a sense had to bring the spectator into account, and artists from Daumier to Picasso (fig. 3) traded on "cropped" subjects to do so.

Lautrec indulged his reputed fondness for humorously ill-matched couples in *Au café*, a painting acquired by his old friend Dr. Bourges (cat. no. 46). The stout proprietor posed in a full frontal view dominates the picture, barely leaving enough room for his gaunt, tall cashier assistant, who is turned away and emotionally distant. Both figures are trapped between the wooden counter and background mirror wall where complementary green tones are reflected. Lautrec devoted fully half of his picture to the counter top and front. Only a glass and bottle, whose shapes mimic those of the figures, interrupt the broad expanse of polished wood. Yet those simple accessories are painted economically, with dazzling virtuosity. The glass is only a grouping of white highlights around an imaginary perimeter, and the bottle is drawn asymmetrically, as if wobbling, to suggest its volume. The proprietor's hands, in particular the one behind the glass, are suggested by the crudest ciphers for fingers and fists. Perhaps most extraordinary is the wood counter. Lautrec left the majority of his buffed-tone board ground unpainted and placed thinly scumbled streaks of brown and green to evoke polished woodgrain and shadowy reflections. However sparse Lautrec's means, his foreground is as loaded with recorded observation as the overcrowded booth imprisoning this odd couple.

C.F.S.

Fig. 2
Toulouse-Lautrec, *Monsieur Boileau at the café*
1893, 0.80 x 0.64 m., gouache on cardboard
The Cleveland Museum of Art, Hinman B. Hurlbut Collection

Fig. 3
Picasso, *The café*
1901, 0.29 x 0.45 m., pastel
Private collection

96

À la toilette: Madame Poupoule

At her dressing table: Madame Poupoule

1898

0.608, 0.496 m.; 24, 19½ in.

Oil on panel

Dortu, 1971: P.668

Musée d'Albi

In 1898 Lautrec painted a prostitute known as Madame Poupoule ("fast chick") sitting at her dressing table and contemplating her mirrored image. The theme was a fairly common one for "naturalist" painters of modern life during the 1870s and 1880s, and Lautrec must have been familiar with works of this type by Courbet, Manet (fig. 1) and Seurat (fig. 2), to name only a few. Lautrec himself had executed a picture of the same motif nearly a decade earlier in 1889 (fig. 3).

Both Manet and Seurat seem to have been preoccupied with formal, decorative qualities in their paintings, playing off the hour-glass shapes of their corseted models with the rhythmic curves of furniture, and suggesting femininity through the use of soft, pastel colors. Lautrec, however, was throughout his career concerned with expressing truths of a psychological nature, and his interpretations of the themes of his older contemporaries always explored the emotional content of experience as well as the visual beauty of forms and colors. In his 1889 picture (fig. 3) he stressed the deliberate, conscious artifice of a woman making up before a mirror, rejecting the gentle grace and elegance of Manet and Seurat in favor of a seedier realism. Every detail is organized to suggest the casual disorder of real life which his predecessors ignored: the jagged clutter of background paraphernalia, the awkward angularity and tilt of the mirror, and the model's slouching pose and unkempt hair.

Fig. 2
Seurat, *Woman powdering herself*
1889-1890, 0.25 x 0.16 m., oil on canvas
Courtauld Institute of Art, London

Fig. 1
Manet, *Before the mirror*
1876, 0.92 x 0.72 m., oil on canvas
The Solomon R. Guggenheim Museum, New York
The Justin K. Thannhauser Collection

By 1898 Lautrec's sensibilities had changed, and he depicts Madame Poupoule in a mood of quiet introspection. Beginning with the brothel pictures of 1893 and continuing throughout the rest of his career, he seems to have become increasingly sensitive to the poignant aspects of human vanities and emotions. While his initial youthful contacts with the Parisian demi-monde of prostitutes and cabaret dancers inspired him to evoke in his art the intoxicating revelry of their frenzied nightlife, his later work tends to portray these women not as exotic symbols of decadence but as isolated, melancholy human beings.

Lautrec depicted Madame Poupoule here in an atmosphere of dreamy reverie. While the model of his 1889 picture leans forward to paint herself, Madame Poupoule seems lost in inner contemplation. Her hands plucking idly at her comb, the bitter twist of her mouth and the droop of her eyelids suggest the disillusioned nature of her self-examination. Lautrec has accentuated her introspection by reducing and simplifying the setting and accoutrements of his earlier work, and by veiling his model's face with a rippling curtain of hair. The complex rhythms and contrasting accents of the 1889 painting are here replaced by an elegant, simplified structure of interlocking triangles, which seem to barricade Madame Poupoule in isolation in much the same way as Mademoiselle Margouin is blockaded by hats (see cat. no. 101). Lautrec's high-keyed color harmonies of complementary reds and greens, oranges and blues create a shimmering, jeweled effect that contrasts strangely with the subdued subject, transforming an ordinary and melancholy moment into a vision of unsettling beauty.

Lautrec evidently found Madame Poupoule an evocative and moving model, for he painted her again in 1899 (cat. no. 97), 1900, and shortly before his death in 1901. Each picture depicts her in isolated meditation, either standing by a disheveled bed or sitting before her mirror. Lautrec's second portrayal of her at her dressing table (fig. 4) brings her even more closely under the spectator's gaze, and he has deepened the sense of her lonely colloquy by curtaining her eyes completely and repositioning the mirror to confront her not with her own reflection, but with a blank expanse of dark shadows. Lautrec's color scheme has shifted here to a deeper palette of purples and greens, evoking a mood of heavy melancholy which was brought to an ultimate pitch of intensity in his final study of her in 1901 (cat. no. 108).

N.E.M.

Fig. 3
Toulouse-Lautrec, *Woman at her dressing table*
1889, 0.45 x 0.54 m., oil on board
Private collection

Fig. 4
Toulouse-Lautrec, *The dressing table*
1900, 0.49 x 0.60 m., oil on panel
Private collection

97

**Le coucher, ou Femme en chemise
devant un lit**

Going to bed, or Woman in nightgown
in front of a bed

1899

Oil on panel

0.61, 0.50 m.; 24, 19¾ in.

Dortu, 1971: P.678

The Phillips Family Collection

According to Joyant, Lautrec painted this extraordinary work in 1899 from a prostitute model called Madame Poupoule ("fast chick"). Judging from the close relationship between the painting and several of Lautrec's brothel pictures from 1892-1895 (P.498 and P.557), the pictorial idea of a semi-draped female figure set against a dim background, although developed earlier, continued to fascinate him. In 1897 he had painted a standing nude before her boudoir mirror (P.637). Related to the earlier brothel paintings, this picture closely foreshadows *Madame Poupoule*, for Lautrec now used only one figure, placed centrally in his composition. It was two years afterwards, however, when painting *Madame Poupoule*, that Lautrec finally reduced his pictorial idea to its essential and achieved one of his most gracefully evocative masterpieces.

As he had done frequently since painting his first female nude in 1882 (cat. no. 13), Lautrec placed his model in profile at the very center of his composition, in the attitude of an antique statue such as the *Venus de Medici*. The "sculpted" quality of the woman's body is emphasized by Lautrec's treatment of the background, whose hazy and diffuse homogeneity contrasts strongly with the clearly defined volume of her form. Lautrec's choice of colors is equally important in establishing the mood and formal decorative power of this image. The yellow-green tones of the model's body, intensified by Lautrec's use of complementary shades of orange-brown shot with violet in the background, are almost phosphorescent and mordant, creating a slightly hallucinatory effect. The wood panel support on which Lautrec chose to paint the picture enhances its dominant warm tonality where it shows through his transparent washes of thin paint. The combination of pensive profile pose and subdued background creates a delicate mood of introspective reverie, a mixture of substance and dream with an underlying suggestion of a traditional "vanitas" theme.

Lautrec's initial inspiration probably came from the well-known pictures of bathers which Renoir created beginning around 1887 (fig. 1). These images were in turn

Fig. 1
Renoir, *Bather*
1888, 0.81 x 0.65 m., oil on canvas
Private collection

possibly influenced by Puvis de Chavannes' naïve style or that of the antique and Renaissance art Renoir had encountered on a recent trip to Italy. Renoir juxtaposed sculpturally modeled female nudes against decoratively simplified settings rendered with loose brushwork. Several of these "bathers" were cropped just above the knees, since Renoir had posed them standing in water. Lautrec, who spent much time in Renoir's studio during this period (Natanson, 1951, p. 15), began to crop the lower extremities of his own figures at the bottom edge of his canvases beginning in 1888. Like Renoir's bathers, *Madame Poupoule* seems to float in a space made of an altogether different element, the unsubstantiality of which accentuates the beauty of the female form.

Unlike Renoir's pictures, however, Lautrec's evokes a moral introspection by his use of a sexually suggestive setting and the restrained background. These call to mind allegorically conceived pictures of women contemplating their existence, such as Antoine Wiertz's *La Belle Rosine* (fig. 2), in which a semi-draped young woman posed similarly to Madame Poupoule contemplates a skeleton in the artist's atelier. Lautrec surely knew Wiertz's picture from the almost annual trips he made to Brussels between 1890 and 1897, during the course of which he studied the local museums intently (Joyant, I, p. 168). Another possible source for the figure of Madame Poupoule is the allegorical central female in Courbet's famous *L'Atelier* (fig. 3). *Madame Poupoule* suggests a similar allegory, but with a poetically concentrated and elegant economy of means comparable to that of Redon. Munch's 1906 version of a similar theme seems clearly indebted to Lautrec's example (fig. 4).

N.E.M. & C.F.S.

Fig. 2
Wiertz, *The beautiful Rosine*
c. 1829, 0.14 x 0.10 m., oil on canvas
Musée Wiertz, Brussels

Fig. 3
Courbet, *The studio of the artist* (detail)
1855, oil on canvas
Musée du Louvre, Paris

Fig. 4
Munch, *Model by the bed*
1906, 0.63 x 0.60 m., oil on canvas
Rolf Stenersens Sammlung

98

Aux courses

At the racetrack

1899

0.46, 0.55 m.; 18⅛, 21¾ in.

Oil on canvas

Dortu, 1971: P.683

Musée d'Albi

Between 1898 and 1901 Lautrec returned a number of times to the themes of riders, carriages and the racetrack which had dominated his boyhood and earliest years in Paris, but had disappeared from his repertoire while he developed the principal preoccupations of his mature career. Whereas Lautrec's early depiction of a racetrack (cat. no. 4) was inspired by the "naturalist" examples of Manet and Degas, by 1898 (fig. 1) his interest in capturing the activity and movement of the track had shifted to a desire to suggest the relationship between the spectator and his milieu. Always intensely aware of his own role as an observer of life, Lautrec was very sensitive to the varieties of situations in which people watching the activities of others became a spectacle in themselves.

Like his contemporary Jean-Louis Forain (fig. 2), Lautrec devoted many works to the study of the spectator who remains somewhat aloof from the events under his gaze.

Fig. 1
Toulouse-Lautrec, *Émilie*
c. 1898, 0.41 x 0.33 m., oil on panel
The Metropolitan Museum of Art, New York

In all these related works (for example, fig. 3) Lautrec creates this sense of the separation between observers and things observed by closely juxtaposing large figures in the foreground with the much smaller forms seen in the distance. By also turning his onlookers' backs to the viewer, he sets up an additional relationship between the spectator of the picture and the spectator depicted, and initiates a flow of glances beginning outside the picture frame and moving through the pictorial space to come to rest on the spectacle in the distant background.

As was true in all his work, Lautrec's desire to suggest experience was matched by his concern for achieving decorative effects of color and formal relationships. The flat silhouettes of his figures in their simplified garb create the masses and vertical accents of these very reduced compositions. They are subtly balanced by the minimal horizontal and diagonal elements of landscape, horses, or details of clothing, all adjusted to unify figures with setting and foreground with background through a series of formal repetitions and oppositions. Lautrec's palette in *Aux courses* plays off the rich, warm russets and reds of the horse and the woman's hair with the vibrant green of the grass and the cool blues and greys of the spectators' clothes and the background hills and sky. His color relationships are so subtle that he has managed simultaneously to use a range of strong, contrasting tones, and yet create the effect of the subdued light of a cloudy autumnal day.

N.E.M.

Fig. 2
Forain, *The racetrack*
date unknown, 1.15 x 0.89 m., oil on canvas
Private collection

Fig. 3
Toulouse-Lautrec, *In the Bois de Boulogne*
1901, 0.55 x 0.46 m., oil on board
Private collection

99

Repos pendant le bal masqué

Interlude during the masked ball

c. 1899

0.56, 0.39 m.; 22, 15½ in.

Peinture à l'essence on board

Dortu, 1971: P.695

The Denver Art Museum; The T. Edward
and Tullah Hanley Memorial Gift to the
People of Denver and the Area

Lautrec's cousin and devoted companion, Dr. Gabriel Tapié de Céleyran, was among his favorite models. His giraffe-like anatomy and withdrawn personality were comical contrasts to those of the artist, as the double-portrait at the center of *Au Moulin Rouge* (cat. no. 52) testifies. It seems as if Lautrec took particular delight late in the 1890s to have the dignified doctor pose for two of his most rambunctious pictures. Both depict Gabriel as a Casanova aggressing a voluptuous woman of the world who is primping in a mirror. Were it not for the pictures' different dimensions, they would constitute pendants.

Whereas for the larger work (fig. 1) Gabriel lunges forward to grasp the haunches of a woman in under-clothing, in this picture his pluck is more subdued. He keeps his oversized gloved hand on his lap, while leaning to watch his red-headed companion. She leers in a mirror at the reflection of an eyes-and-nose mask which she is adjusting. The cackling, bare-breasted mirror reflection is menacing, and it is a sharp contrast to Gabriel's polite joviality, mercilessly exaggerated here by Lautrec, who posed Gabriel with a red-nosed clown's mask.

Lautrec outlined the woman's body boldly under a sheer, black grown. Her outthrust abdomen and clenched buttocks are scandalously alluring. Their proximity to Gabriel's hand suggests that he is contemplating an act altogether naughty and out of character. It is as if Lautrec wanted to parody his own slightly earlier portrait of Maxime Dethomas (fig. 2), another timid, withdrawn friend (Coquiot, p. 123). The seated Dethomas also con-fronts a venal masked woman, his cane standing erectly phallic to symbolize his arousal. Gabriel, however, made an even better model for Lautrec, whose developed think-ing now represented the theme more robustly and with deeper psychological insight.

C.F.S.

Fig. 1
Toulouse-Lautrec, *In the dressing room at Armenonville*
1899, 0.67 x 0.52 m., peinture à l'essence on board
Private collection

Fig. 2
Toulouse-Lautrec, *Maxime Dethomas at the Opéra ball*
1896, peinture à l'essence on board
National Gallery of Art, Washington, D.C.
Chester Dale Collection

100

Chez la blanchisseuse

At the laundress'

1900-1901

0.80, 0.58 m.; 31½, 22⅞ in.

Oil on canvas

Dortu, 1971: P.267

Mrs. Leon Fromer

According to Joyant, Lautrec painted this small scene of the interior of a laundry in 1886 while still a student at Cormon's. However, both the subject matter and style would seem to indicate a later date. In 1886 Lautrec still modelled his figures fairly volumetrically with dense shadows and interior detail, the technique taught by Cormon as a part of academic training (see cat. no. 15). This picture has the flatness and simplified linear outlines Lautrec developed during the 1890s, and in both composition and drawing style it most closely resembles the pictures he executed between 1897 and 1900 (cat. nos. 92, 102). In 1886 Lautrec was also just beginning to frequent the theater and cafés in search of modern-life subjects and, in addition to portraits, his output of that year was restricted to these themes. This unusual depiction of a laundry seems unrelated to his earlier work.

The laundry motif was one which had been studied by Lautrec's idol, Degas, in a series of pictures dating from 1882. It is quite possible that Lautrec saw one or more of these at some time, since his own version of the theme has certain compositional similarities to at least one of Degas' renditions (fig. 1). For example, both artists fill the foreground with an obliquely angled table, the implied extension of which beyond the picture frame creates a sense of spectator participation in the scene and adds to its quality of immediacy. Lautrec has also incorporated Degas' telling details of the neatly folded shirt on the table and the laundry hanging in the background, both of which serve the dual purposes of characterizing the setting and structuring empty areas of composition. Finally, each artist has balanced the diagonally set table with a series of vertical doors or windows, linking foreground and background through the repetition of geometric forms which act as a matrix for the figures.

Lautrec's painting differs from Degas' primarily in his choice of the moment to depict. Degas was usually interested in capturing characteristic activities, while Lautrec frequently preferred to portray truths of a more psychological nature. He has seized a moment of inanition, a lull in the laundress' routine during which she leans slouched with weariness against the table, holding a glass of green absinthe. Her face partially concealed in *profil perdu*, she projects a sense of listless apathy and seems only partially attentive to the oddly intense encounter in progress at the rear of the room. Juxtaposed so directly with the laundress' face as to make her inattention even more pointed, a couple is engaged in some private confabulation. The close proximity of their forms and the woman's intimate gesture make it unlikely that this is a business transaction regarding a client's laundry. The scene is strongly reminiscent of passages in Zola's famous novel *L'Assommoir (The drinking den)* of 1877, which traces the moral decline of a Parisian laundress. All the details of Lautrec's picture have their counterparts in Zola's descriptions of surreptitious assignations in the steamy laundry, where natural jealousies and delicate feelings for propriety are dulled by grinding toil and blunted by drink, leaving only resignation or despair. The overall color scheme evokes this dismal atmosphere by its grayish-white suggestions of steam and melancholy, and the low-keyed jangle of purple, green, and orange-brown accents. This color combination and the extensive use of white relates to Lautrec's works of the late 1890s (see cat. no. 95).

In 1900 Lautrec executed a panel painting as a study for the theater program of a dramatic version of *L'Assommoir* (P.713). While depicting a bar scene instead of a laundry, the works appear closely related in feeling and style, and both settings are common to Zola's novel. Since Lautrec never painted pictures on literary themes unless commissioned to do so, it seems likely that he executed this unusual scene of a laundry around the same time and for the same project as his depiction of the bar for *L'Assommoir*. Thadée Natanson (1951, p. 163) recalled that Lautrec read Zola's novels avidly, and certainly this work bears a strong resemblance to the author's powerful depictions of the harsh realities of working-class life.

N.E.M.

Fig. 1
Degas, *Woman ironing*
1882, 0.81 x 0.65 m., oil on canvas
National Gallery of Art, Washington, D.C.
Collection of Mr. and Mrs. Paul Mellon

101

La modiste: Mademoiselle Margouin

The milliner: Miss Margouin

1900

0.61, 0.493 m.; 24, 19½ in.

Oil on panel

Dortu, 1971: P.716

Musée d'Albi

In 1900, after Lautrec was released from the sanitorium to which he had been committed following his physical and mental collapse, his friends tried to interest him in projects which would keep him away from the alcoholic temptations of bars and cabarets (Joyant 1, pp. 224-7). Among the various environments suggested was that of a milliner's shop, for Lautrec loved costume and was intrigued by the atmosphere of feminine establishments. He dutifully spent some time at a fashionable shop, made a few sketches, and produced this single powerful painting before losing interest in the enterprise. Possibly he found the milieu too conventional and the customers too colorless in comparison with the exotic and bizarre subjects he had pursued for the previous fifteen years.

According to Joyant, Lautrec's model at the milliner's was Mademoiselle Margouin, an assistant to the owner. Presumably he chose her because of her magnificent red-gold hair, always his irresistible preference in models. While the motif of a hat shop was popular with modern-life painters of the 1870s and 1880s and had been explored many times by artists such as Manet (fig. 1), Renoir and Degas (fig. 2), Lautrec as always endowed an ordinary "naturalist" subject with a dimension of unexpected enchantment. Manet and Degas' bold decorative images of silhouetted shapes still convey the effect of conventional environments, but Lautrec has transformed his shop into a mysterious realm of dark shadows and eerily glowing color.

Always an enthusiastic devotee of extravagant hats, Lautrec had over the years incorporated a good deal of unusual headgear into his paintings. In *La modiste*, however, he has ignored the potential for amusing effects inherent in his subject and chosen instead to evoke some sense of the intriguing, transfiguring nature of hats. Mademoiselle Margouin looms out of a dim interior, hemmed in by the dark, empty shelves behind her and the ambiguous floating shapes of the hats which surround her. Having no specific form of their own, they echo the contours of the model's heavy mass of russet hair, itself oddly hatlike in the arrangement of its folds and twists. Her dress also repeats the puffed shapes of hats and hair, the elegant cascade of the ruffled frill at her neck adding an accent of bravura decoration which balances the seriousness of the model's face and the gloomy obscurity of the interior. Lautrec's incandescent color combination of orange and blue-green, yellow and purple intensifies the almost hallucinatory effect of this remarkable scene.

N.E.M.

Fig. 1
Manet, *The milliner*
1881, 0.85 x 0.74 m., oil on canvas
Palace of the Legion of Honor, San Francisco

Fig. 2
Degas, *The millinery shop*
c. 1882, 1.00 x 1.10 m., oil on canvas
The Art Institute of Chicago
Mr. and Mrs. Lewis Larned Coburn Memorial Collection 33.428

102

Messaline descend l'escalier bordé de figurantes

Messaline descends a staircase lined with attendants

1900

1.00, 0.73 m.; 39½, 29 in.

Oil on canvas

Dortu, 1971: P.704

Los Angeles County Museum of Art; Mr. and Mrs. George Gard De Sylva Collection (M.A.)

During the winter of 1900-1901 Lautrec retired to Bordeaux, where he concentrated on pictures inspired by productions at the Grand Théâtre. He was particularly drawn to Isidore de Lara's operetta *Messaline,* upon which he based six oil paintings (figs. 1 and 2; P.705, P.706, P.708; D. 4637-D. 4639) representing at least five separate episodes from the operetta, as if he intended a series. As always, Lautrec took pains gathering visual documentation. He wrote to a friend in Paris asking for photographs of the production (Joyant, I, p. 234). Whether or not they were available, he pressed forward with the paintings, with which he was "very satisfied" when he wrote to Joyant (I, p. 230) in April 1901, shortly before returning to Paris.

Lautrec's motivations for undertaking the project must have been numerous. He had frequently painted performers on stage (cat. no. 37), most recently in the ballet of

Fig. 1
Toulouse-Lautrec, *Messaline*
1900, 0.92 x 0.68 m., oil on canvas
Sammlung E. G. Bührle, Zurich

Chilpéric (P.627). Typically the performer aroused his interest to a greater degree than the play. Consequently, perhaps Lautrec found Mlle Ganne, who sang Messaline, to be good pictorial material, for she appears in at least five of his paintings. In this case, however, the play itself may have had significance for Lautrec. Based upon Juvenal's sixth and tenth satires, or upon Gautier's adaptation of them, *Messaline* recounts the tragedy of Emperor Claudius' faithless wife, whose lust knew no moderation. The imperious whore is the counterpart to the brazen queens of Montmartre who fascinated Lautrec. Moreover, two artists associated with him came to the Messaline theme at almost the same time. Beardsley began a series of illustrations to Juvenal's sixth satire in 1896. Although never culminated as a series, several of the drawings were published in 1899 (fig. 3). Lautrec likely saw these, and in addition may have known that Alfred Jarry, for whom he prepared stage sets in 1896, was now writing *Messaline* as a novel, which he published in 1901.

This painting depicts the first act, set in the imperial Roman gardens at dawn. Stage directions call for a central staircase leading downstage from the palace. Columniated hemicycles extend left and right from the foot of the staircase to the stage wings. The left hemicycle is roughly indicated in this picture, which Lautrec seems to have taken from a box above to the right. (Different pictures in the series are taken from a variety of viewpoints.)

For her grand entrance Messaline wears a brilliant red dress, emblematic of her nymphomania. Eight identically dressed female attendants line the left side of the stairway which she descends, each playing a lyre and wearing large, vivid pink flowers in her hair like horns. The more distant of these figures are barely indicated except for two dots for the floral headdress. The women's green gowns and the artificially colored grass intensify the effect of Messaline's red dress. The soldiers at attention, placed in characteristic Lautrec fashion in the foreground corner, are brutish automata worthy of Max Beckmann, and their abrupt juxtaposition with Messaline, viewed on an oblique angle, adds greatly to the expression of suspense. It is they who shall yield to her appetite and finally execute her during the course of this sensationalist psychodrama, which differs only in degree from the sexually charged encounters of Lautrec's best cabaret and brothel pictures.

C.F.S.

Fig. 2
Toulouse-Lautrec, *Messaline*
1900, 0.46 x 0.61 m., oil on canvas
Musée d'Albi

Fig. 3
Beardsley, *Messalina returning home*
1895, 0.28 x 0.18 m., pencil and ink, later tinted with watercolor
The Tate Gallery, London

103

Le violoniste Dancla

Dancla, the violinist

1900

0.92, 0.672 m.; 37, 27 in.

Oil on canvas

Dortu, 1971: P.711

C. van der Waals-Koenigs

According to Joyant (I, p. 300) Lautrec painted his portrait of the violinist Dancla towards the end of 1900 while retired at Bordeaux. Presumably Dancla and a chamber ensemble were performing there. Already in his early eighties, Dancla had a celebrated reputation as a composer and performer of chamber music.

Lautrec, who was deeply moved by classical music, developed the portrait from a group of caricature-like sketches (D. 4.658, D. 4.693). These studied the musician's facial features and the rhythmic movements of his hands and body, all of which Lautrec carefully translated into the finished portrait.

Dancla's energetic movements suggest a solo, since even a cropped view of the conductor indicates that he is relaxed in comparison. Nonetheless, the interconnected black forms of his elbow, the music stand and Dancla himself indicate collaboration. The conductor is turned towards the other members of the ensemble whom Lautrec omitted from the portrait. Their visual absence corresponds to the long rests in the score, during which they remain unnoticed while the attention of the audience turns to Dancla. His reddish-brown violin sounds a note which is amplified by the rich color of the floor and deepened by the contrast with the black tuxedos. Asymmetrical and fragmentary, Lautrec's composition evokes the aged musician's virtuosity, which dominated both visual and aural attention.

C.F.S.

104

M. Maurice Joyant—En baie de Somme

Mr. Maurice Joyant-On the bay of
Somme

1900

1.168, 0.81 m.; 46, 32 in.

Oil on panel

Dortu, 1971: P.702

Musée d'Albi

Maurice Joyant (1864-1930) was Lautrec's closest friend, his art dealer, and, after the painter's death, his most important biographer. He played a crucial role in the creation of the museum dedicated to Lautrec in Albi, to which he donated many important works including this portrait. Lautrec and Joyant were schoolmates whose close acquaintance was renewed in Paris in 1888. When two years later Joyant filled the position vacated by Théo Van Gogh as director of the Boussod and Valadon gallery, he assumed an active involvement in the management of Lautrec's career. For example, he arranged all the most important exhibitions of Lautrec's work during his lifetime.

Generally fond of costumes, Lautrec owned a bright yellow weatherized raincoat and "sou'wester" cap (Sert, p. 51), not simply because they were American but because, like his favorite companions Joyant and Dr. Tapié de Céleyran, he was an avid hunter and fisherman. He wanted to use the costume in a portrait and Joyant agreed to pose. The model recorded fascinating details about the genesis of the picture (Joyant, II, p. 46 and p. 64). For example, he explained that Lautrec typically "incubated" a pictorial idea over a long period of time during which he discussed the projected work and planned its details. In the case of this portrait, Lautrec's preliminary thoughts began two years prior to its execution in the summer of 1900. At some point Lautrec investigated the relative size of the figure within his composition in four pencil drawings (D.4.632-4.635). As Joyant recalled, however, once Lautrec was satisfied with his idea he set about its accomplishment "tyranically." As was his habit, Lautrec required numerous (in this case no fewer than seventy-five), rather short sittings from a model. He blocked in the sail and the boat's prow quickly, then concentrated on the figure. Evidently he hoped to obtain certain precise technical details before proceeding further with the background, but never getting them, he left it broadly and imprecisely painted. Eager to have the portrait "completed," Joyant sent someone to the site in Crotoy to prepare working photographs, but Lautrec never used them (Jedlicka, p. 383).

Joyant's figure, however, is carefully worked. The slick, rubbery surface of the golden raincoat, streaked with complementary deep blue and green shadows and reflections, has the magnificence of some Japanese warlord's armor. Executed in profile, Joyant stares intently out at something beyond the picture frame, as so many of Lautrec's models do. There are few precedents for Lautrec's mock-epic portrait of Joyant, except for Manet's misunderstood portrait of M. Pertuiset (1881, Sao Paolo). Perhaps this portrait of Joyant, the slightly earlier one of Oscar Wilde as a Regency "swell" (P.574) and the slightly later one of Paul Viaud dressed as an admiral (P.722), all explore and reanimate the swaggered poses commonplace in the grand style of eighteenth-century English portraiture. Indeed, Rivoire divulged (April 1902, p. 260) that at the end of Lautrec's life he desired to devote himself solely to portraits painted in the grand tradition.

C.F.S.

105

Paul Viaud—Taussat—Arcachon

1900

0.79, 0.40 m.; 31⅛, 15⅞ in.

Peinture à l'essence on board

Dortu, 1971: P.709

Private collection

Paul Viaud, a native of Bordeaux, was a family friend who at the request of Lautrec's mother acted as the artist's caretaker after his release from the Madrid-les-Bains asylum in the spring of 1899. Lautrec enjoyed Viaud's company during the brief remainder of his life and used him as a model for several important costume portraits (for example, P.722).

During the summers of 1899 and 1900, the two men went to Lautrec's favorite vacation surroundings on the southwest coast. It was there in a garden in either Taussat or Arcachon that Lautrec undertook this painting in August or September of 1900. Although the pose is one Lautrec has developed in an earlier portrait (cat. no. 46), the painter had neglected rustically dressed models since the early 1880s. For Viaud's portrait he returned to this less urbane genre, one more frequently associated with works by Raffaëlli, Van Gogh, Picasso or even Cézanne.

The tall, narrow format, probably Oriental in inspiration, had been among Lautrec's favorites since the later 1880s (cat. nos. 33, 81). In every case Lautrec adjusted his figure to the support, so that both reciprocally reinforced the picture's verticality. For example, in this portrait Viaud's meditative pose is dignified and monumentalized by its position within the complementary format. In addition, every element of the background is orchestrated to reiterate Viaud's silhouette. The roofline of the building at the right continues the line of Viaud's chest, while the smaller tree continues the outline of his left leg. The larger tree, of course, repeats the vertical accent of his figure as a whole.

The refined relationships among disparate details of the painting establish a strong formal structure, within which Lautrec could apply color rather loosely. Long, thin strokes indicate the shed and Viaud's clothing, and shorter ones suggest leaves and dew-sparkled grass, although the trees and ground are barely defined by drawing. By contrast to the loosely handled setting, Viaud's beautifully and fully modelled head stands out in relief. Lautrec further emphasized the head's central importance in his picture by placing the red triangle of the shed's roof so that it draws the eye to the introspective Viaud.

C.F.S.

106

Portrait d'homme: M. G. de Villechenon

1900

0.81, 0.62 m.; 32, 24½ in.

Oil on canvas

Dortu, 1971: P.698

Neue Pinakothek; Munich

Lautrec's portrait of Georges de Villechenon is one of a group of seven conventionally posed male portraits produced during the last three years of his life. This painting is close to Lautrec's portraits of Lucien Guitry and André Rivoire (cat. no. 107) in composition, and in all of them Lautrec expressed wit and humor through a wrily arched eyebrow and a slightly smiling mouth.

E.M.M.

107

M. André Rivoire

1901

0.575, 0.46 m.; 22⅝, 18⅛ in.

Oil on canvas

Dortu, 1971: P.725

Musée du Petit Palais, Paris

During the last year of his life, Lautrec produced a series of four male portraits of which this image of André Rivoire is the most powerful and compelling. Rivoire (1871-1930) was a popular poet and playwright whose works, such as the collection of poems *Le songe d l'amour* and his play *La peur de souffrir,* were published in 1900.

In Lautrec's portrait Rivoire is presented as a broad, muscular type whose strong physical presence is relieved by a wry smile and arched brow indicating his wit and humor. The modelling of his face is achieved by the use of heavy strokes of paint that give it a great sense of volume. The strength of the facial modelling is emphasized by the intense contrast of his livid red ear with the green brushstrokes of the background.

The technique of isolating the sitter against a non-representational background has its roots in traditional European portraiture. Lautrec first used the technique in 1882 when he was a young student doing portraits of workers and studio models (P.152, P.175). In the following years Lautrec used this device for portraits of male sitters who were artists, including Emile Bernard, Charles Conder, H. G. Ibels, Henri Grenier and Romain Coolus. The general effect of this compositional technique is to isolate and therefore emphasize the sitter's personality solely on the evidence of physiognomy. That the style of Rivoire's portrait represented a particular type for Lautrec can be demonstrated by a comparison of this late work with the artist's lithograph of the actor Lucien Guitry which was done six years earlier (fig. 1). The compositions and general pictorial effects of the two portraits are almost as identical to each other as are the faces of the men themselves.

In the *Revue de l'art* of December 1901 and April 1902 Rivoire published a two-part article on Lautrec that included many personal observations about his recently deceased friend. In the first part he described Lautrec's portrait technique and emphasized the importance to the artist of having a thorough understanding of the sitter's character:

"He would never make a portrait without having thought for months, sometimes for years, without having lived in almost daily intimacy with his model. He needed to know not only their traits, but their thoughts, and before beginning the work he always waited patiently as all the secrets of a person were made familiar to him . . . But the execution, as always, was rapid. Two or three sittings, perhaps even one, were sufficient for him" (1901, p. 398).

E.M.M.

Fig. 1
Toulouse-Lautrec, *Lucien Guitry*
1895, 0.29 x 0.24 m., lithograph
The Art Institute of Chicago

108

Femme retroussant sa chemise

Woman adjusting her nightgown

1901

0.56, 0.43 m.; 22⅛, 17 in.

Oil on panel

Dortu, 1971: P.723

Albright-Knox Art Gallery;
Buffalo, New York, Gift of A. Conger
Goodyear

In this picture, Lautrec returned for the last time to a theme which had haunted him since 1894 (cat. no. 72). Like his 1897 *Femme nu devant sa glace* (P.637) and the 1899 portrait of *Madame Poupoule* (cat. no. 97), this painting depicts a partially undressed woman posed meditatively in her boudoir. In all three, the mood of pensive repose evokes a "vanitas" theme.

Lautrec spent the entire period from May 1900 to late April of 1901 visiting familiar country locales and remaining quietly away from the temptations of his Paris life. Sensing that he was close to death, he returned to Paris at the end of April and remained until July, sorting through his paintings and other belongings. During this brief visit he apparently painted several pictures (see cat. no. 98, fig. 3), including *Femme retroussant sa chemise*.

It seems more reasonable to assume that Lautrec made a last visit or series of visits to a favorite brothel, than to imagine that he began a picture from memory in the studio he was dismantling. It is interesting to note that the model for this work closely resembles Madame Poupoule in hairstyle, features, physique, and posture, and that her pose, although reversed, is almost identical to that used for the earlier picture. Perhaps Lautrec returned to visit her and was moved to do another version of his haunting painting of two years before. In both works the model was placed centrally, almost iconically, in a subdued setting against which her flesh stands out emphatically. Both figures are posed in profile and are cropped at the knees to bring them more directly and intimately under the spectator's gaze. Finally, both paintings contain the same allusion to carnal pleasures in the juxtaposition of the woman with a disheveled bed.

The evocative power of this picture derives in part from Lautrec's moody combination of purples, blues and greens. But the real psychological subtlety lies in the disparity between the blatant sexual invitation of the woman's raised chemise and her reflective pose and remote facial expression. The physical and psychological duality of human nature was a theme that had permeated much of Lautrec's art since his earliest representation of a nude (cat. no. 13), but seldom before had he summarized it in a single image of such condensed and simplified expressive force.

N.E.M.

109

Un examen à la faculté de médecine de Paris

An exam at the faculty of medicine in Paris

1901

0.65, 0.81 m.; 25⅝, 31⅞ in.

Oil on canvas

Dortu, 1971: P.727

Musée d'Albi

In 1891 Lautrec's cousin and close friend Gabriel Tapié de Céleyran came to Paris, where he began an internship at the Hôpital International with its founder, the famous surgeon Dr. Jules-Emile Péan. Lautrec spent a good deal of time with Gabriel at the hospital because he was strongly interested in the scenes and personalities he found there. The work that came from these visits included a series of drawings and two paintings of the great Dr. Péan at work (P.384, P.385). These remained the only medical subjects in Lautrec's *oeuvre* until he did this painting of a medical examination in 1901.

The scene commemorates Tapié de Céleyran's oral examination in 1899 for admission to the Faculty of Medicine. Gabriel, portrayed in a serious, professional role, is defending his thesis, "Sur un cas d'elytrocèle postérieure," which he dedicated to the memory of Dr. Péan. Gabriel sits across the table from the board of examiners, three of whom are depicted. The doctor on the far left is obscured by shadow and unidentifiable. The elder physician with white hair who is placed so close to Gabriel's face is Dr. Fournier, and the main figure facing Gabriel is Dr. Robert Wurtz.

Wurtz's figure dominates the composition by its size and by the crimson accents Lautrec has distributed on or around him to attract the spectator's attention. The decoration on his robe and the hat at his elbow serve to draw the viewer's eye, as do the bold red strokes with which Lautrec has delineated his left ear and mouth. As he questions the aspiring doctor, Wurtz's gaze is sharp and intent, his pen poised and ready to take down important notes. The suggestive triangular grouping of Wurtz and Céleyran's hands is emphasized by the white papers on which they are placed, and reflects the structural organization of the three main sitters. The seriousness and tension of the examination is evoked by the dark, somber colors and the ponderous geometry of the composition. The long, high window behind the examiners, while not providing any direct light or distracting outdoor scenes to relieve the concentration below, compresses the figures into a tight space.

This work is the last finished painting that Lautrec produced before his death. An oil study on board shows Dr. Wurtz posing profile right in shirtsleeves and vest, sitting at a table with pen in hand (P.726). This highly finished study and Wurtz's prominence in the *Medical examination* indicate Lautrec's serious interest in portraying the doctor at work. Dr. Wurtz was the first owner of both the sketch and the painting, which were eventually donated to the Albi Museum by one of his relatives.

E.M.M.

Photographic Credits

Acquavella Inc.   Page 295

Georges Beaute   Page 265

Bridgens Photographers, Winnipeg   Page 109

Photographie Bulloz   Pages 119, 171, 251, 295, 322

Goeffrey Clements   Page 100

A. C. Cooper (Colour) Ltd.   Pages 121, 206, 262

Courtesy of Christies, photograph by A. C. Cooper (Colour) Ltd.   Pages 272, 297, 303

Dignimont Collection   Page 125

Photographie GIRAUDON   Pages 258, 271

M. Knoedler & Co., Inc.   Pages 19, 21, 75, 93, 99, 173, 209, 211, 260, 291, 303

Alex Reid & Lefevre Ltd.   Page 243

Antonia Mulas   Page 226

Archives, Musée du Toulouse-Lautrec, Albi   Pages 27, 79, 93, 113, 177, 235, 237, 305, 311

The New York Public Library   Page 187

Oslo kommunes hovedkasse   Page 299

Roger-Viollet   Pages 1, 4, 155, 241

Paul Rosenberg   Page 154

Galerie Schmit   Pages 127, 130, 143, 318

Sotheby Parke Bernet Inc.   Pages 62, 98, 136

Marianne Stevens   Page 159

Wildenstein & Co., Inc.   Pages 28, 171, 228, 266, 276

10,000 copies of this catalog were
Designed by Michael Glass Design
Typeset by Dumar Typesetting, Inc.
Printed by Eastern Press